Also by Thomas Chatterton Williams

Self-Portrait in Black and White

Losing My Cool

SUMMER
OF OUR
DISCONTENT

SUMMER OF OUR DISCONTENT

THE AGE OF
CERTAINTY
AND THE
DEMISE OF
DISCOURSE

THOMAS
CHATTERTON
WILLIAMS

Alfred A. Knopf · New York · 2025

A BORZOI BOOK

FIRST HARDCOVER EDITION PUBLISHED BY ALFRED A. KNOPF 2025

Published by Alfred A. Knopf, a division of Penguin Random House LLC,
1745 Broadway, New York, NY 10019.

Knopf, Borzoi Books, and the colophon are registered trademarks of
Penguin Random House LLC.

Library of Congress Cataloging-in-Publication Data
Names: Williams, Thomas Chatterton, 1981– author.
Title: Summer of our discontent : the age of certainty and the demise of
discourse / Thomas Chatterton Williams.
Description: New York : Alfred A. Knopf, 2025.
Identifiers: LCCN 2024043939 | ISBN 9780593534403 (hardcover) |
ISBN 9780593534410 (ebook)
Subjects: LCSH: Social justice. | Anti-racism.
Classification: LCC HM671 .W545 2025 |
DDC 973.933—dc23/eng/20250411
LC record available at https://lccn.loc.gov/2024043939

penguinrandomhouse.com | aaknopf.com

Printed in the United States of America
1   3   5   7   9   8   6   4   2

The authorized representative in the EU for product safety and compliance
is Penguin Random House Ireland, Morrison Chambers, 32 Nassau Street,
Dublin D02 YH68, Ireland, https://eu-contact.penguin.ie.

For Valentine:

Merci pour tout—toujours.

Epochs which are regressive, and in the process of dissolution, are always subjective, whereas the trend in all progressive epochs is objective.

—GOETHE

I have seen people behave badly with great morality.

—CAMUS

Contents

Preface

There is no doubt that the initial animating spirit of Black Lives Matter, #MeToo, and the thousands of social justice protests since 2020 forced a necessary national (re)consideration of long overdue demands for police reform in particular, as well as broader calls for greater equality and inclusion—and, perhaps above all, the wholehearted extension of dignity and recognition, which sit higher atop Maslow's pyramid of needs than strict physical safety. Just as there is no contradiction between these goods and a maximally tolerant society that is committed to the most robust standards of freedom of expression and viewpoint diversity. On the contrary, the argument has been made in less liberal times and bears repeating today: free speech is the bedrock for all subsequent rights and assurances, particularly those of ethnic, numerical, ideological, and other minorities. This is true in a high-minded way, as the American Civil Liberties Union once exemplified, or as Rosa Luxemburg remarked: "the freedom of speech is meaningless unless it safeguards the freedom of the person who thinks differently," even offensively. But it is also pragmatically true, as Christopher Hitchens highlighted when he argued, "Every time you violate or propose to violate the free speech of someone else, you, *in potencia,* are making a rod for your own back."

It is undeniable that our current technological reality in which even the president can cross unthinkable boundaries* poses new and distinct challenges to such values and to liberalism itself. We must revisit, reassess, and ultimately learn to reaffirm our core beliefs—which have been so gravely tested since the comparative normalcy of the Obama years, but which have always formed the basis of any enduring social progress—so that we may achieve our noblest ideals. *Summer of Our Discontent* is ultimately an argument for why we must resist the mutually assured destruction of identitarianism—even when it comes dressed up in the seductive guise of "antiracism"—and really *believe* in the process of liberalism again, if we are ever to make our multiethnic societies hospitable to ourselves and to the future generations we hope will surpass us. We must, in a sense, reopen—or finally open—the liberal mind, which has been pressed perilously closed by furious, radical, and sophistic forces on both sides of the political and cultural spectrum.

The collective and rapidly evolving cognitive reality enveloping the globe is a fait accompli, and in many ways a distorting, polarizing, and dehumanizing one in the extreme. But that does not mean we are powerless against it. Just as we must return to core tenets

---

* "In Trump's first year in office, tweets from @realdonaldtrump have cut the cost of an Air Force contract, undermined White House messaging, forced federal agencies to rebuke them, stoked a congressional investigation, spurred the former director of the FBI to leak a damaging memo, possibly led to the appointment of a special counsel, created new legal trouble for the White House, announced a new military policy to the surprise of the Pentagon, upended a Republican plan to gut an ethics office, nearly derailed two bills the White House backed and been cited by multiple judges ruling against the Administration on several issues." "Donald Trump's Tweets Really Matter. These 27 Examples Prove It," *Time,* Jan. 18, 2018.

of the open society in rejecting even (short-term) advantageous authoritarian impulses to silence and subdue those with whom we disagree and vie for influence, prestige, and recognition, we must also return to our fundamental political unit, which has always been the family. So many of our seemingly most intractable problems arise in no small part from having learned to see and understand ourselves as part of overwhelming, monolithic abstractions (enormous categorizations of color, sex, gender, race, religion), mistaking our own interests for the purported ends of the identity bloc we've been arbitrarily assigned to. This is true across the culture, whether the ill-conceived identity politics of the left or the spiteful populism of the right. And it is a fact that it is most certainly rooted in the exploitative invention of whiteness, which in turn produced and necessitated blackness and other purported deviations. But we are never going to transcend the racism this historical oppression conjured by reinforcing those same categories it both establishes and continues to feed on.

The way forward begins by stepping out of the rhetorical, out of the abstract, out of the strictly historical, and into the specificity of the present—which, thankfully, is far more complicated and dynamic than oversimplified, dualistic tales of black and white, oppressor and oppressed, colonist and indigenous, can ever account for—and back into what we directly control. Without a doubt, social institutions matter. We *need* concrete policies: police reform, a floor of universal dignity that expands access to health care, day care, and quality public education. One of the most important and potentially transformative practical arguments to gain traction in recent years has been the case for reparations for descendants of slavery and Jim Crow. A full imaginative healing remains improbable so long as so many of us continue to live on such unequal terms—so long as material conditions, no matter how persuasively, are expressed and understood primarily through the limiting language of racial identity.

A crucial dimension of 2020's reckoning that I will return to throughout this book remains, half a decade later, conspicuously underarticulated:* the simple fact that George Floyd was a poor man. That was the most salient fact about his life. Reparations not for *race*—not for some ambient, transnational state of metaphysical "blackness"—but for a specific community of people and their descendants in the United States who can be shown to have been harmed by measurable policies and practices, usually in the housing sector, are not without enormous risk and potential for political blowback. But if conceived and executed properly, and narrowly, and combined with supplementary programs and initiatives that lift *all* Americans stuck at the bottom rungs of our flawed but nonetheless largely admirable† meritocracy, they could help close the ignominious wealth gap that does more than anything else to prevent people from meeting each other as equals.

But even such an ambitious effort as that would not solve everything. How could it? The fundamental political unit, going back to Aristotle, remains the family. That is the foundation upon which the health of the community (whether heterogeneous or homogeneous) is formed, and there is no getting around this through social engineering or positive discrimination. At this moment when our focus has so powerfully shifted to the macro level—to the institu-

---

* Or, even when it is discussed at length by anti-identitarian leftists such as Adolph Reed and Bernie Sanders, it still gets shouted down and dismissed.
† What other country has world-class schools like Stanford, Harvard, Berkeley, and many dozens of other top-tier institutions that, as a matter of course, year after year, propel countless first-generation and foreign-born students to the heights of their respective societies? This certainly is far less common in France.

tions and systems and invisible structures—fathers and mothers, aunts and uncles, big sisters and older brothers, are going to have to inculcate the values, practices, and habits that prepare their children to make the exertions necessary in this competitive, globalized society. And yet the inexorable truth is that reality is still unequal. So long as we are free, there will always be gaps—some of them critical—that both the state and private enterprise are powerless to mend for us. It has been disastrous for the left to cede this most important realm of the political to "conservatives," who so often invoke the family cynically,* but invoke it nonetheless. Reparations, health care, child care, high-quality public school options—these are valuable goods not in themselves but only insofar as they are useful tools for real flesh-and-blood families to flourish. This is why it will never be sufficient to dismantle police departments if we wish to make our most vulnerable communities safer, or to abolish entrance examinations if we wish to bolster authentic equality, any more than it would make sense—as President Trump so foolishly recommended—to do away with COVID-19 testing if we wish to lower the rate of coronavirus infection.†

The summer of 2020 changed us. Like the Trump presidency of which it marked the beginning of a brief intermission, it has changed us in deep and complicated ways that are still unfolding.

* Momentarily, forget about Trump. Perhaps the most influential figure on the right, Elon Musk, has, as of this writing, fathered thirteen children out of wedlock by four different mothers.

† This logic was strangely echoed in a comment Jeanelle Austin, the leader of the George Floyd Global Memorial, had made to me in Minnesota when I asked her about the reality of disproportionate violence within predominantly black neighborhoods like the one in which George Floyd was murdered. "I don't think that there's more violence in the black community than there is in the white community," she told me. "I just think we are counted more frequently than white folks are counted."

We could not return to the honeymoon phase of the early Obama era if we wanted to, and I suspect that an overwhelming majority of us, knowing what we know now, wouldn't wish to do that, either. So far, the alterations have been disorienting and painful—above all chaotic. But there is always opportunity in chaos. Reinvestment in lived community as opposed to virtual, national, and global pseudo-communities (connected through shared and often imagined grievances) will be paramount. As will genuine integration—not as stereotypes or avatars of broad social categories, but as living individuals, in all our fullness and contradiction.

The spectacle of the death of George Floyd and the stasis of the pandemic provided an unusually sustained interest in national and even international renewal and betterment. This potential good carried with it one terrible danger: that in our zest to correct these undeniable and manifold wrongs we became so attuned to, we might have exacerbated a great many of them in the process—introducing even more damaging feedback loops we now find ourselves trapped in.

The progressive development of the collective consciousness of the West will not be attained through the negative forces of guilt and resentment. It will not be spelled out by means of a fatally subjective, self-styled "moral clarity" that is forever backward-facing—a national storytelling project that both guarantees division and verges on embittered determinism. We need objective goals again, both grander and, paradoxically, far more modest than "antiracism" could ever be. "Antiracism," "social justice"—these are worthy values, certainly, but there are also others that demand our attention and that we have damningly neglected. Truth, excellence, plain-old unqualified justice—these deserve our utmost interest. To pursue them will require all people of goodwill to collaboratively articulate something far more difficult than reflexive recrimination; we will also need *positive* visions, practices, and stories about ourselves and one another that do not shy away from past injustices but do not mire us in them either. We will have to find convincing ways for all of us to contribute and move forward, beyond a paralyzed state of permanent anger or contrition. This will require new political strategies, as Francis Fukuyama has argued, in which "identity is seen as a mobilizational tool to demand inclusion in a broader liberal order," and nothing like an end in its own right. These strategies will honor and engage with people as *individuals* with rich and varied backgrounds, not as "ascriptive groups" or abstractions. And so we will also need capable, honest, and courageous journalists, artists, intellectuals, activists, and political and institutional leaders who will win for all of us that shared society in which all are equally invested and, inevitably, all are held equally responsible.

We are, in a very real sense, immensely fortunate to have made it through the extraordinary racial, social, and epidemiological upheaval and tribulation of the summer of 2020 and its punishing, protracted aftermath, and to have emerged with the opportunity to disabuse ourselves of what have proven to be some intensely seductive illusions, however painful the process of disillusionment has been and will surely continue to be. Having put, even temporarily, into practice so many of our most unproven, fantastical, and ambitious *theories,* we find ourselves free at last to abandon the contentious limbo of conjecture and to step back into a hard-won lucidity.*

What we can say with absolute certainty, and what remains at the heart of this book's inquiry: it is no victory at all simply to lose together in a more equitable fashion.

---

* A clear-sightedness that will be all the more necessary under the second, far more emboldened administration of Donald Trump.

SUMMER
OF OUR
DISCONTENT

Prologue

Like the events of September 11, for the rest of my life I am going to remember exactly where I was the moment I first watched it. It was a Tuesday afternoon in the rural west of France, where we'd gone into quarantine seven weeks prior. By that point, days were indistinguishable, but the sheer repetitiveness of the new reality had months ago ceased to be a nuisance and had shifted instead into something like reassurance. It had been unseasonably sunny the whole of confinement. I'd spent the morning exercising and reading, aware of my good fortune to be able to work remotely. In many ways it was a healthier existence than the one we'd left behind in the density of Paris. After clearing the family lunch from the table, I heard the children's voices in the yard as I took my coffee up to my borrowed office. I don't know when the habit would have solidified—a few years prior—but the new normal meant that I went not to my email or the home page of *The New York Times* but straight to Twitter.

A post from CBS News at 1:21 p.m. my time snapped me from the mild solipsism of confinement. "Video shows Minneapolis cop with knee on neck of motionless, moaning man," read the text above an astonishing image. Within the numbing flood of bad news and stress that is the lifeblood of social media, and at a juncture in an appalling campaign when the president of the United States had spent the Memorial Day weekend attacking the physical appearances of various female opponents—a time when the U.S. death toll from the novel coronavirus was fast closing in on the symbolic, previously unthinkable 100,000 mark—this picture was orders of magnitude more upsetting. If it wasn't clear on that first agonizing click, it became so within the hours and days that followed: for America, and indeed for large swaths of the world, it was the visual quintessence of a centuries-long and cancerous history—a tortured transatlantic oppression rendered in flesh and pixels.

From that moment on, there would be two George Floyds, related but not identical, and it has become necessary to separate them. On the one hand, there was the son and the brother, certainly down on his luck that long weekend, unemployed and carrying methamphetamines and fentanyl in his system. This man was in a bad way when law enforcement encountered him dozing in a parked car, having passed a counterfeit banknote moments earlier—a petty crime that even the cashier seemed embarrassed to have reported. This George Floyd had survived an early bout of COVID-19, only to be asphyxiated in broad daylight by an officer he'd once worked side by side with in his bouncer days at El Nuevo Rodeo nightclub. That mortal man's biography, his early life as a promising high school athlete on an elite football squad in Houston, Texas, his scattered efforts as an aspiring rapper in that city's "screw" scene afterward, and his practically unmentionable and half-hearted criminal career as someone who had allowed himself to be party to the robbery and pistol-whipping of a pregnant woman in her own apartment, fixed him in a specific time and place within the very real, painful, and transformative discourse around systemic poverty and racism, crime and punishment, Black Lives Matter, police violence, the limitations of the first black presidency and its immediate succession by what has been ruefully termed "the first white presidency."*

On the other hand, there is the immortalized George Floyd, whose death exists in footage, on wretched loop in our brains, and can be instantaneously conjured on our screens as a discrete and profoundly shareable cultural unit. This latter technological aspect, informed by but also divorced from and transcending its particular subject, cannot be overestimated. A "meme," as the British evolutionary biologist Richard Dawkins defined it, "is an idea, behavior, or style that spreads by means of imitation from person to person within a culture and often carries symbolic meaning representing a particular phenomenon or theme." The idea, simmering for years without reaching a rolling boil, of intransigent black pain and suffocating white supremacy—two definitive poles of an irredeemable American, and by extension European, and in a certain

---

* "It is insufficient to state the obvious of Donald Trump: that he is a white man who would not be president were it not for this fact. With one immediate exception, Trump's predecessors made their way to high office through the passive power of whiteness—that bloody heirloom which cannot ensure mastery of all events but can conjure a tailwind for most of them. Land theft and human plunder cleared the grounds for Trump's forefathers and barred others from it. Once upon the field, these men became soldiers, statesmen, and scholars; held court in Paris; presided at Princeton; advanced into the Wilderness and then into the White House. Their individual triumphs made this exclusive party seem above America's founding sins, and it was forgotten that the former was in fact bound to the latter, that all their victories had transpired on cleared grounds. No such elegant detachment can be attributed to Donald Trump—a president who, more than any other, has made the awful inheritance explicit." Ta-Nehisi Coates, "The First White President," *Atlantic,* Oct. 2017.

telling, ultimately *metaphysical,** order—was what the entire world encountered in that eight-minute and forty-six-second clip (in fact, as prosecutors later made clear, Derek Chauvin knelt on Floyd for nine minutes and twenty-nine seconds).[†]

"This is plain, coldblooded murder," I quote-tweeted the CBS News post, immediately ricocheting it back into the ether to fulfill my insignificant yet essential role in the viral-making process. The truth is that people seldom have ideas, but ideas—and the intimations of such, their prerational moods, assumptions, and gestures—very certainly have people. They are contagious, ripping through

---

* From the Oxford Bibliographies entry on "Afro-pessimism," by Patrice Douglass, Selamawit D. Terrefe, Frank B. Wilderson: "Afro-pessimism is a lens of interpretation that accounts for civil society's dependence on antiblack violence—a regime of violence that positions black people as internal enemies of civil society, and cannot be analogized with the regimes of violence that disciplines the Marxist subaltern, the postcolonial subaltern, the colored but nonblack Western immigrant, the nonblack queer, or the nonblack woman." The authors explain that while "it is assumed all sentient beings are human beings," Afro-pessimists such as themselves "argue that critical theory's lumping of blacks into the category of the human (so that black suffering is theorized as homologous to the suffering of, say, Native Americans or workers or nonblack queers, or nonblack women) is critical theory's besetting hobble." In their view, "the black (or slave) is an unspoken and/or unthought sentience for whom the transformative powers of discursive capacity are foreclosed ab initio—and that violence is at the heart of this foreclosure." And so we are left with what they call, rather alarmingly, "a structural antagonism between humans and blacks."

† The meme of white supremacy/black victimization has become so widespread and axiomatically true over the past few years that, as I write, even the violent and sometimes deadly anti-Asian hate crimes shown to be carried out by black assailants are nonetheless described not as racism but as acts of "white supremacy," too. And the deadly beating of Tyre Nichols in Memphis in January 2023 at the hands of five black policemen was also widely described as yet another instance of anti-black racism—even white supremacy.

populations that are sometimes asymptomatic until there is a further crucial mutation. None of this is to say that they are necessarily sinister. They simply inhabit us—at different times and places, individually and collectively—like personalities. Whether they are good or bad—or neutral or some hybrid of the two—is clear only in retrospect, after their course has been exhausted. In the moment, emotion and solidarity can blind as well as ennoble us. Hegel put it aptly: "The owl of Minerva spreads its wings only with the falling of the dusk." Wisdom and understanding follow events. Has enough time passed now to begin to ask ourselves some questions? *What exactly did we see in that video?* Or, perhaps more to the point: *What is the seminal meme in the Western tradition that this video so powerfully tapped into?*

As America began to wake up, and I left my desk and returned to it and the saddening spectacle in Minneapolis, as the nation's grief and fury began to concentrate around a midwestern Golgotha, the Christlike dimensions of that horizontal crucifixion started to take root in the subconscious. Had Floyd not, in some viscerally apparent way, borne the awful weight of his society's racial sins on his very own neck and shoulders? And had that weight—all of ours massed and taken together—not in turn crushed him? A man died for us on that squalid pavement, not asking why his father had forsaken him but, shatteringly, calling for his deceased mother. The lethargic executioner, operating solely on the authority that we collectively grant him and resigned to a haunting impassiveness, had washed his hands of the matter—had buried them deep inside his pockets.

Paradigm shifts occur much the same way Hemingway described going broke: "gradually and then suddenly." All of us rely on mental frameworks to make the world legible until, from one moment to the next, they suddenly fail to do so. We fumble around blindly in the dark until a new framework takes over. The death of George Floyd on May 25, 2020, in Minneapolis touched on every single aspect of our public lives and much of our interior ones also. During the season of rebellion and reckoning that followed, nearly eight thousand Black Lives Matter demonstrations took place across the nation—not to mention the mass protests that erupted internationally in places as far away as Paris, Amsterdam, London, Seoul, Taiwan, and Helsinki. All told, millions of people rose up worldwide, disgusted by what they saw in mind-boggling unison. It is no exaggeration to say that these were the largest manifestations against racism in the history of humanity—yet such an abstract truth, like the scale and suffering of a pandemic, remains difficult to wrap our minds around entirely.

Why did this mass attunement to racialized injustice happen—why then and not on any number of previous occasions? Recent history is inundated with them. Why did the reaction transcend national boundaries? Why, to cite just one of countless such examples, were students at Oxford University in the U.K. suddenly granted "special consideration" in their final examinations solely because of *this* American travesty?* In 2014, we watched in dis-

---

* There had been for years an active and ongoing campaign of ethnic cleansing verging on genocide against the Uighur population in China; a decade-long civil war in Syria had claimed between 388,650 and 594,000 lives as of March 2021, with another 6.1 million men, women, and children violently displaced, leading to a refugee crisis spanning western Europe; and in October 2018 the *Washington Post* columnist Jamal Khashoggi was dismembered in the Saudi embassy in Istanbul. Yet none of these violations or countless other highly publicized atrocities from around the world prompted the heads of Oxford's colleges to sign an open letter declaring, as they did after the killing of George Floyd, "Any student taking university assessments who feels their performance

belief as Officer Daniel Pantaleo dragged Eric Garner to the sun-drenched Staten Island sidewalk for the crime of peddling loose cigarettes, compressing the unarmed man's windpipe beneath his straightened forearm, deafening himself to the dying man's pro-testations. That was when we first heard the wrenching phrase—"I can't breathe"—that Floyd would echo in Minneapolis (and pro-testers in Paris would learn to chant in English). It soon became a T-shirt that LeBron James could warm up in, a pithy slogan. We applauded his consciousness and were troubled by the footage, but unbridled outrage remained limited and sporadic. Two years later, when Philando Castile bled out on Facebook Live, we felt sickened. The footage was abysmal. A father destroyed in front of his daugh-ter and girlfriend for no plausible reason. Castile had done nothing wrong; in fact he'd done everything right—calmly announcing up front that he was carrying a licensed firearm—and it was difficult to fathom why he'd been stopped some fifty-two times prior to that fatal encounter. Still, our lives remained busy and we resumed them. By May 2020, however, stuck in our houses and clasping our screens while the world outside our windows took on ever more menacing dimensions, a recording of a fatal confrontation in Geor-gia held our attention. What happened to Ahmaud Arbery looked strikingly, anachronistically like a lynching—a lynching that had been covered up for months, much like the news of a young medic named Breonna Taylor, roused from her sleep and shot to death by police in Kentucky. All of this, and more, began to form a context.

"To draw momentous conclusions from a single video shot on the sidewalks of Minneapolis might seem excessive," Paul Berman wrote in the journal *Liberties*. "Yet that is how it is with the historic

---

has been affected should submit a self-assessment mitigating circumstances form after their final examination or assessment."

moments of overnight political conversion. There were four million slaves in 1854, but the arrest of a single one proved to be the incendiary event."* For a not insignificant portion of the American left and center—and also some of the right—who were sidelined from normal life, homeschooling and working remotely or panicking about not working, and who were being antagonized into a near-constant state of anxiety by a singularly juvenile and polarizing president who seemed not only not to grasp the severity of the pandemic but even to revel in tempting catastrophe—as he had after Charlottesville, come to think of it—the possibility that the country had a malignant racial sickness began to seem undeniable. Many of these people understood themselves to be white and were newly alive to their own physical and spiritual vulnerability but also freshly aware of the disproportionate toll COVID-19 had been taking on communities they did not belong to. That discrepancy, a consistent theme in the mainstream media's coverage in those early weeks and months,[†] seemed to suggest problems of a more systemic nature. In the ghoulish and farcical figure of Donald Trump, and in the unfolding epidemiological scandal, as Berman argued so powerfully, many of these same people could see for themselves with sudden and blinding clarity the way that they, too, had been and were continuing to be lied to about the sturdiness of their institutions, about the professionalism and objectivity of their law enforce-

---

* A nineteen-year-old named Anthony Burns, escaping slavery in Virginia and fleeing to Massachusetts, was arrested in Boston in May 1854 under the Fugitive Slave Act of 1850. His arrest and return to Virginia sparked protests in Boston and drew national attention, galvanizing the abolitionist movement.

† "The old African-American aphorism 'When white America catches a cold, black America gets pneumonia' has a new, morbid twist: when white America catches the novel coronavirus, black Americans die." Keeanga-Yamahtta Taylor, "The Black Plague," *New Yorker,* April 16, 2020.

ment agents and political leaders, about the general state of social progress in their society. They could intuit what was happening to people like George Floyd more clearly now, in large part, because of the simple fact that they were seeing what was happening to themselves and others like them in the eerie new half-light of the pandemic.

Perhaps more significantly, as commentators have pointed out since the advent of the Black Lives Matter movement following the deaths of two teenagers, Trayvon Martin in 2012 and especially Michael Brown two years later, there has been for some time now the heat of religious fervor* simmering beneath our secular social justice rhetoric. In particular, the all-encompassing original sin of "whiteness"† had taken hold in the popular imagination. By the end of May 2020, an enormous number of Americans had been staring at their smartphones and televisions and computers in quarantine as fellow citizens who could not afford to stop working braved the contagion and delivered their groceries and other necessities as well as more frivolous packages—a great many of the latter group, of course, peering out from surgical masks that half-concealed black and brown faces. Many of the Americans with a sudden surplus of

* One critical element of religious fervor of course being blind faith in what cannot be proven with empirical evidence—indeed, at times, a fanatical belief in that which empirical evidence directly contradicts. The "Hands up, don't shoot!" mantra popularized by Black Lives Matter after Michael Brown's killing, which became a rallying cry for the nascent social justice movement, was one such instance. It would help plant the seeds of racial cynicism in large swaths of the country that would blossom years later.

† Flawed and confusingly worded as it may be, a national survey of a thousand American adults conducted on February 13–15, 2023, by Rasmussen Reports, asked the question, "Do you agree or disagree with this statement: 'It's OK to be white.'" To which some 20 percent of self-identified white Americans responded that it was *not,* or that they weren't sure.

time to reflect on themselves became unusually, collectively alive to the possibility that they, too, were implicated in the entire constellation of processes and implicit biases that could allow a madman to gamble with the health of the body politic with the same startling lack of concern that a policeman could evince while chicken winging a handcuffed, writhing civilian. This was an extraordinary, not at all inevitable conclusion for so many to arrive at so swiftly, but one that didn't come from nowhere either.

O f course, there were signs of expanding fracture beforehand. On the left, significant numbers of mostly white millennials saddled with student loan debt and entering a contracting job market had found themselves newly radicalized by the Great Recession of 2008 and the disorganized, short-lived, but galvanizing Occupy Wall Street movement that sprang up in response to it. This unprecedentedly educated cohort—emblematic of Peter Turchin's notion of "the overproduction of elites"—began to rethink some of the central tenets of late capitalism and to register views that were more approving of social democracy and even Marxism than the country had seen in generations. Though the United States would spend the first two decades of the twenty-first century enmeshed in punishing, far-flung wars, the realities of an all-volunteer military (essentially an undereducated mercenary underclass) meant that these relatively privileged Americans were divorced from the burdens and sacrifices of service that previous generations had been forced to shoulder. One powerful consequence of this, we can see now, was that many of them would spend the coming decades processing and sublimating some highly complex feelings of guilt and shame about their comparative safety and security.

For non-whites, even though the mixed-race population has

become the fastest-growing segment of the American demos and, in real terms, a disproportionate but statistically small and decreasing number of unarmed black civilians were killed by police annually (typically between fifteen and twenty-five per year from a population exceeding forty million, according to *The Washington Post's* "Fatal Force" database)—and indeed other quality-of-life markers have been equalizing for significant numbers of black people since the civil rights movement* —the death of Martin followed by Brown (regardless of the specific contingencies of that case), and a high-profile slate of videotaped police and vigilante killings that converged with the proliferation of camera-equipped smartphones and the pervasiveness of social media,† thwarted any self-

---

* For example, as Adolph Reed Jr. and Walter Benn Michaels observe in "The Trouble with Disparity," the notion of a neatly racialized color-caste system can be deceptive: "The top 10 percent of white people have 75 percent of white wealth; the top 20 percent have virtually all of it. And the same is true for black wealth. The top 10 percent of black households hold 75 percent of black wealth. That means, as Matt Bruenig of the People's Policy Project recently noted, 'the overall racial wealth disparity is driven almost entirely by the disparity between the wealthiest 10 percent of white people and the wealthiest 10 percent of black people.' While Bruenig is clear that a discernible wealth gap exists across class levels, he explored the impact of eliminating the gap between the bottom 90 percent of each group and found that after doing so 77.5 percent of the overall gap would remain. He then examined the effect of eliminating the wealth gap between the bottom 50 percent—the median point—of each population and found that doing so would eliminate only 3 percent of the racial gap. So, 97 percent of the racial wealth gap exists among the wealthiest half of each population."

† At the same time, we remained selective about which atrocities would captivate our attention and stoke our moral indignation. For instance, the case of Tony Timpa bears striking similarities to the killing of George Floyd. Timpa, an unarmed thirty-two-year-old white man suffering from schizophrenia, was killed in Dallas on August 10, 2016, by the police officer Dustin Dillard after requesting aid for a mental breakdown. As a report in *Reason* magazine

congratulatory sense of the inevitability of social progress still alive in the first half of Obama's second administration.

In both instances, then, what stood out was a "revolution of rising expectations" that seemed, at least in part, to have played a decisive role in the blooming discontent that had metastasized throughout the entirety of Trump's first term and especially during the pandemic year of 2020. As far back as 1856, however, Alexis de Tocqueville observed that unfulfilled, rising expectations create unstable political situations. This explains why, for example, the strongholds of the French Revolution were in regions where standards of living had been *improving,* not the reverse. "It is not always by going from bad to worse that a society falls into a revolution," Tocqueville wrote in *L'ancien régime et la révolution.* "It happens

---

explained, two security guards had already handcuffed and detained Timpa before police arrived on the scene. Yet "the officers re-handcuffed him and zip-tied his feet, with Dillard and [Officer Danny] Vasquez holding him in the prone position facedown. Vasquez stopped applying force about two minutes thereafter, while Dillard pressed his knee, with some additional help from his hands, into Timpa's back for approximately fourteen minutes and seven seconds.

"Timpa initially resisted the restraint, yelling for help and thrusting his shoulder upward; his activity gradually peters out over the course of the body camera footage. Toward the latter third of the video, his pushing becomes twitching, his speech slurs, and for the final few minutes, he is limp. Vasquez and [Senior Corporal Raymond] Dominguez are heard mocking Timpa nearby, comparing him to a schoolboy who they taunt with 'new shoes,' 'waffles' ('tutti-frutti' flavor), and 'scrambled eggs' to excite him out of bed." Video of the encounter exists online, though it was never shared broadly. There were no widespread social media campaigns around his death to raise awareness of police brutality. It took more than three years for footage of the incident to be released, and the officers involved returned to active duty. Billy Binion, "Tony Timpa Wrongful Death Trial Ends with 2 out of 3 Cops Getting Qualified Immunity," *Reason,* Sept. 27, 2023.

most often that a people, which has supported without complaint, as if they were not felt, the most oppressive laws, violently throws them off as soon as their weight is lightened."

On the right side of the political spectrum, even as liberals lamented the supposed intractability of structural racism, classism, and patriarchy, the sheer symbolic power of witnessing an apex-level family of black meritocrats inhabit the White House—an event that, to some people's chagrin, seriously undermined the claim that the nation was irredeemably white supremacist—seems to have driven a not insignificant segment of the population to despair, and to seek a crude but effective "populist" champion in the figure of Donald Trump to avenge that loss of status. Here, too, however, the angriest and most organized among them were not the white poor, the downtrodden increasingly given to what sociologists have dubbed "deaths of despair" (induced by hopelessness mingled with too-easy access to guns, opioids, and alcohol), but rather the various tiers of middle classes, whose fortunes might not have been declining in real terms—indeed, might actually have been rising*— but were declining *in relation* to other groups historically perceived as inferior and increasingly seeking recognition.[†]

---

* As they also continued to rise under President Biden.

[†] "Between two generations, Americans' ability to break into the middle class has changed. Race has come to play a smaller role in upward mobility, while economic class plays a larger role," according to an in-depth report published in *The New York Times*. "Researchers found that black millennials born to low-income parents had an easier time rising than the previous black generation did. At the same time, white millennials born to poor parents had a harder time than their white Gen X counterparts. Black people still, on average, make less money than white people, and the overall income gap remains large. But it has narrowed for black and white Americans born poor—by about 30 percent." "Who Can Achieve the American Dream? Race Matters Less Than It Used To," *New York Times,* July 25, 2024.

By the time the world ground to a halt in the spring of 2020, there had been a long-festering, multifaceted need—a need felt in multiple, previously estranged corners of the American (and global) polity—to revolt against *something*. And no matter how high the frustrations piled, or how unacceptable the trade-offs seemed, during what was incessantly billed as the most important election year in U.S. history—in a certain feverishly persuasive telling, the single event that would fundamentally determine whether the nation itself would even remain a democracy or slide into genuine fascism—it remained politically unrespectable to rebel against stay-at-home orders or any of the other hastily conceived and sometimes contradictory new restrictions, the rejection of which had become irredeemably linked with Trump and his supporters. The latter's very reluctance to prioritize a flattened curve at a moment when the left-of-center mainstream had coalesced around a narrative of COVID-19 as a racially discerning "Black Plague," as a *New Yorker* essay labeled it, opened a new and volatile front in the cold civil war of intra-white status jockeying. It created an opportunity for "those who see themselves as (for lack of a better term) upper-whites," as Reihan Salam has termed them, "to disaffiliate themselves from those they've deemed lower-whites." This in turn made it necessary to suppress dispassionate scientific probability and the aspiration to objective truth in favor of emotional, bitterly partisan team politics. And so what had started understandably and even nobly as regard for specific communities with racially correlated but variegated vulnerabilities—dense living conditions, high rates of comorbidities, disproportionate representation in fields designated "essential work," lack of quality health care, and, not insignificantly, distrust of medical institutions—would soon give way to something intensely different: a full-blown moral panic that, in retrospect, it is possible to say with no exaggeration, touched on every facet of our collective, mediated existence and spawned a vicious counter-reaction from the authoritarian right that further erodes our liberal democracy.

S*ummer of Our Discontent* is the story of this dramatic and not inevitable turn in consciousness, encapsulated in these generation-defining twin calamities, which reshaped not just American life in the third decade of the twenty-first century but also the networked, internet-driven monoculture that huge swaths of the planet increasingly inhabit. Any attempt to make sense of the recent past is not without risk. The aim here is not so much a definitive account of an era I view as more or less beginning in the second Obama administration and concluding in the fall of 2023, after Hamas's attack on Israel, as it is a broader analysis of the evolving manners, mores, taboos, and consequences of the recent American social justice orthodoxy—"antiracism,"* or "wokeness"† more broadly—that came in from the discursive margins and went global.

It is a deep irony that, even with a discourse rooted in the ideals of "diversity, equity, and inclusion," the United States cannot help but throw its customary weight around in new and paradoxical

---

* I put this in quotation marks for the simple fact that this term is no longer generic or self-evident but refers to a specific set of attitudes, beliefs, and assumptions and excludes others—for example, color blindness—that have in previous eras been associated with the notion.

† As I wrote in *The Guardian,* I do not like to use the term "woke," which is not, and has not been for some time now, a viable descriptor for anyone who is critical of the many serious excesses of the social justice left yet remains interested in reaching beyond their own echo chamber.

ways: while the rest of the world might have lamented the decline of American stewardship, prestige, and status under the Trump administration (and may yet do so again under Trump 2.0), the new soft power of identitarian social orthodoxy only underscores the extent to which U.S. cultural imperialism remains a destabilizing force to contend with in the global arena.

Much popular writing touching on any aspect of race and identity* in recent years has proceeded from the central premise of reiterating the dismal litany of historical abuses that blacks as a group have endured in the four centuries since the first ships holding slaves eased into New World shores following the incursion of Europeans into the African continent almost six hundred years ago. One of this movement's chief achievements has been the fusion of tragedies past and present along a flattened continuum of pain. I am often exasperated by this tendency, even as I grasp and empathize with the complex emotional and psychological forces that propel it.

I myself am the son of a black man from the segregated South who is old enough to be my grandfather and whose own grandfather was born in the year of the Emancipation Proclamation. My parents were married three years after the 1967 *Loving v. Virginia* verdict abolished the so-called racial integrity laws that prohibited "miscegenation." My mother lost social standing over her willingness to recognize my father's humanity. My older brother had his teeth knocked clean out of his mouth by the Maglite of a furious white police officer who had crossed the threshold of his own home. The story of American racism is not merely an abstraction for me. It is something both tangible *and* intellectual, an epistemology I have lived and grappled with my entire life. The stories of past injustice that so frequently emerge today as news have never been news to

* Not just blackness, but increasingly any historically marginalized category.

me. The barbarity of race—racism, too, to be sure, but the fuel it feeds on is the lie of race—is a living, breathing reality that has addressed me in my own home through the beloved voice of my father and, much more tellingly, through his silences.

From my vantage as an American descendant of both enslaved Africans and European immigrants, now raising children that most people would and do mistake for "white" in Paris, I have spent the past decade and then some watching the world's two "universal" societies reckon in competing, contradictory, and sometimes complementary ways with loaded and subjective questions of modern identity and civil liberty. Both societies possess their own distinct yet interrelated foundations of slavery and colonialism, and both now struggle to achieve more inclusive and equitable multiethnic democracies without unraveling in the process. Living as an insider-outsider in these two particular countries has afforded me a more expansive and, I believe, thoroughly empathetic view of what has transpired and what is being fought for. Some years contain whole epochs within them, in all their contradiction, possibility, and peril. The summer of 2020 was the climax of this story, not its beginning nor its culmination. My aim now is to retrace the radical and profound intellectual and social history of that year's rupture in order to reveal the foundational actions and ideas that produced it.

Our liberal Western democracies, run through the supercollider of identity, risk collapsing on themselves. The temptation of coercive, illiberal solutions from the left and the right has never been greater in my lifetime. We find ourselves now overwhelmed by paralyzing, highly subjective notions of grievance and the toxic, reactionary backlash they are said to validate. Escaping both traps means consciously de-emphasizing zero-sum tribal oppositions and keeping faith with the objective democratic values of the liberal society that can be extended ever more universally to safeguard all human dignity. What follows is a history of a period that has been profoundly affected by a movement for social justice, which starts from a fertile vision of the world in which no one is diminished yet falters in its attempts to arrive at such an arrangement by means of calamitous shortcuts—ultimately distorting the centuries-long arc of moral progress as it advances. In ways both obvious and subtle, it is in that warp that fresh injustices fester.

CHAPTER ONE

The First "Black" President
and the Failure (or Fear) of Post-racialism

In the spring of 2023, I took a visiting position at a small liberal arts college in the Hudson valley, two hours north of New York City. I'd arrived to teach two undergraduate courses, one an elective devoted solely to the works of Albert Camus, a course that practically enrolled itself. The moment it was listed, I began to receive eager notes of inquiry from students returning from study abroad and happy to linger in the sun-drenched imagescapes of the absurd. The other class proved a much tougher sell, specifically, and to my dismay, with regard to the smattering of eligible students who would have marked the "black" box on their admissions forms. This second class satisfied a curricular requirement and revolved around a core of texts I have been reading, rereading, teaching, and contemplating for most of my adult life. These pivotal books, articles, and essays—by authors ranging from Frederick Douglass to James Weldon Johnson, Richard Wright, Ralph Ellison, and James Baldwin to Albert Murray, Henry Louis Gates Jr., and Adrian Piper— had shaped and refined my thinking about the idea of America, the multihued, regionally distinguished, and fundamentally mongrel populations that inhabit it, and the yet to be perfected flesh-

and-blood nation of the future we might one day bring forth in unison.

"Because if you think back on that moment of the most wildly transformative hope and aspiration, for a while at least the country really did seem to *want* to be better," I said before trailing off. An oblong conference table ringed with blank stares met my enthusiasm as the conversation turned to what seemed to me to be the earth-shattering political achievements of the still unfolding present. For my students, however, it was nothing but the vaguest rumor of an abstract history. "Professor," a diligent girl from Queens who described herself as Latina and applied a no-nonsense activist lens and corresponding set of vocabulary to most engagements voiced what all her classmates must have been thinking. "I was four years old in 2008. I don't know what you're talking about!"

It was not simply that these smart and earnest nineteen- and twenty-year-olds were as removed from the era in question as, I realized, I would have been in their place from Iran-Contra. There was a deeper unfamiliarity still. Race pessimism, or even a kind of mass learned helplessness, was the weather that enveloped them. They took for granted what James Baldwin lamented as "the insistence that it is . . . categorization alone which is real and which cannot be transcended." That was common sense to them. Very few could intuit the optimism in, nor even—not quite—the *desire for,* racial transcendence I still took for granted. (The one most seemingly able to do this was a single foreign student from Europe, enamored of black music and sports culture as well as of his nonwhite girlfriend.) If I wanted them to be able to imagine this alternative future, even fancifully, it struck me then, I was going to have to convey to them a sense of what we had once been promised and sorely felt to have slipped from our clutches. Through their lack of familiarity, I began to understand how difficult it is even to recall that more innocent and in retrospect frightfully naive moment in American—and to a certain extent western European—culture, when the ascent and election of Barack Hussein Obama to the U.S. presidency momentarily seemed to herald not only the end of the cinematically violent and tumultuous Bush era, which had begun in terror and closed in financial ruin, but also the dawn of a whole new so-called post-racial, genuinely progressive epoch of multiethnic social harmony and human flourishing. For the period stretching from roughly 2008, when then-candidate Obama drew an unthinkable crowd of some 200,000 native Germans in Berlin, until 2012, when an unarmed seventeen-year-old black boy was stalked, confronted, and gratuitously gunned down by a vigilante while walking home from a convenience store in Sanford, Florida, it seemed as though things really had improved, however incrementally, and that the "arc" of the "moral universe" that the nineteenth-century transcendentalist Theodore Parker had spoken of, and Martin Luther King Jr. and Obama himself had both so memorably invoked, really did "bend towards justice." It seemed that it might even bend all the way toward serenity and ever-increasing personal and collective satisfaction and mutual acceptance.

The comedown was precipitous; the national disappointment as swift as it was severe and enduring. And it defined the cultural discourse, beyond mere electoral politics to the #BlackLivesMatter movement on social media, the #OscarsSoWhite campaign at the Academy Awards, and the "Afro-pessimist" school of thought that so powerfully altered the mood of art making in general* and magazine and literary publishing in particular. The paradox of rising expectations as well as innovations in communications technology helps explain why discontent has exploded even as life in the United

---

* The movie *Get Out* is the comical embodiment of this sensibility.

States in real terms has never been better—or fairer—for black people and other historically disadvantaged minority communities.

According to the U.S. Census Bureau, poverty rates for blacks and Hispanics reached historic lows in 2019. Since 2008, median household income had increased 14.1 percent for black households, 24.3 percent for Latino households, 11.1 percent for non-Hispanic white households, and 25.7 percent for Asian households. It is necessary to acknowledge such gains even as we refuse to gloss over the persistence of ongoing disparities among and within groups or to dismiss the tenacity with which the racial wealth gap still clings to American families. In roughly the same period, from 2010 to 2021, the status dropout rate, or the percentage of sixteen-to-twenty-four-year-olds who are not enrolled in school and have not earned a high school credential (either a diploma or an equivalency credential such as a GED certificate), declined dramatically, from 16.7 to 7.8 percent for Latinos, and from 10.3 to 5.9 percent for blacks, putting the latter group close to the rate of whites, who went from 5.3 to 4.1 percent. The Census Bureau reports that black high school attainment (at 88 percent) is now nearly on par with the national average, an enormous gain considering that in 1940, when the organization began collecting data, only 7 percent of blacks achieved a high school degree (compared with 24 percent for the nation as a whole). Beyond the presidential level, the Joint Center for Political and Economic Studies reports that the number of black elected officials grew by 173 percent, from 4,912 in 1970 to 13,400 in 2019. About a quarter of voting members (23 percent) in both houses of Congress are racial or ethnic minorities, "making the 117th Congress the most racially and ethnically diverse in history," according to Pew. "This represents a 97 percent increase over the 107th Congress of 2001–03." And, according to the Centers for Disease Control and Prevention, "in 1999, there was a 33 percent higher age-adjusted death rate for blacks compared to whites. By 2015, this gap had narrowed to 16 percent." The report continues: "Between 1999 and 2015, the age-adjusted death rate declined by 25 percent for blacks and 14 percent for whites. There were 284 fewer deaths per 100,000 blacks in 2015 compared to 1999, and 120 fewer deaths per 100,000 whites. Among those aged 65 years and older, there was actually a crossover where blacks had slightly lower age-adjusted death rates than whites starting in 2010." These bland numbers represent cold, hard (and hard-won) facts—not moods or feelings.

Yet again, Tocqueville has much to say. The effect he observed in France after the revolution was also evident during his American travels. As he writes in *Democracy in America,*

> The hatred that men bear to privilege increases in proportion as privileges become fewer and less considerable, so that democratic passions would seem to burn most fiercely just when they have least fuel. . . . When all conditions are unequal, no inequality is so great as to offend the eye, whereas the slightest dissimilarity is odious in the midst of general uniformity; the more complete this uniformity is, the more insupportable the sight of such a difference becomes. Hence it is natural that the love of equality should constantly increase together with equality itself, and that it should grow by what it feeds on.

The promise of Obama was never supposed to be merely incremental or reducible to the realm of statistics, percentages on paper filed away in dusty cabinets at the Centers for Disease Control; on all sides of the political spectrum, the first black president was supposed to be at once tangibly redemptive and symbolically larger than life*—unimpeachably so—to make possible the immediate transcendence, in both theory and practice, of racial identity (and therefore racism and its twisted legacies) once and for all. It was a globally attractive vision so seductive, in fact, it earned the president-elect the Nobel Peace Prize a priori. In retrospect, such a hyperinflated vision would pop when it brushed too many times against reality's jagged grain. But was that preordained?

I was ten years old in 1991 when, lying in my bedroom flipping through cable TV channels, I glimpsed the blurred mass of furious shadows pummeling the poor figure—"swarming" him in LAPD-speak—into the Southern California pavement. George Holliday had captured the grainy atrocity on his handheld camcorder from his apartment unit across the street in Lake View Terrace and shared it with local TV stations before it went national. In total, eight officers mercilessly pounded Rodney King—a twenty-five-year-old black motorist with a prior conviction who was trying to outrun a DUI—in the form of thirty-three baton strikes and seven boot kicks, across his bruised and lacerated body and head. As the footage overtook my regular MTV programming, I could not believe what I was seeing. Prior to that moment, I had never watched anything similar that wasn't billing itself as fiction. Of course, I had heard stories of what I'd later learn was called police brutality,

---

* Asked about his views on reparations in 2019, the then Senate majority leader, Mitch McConnell, derisively quipped that reparations had already been paid in the form of the election of Barack Obama! "We tried to deal with our original sin of slavery by fighting a Civil War, by passing landmark civil rights legislation, elected an African American president," McConnell said. Lucas Aulbach, "Mitch McConnell: We Paid for 'Sin of Slavery' by Electing Obama," *Courier Journal,* June 19, 2019.

had witnessed my father tense up and assume a level of vigilant alertness in interactions with law enforcement officers that I knew even as a young boy was unjust—and I had already learned from my brother and my school friends the chorus to "Fuck tha Police," N.W.A's anthem of rebellion and disrespect. I had grasped the logic behind it. Nevertheless, what happened to King was an outlier, not just in the realm of my own idiosyncratic experience, but within the larger media landscape too. The chiaroscuro swirl of the pitch-dark night shot through by headlights was itself anachronistic, reminiscent of the black-and-white footage of violence against blacks during the civil rights movement. The scene was so extremely affecting in no small part because it was so singular. Even as the subsequent rioting engulfed the ghettos of Los Angeles, and images of even more spectacular racialized violence beamed into my bedroom yet again, these events felt no more ubiquitous or definitive of the nature of American society than scenes from a movie or a first-person shooter game.

Four years later, the next time a story of interracial violence and injustice consumed my consciousness, and that of everyone (of any color) around me, was during the made-for-TV murder trial of O. J. Simpson. This is not to say there hadn't always been uncountable other, more or less famous and disturbing incidents closer to home that generated coverage and outrage—from the death of Michael Griffith in Howard Beach, Queens, to the murder of Yusef Hawkins in Bensonhurst, Brooklyn, to the Crown Heights race riot—but those remained parochial. None of them could capture the national imagination and hold it at any length. The spectacle of the Simpson trial marked a hinge point, certainly in my own evolving understanding of my country and my friends' and my racialized place inside it. Those of us who considered ourselves black and Latino pumped our fists and embraced each other in the corridors of our suburban New Jersey interparochial school when news of the verdict reached us there, a reaction that stunned and baffled and possibly even wounded our white instructors and classmates.

Since then, I believe I have only ever witnessed two other equivalent impromptu celebrations among complete strangers: walking the streets of Brooklyn the night of the election of Barack Obama in November 2008 and sitting at a packed café in Paris at the moment of victory for the white, black, and Arab French national team during the World Cup in July 2018. In all three instances, the sense of jubilation and of common belonging to a righteous coalition was at that same extraordinarily elevated pitch. What those of our community who did not share our glee were unable to fathom was the sense the O.J. acquittal instilled in us of having, in some perverse sense, finally drawn even, of achieving some form of racial parity, albeit apophatically, through the appalling absence of punishment rather than, strictly speaking, the presence of justice. We sensed the flaw here, but it did not sufficiently bother us; we'd take the victory, however we could define it.

Looking back, it is instructive to pair that distorted celebration with the multiethnic triumph that followed only thirteen years later, a measure of how far we'd traveled both as disparate individuals and as a more or less unified nation, when we came together to elect one man who unambiguously resembled what is reductively called black in this society—even if his ancestry had eschewed the all-American institution of slavery—to the office of the presidency. Here, at last, was what we all could recognize as the highest and heretofore rarest form of positive equality—or so it seemed.

Three days after the election, on November 7, 2008, Gallup published research revealing unprecedented levels of optimism, patriotism, and bipartisan goodwill in the wake of Obama's decisive victory. In response to one poll, more than two-thirds of Americans said Obama's election was either "the most important advance for blacks in the past 100 years" (33 percent) or "among the two or three most important such advances" (38 percent). Only 10 percent of respondents said it was "not important." What's more, over half of all McCain voters described the election as one of the most important advances in a century. In the hours after Obama was elected, some 67 percent of Americans said that "a solution to relations between blacks and whites will eventually be worked out." According to Gallup, this was the highest value the organization had ever measured on the question. By contrast, just 30 percent of respondents maintained that race relations would remain a permanent problem. Perhaps most revealing—and it would be hard to believe these abstract stats if every specific conversation I'd had at the time did not surpass the optimism embedded inside them—seven out of ten Americans maintained, on November 5, 2008, that race relations would improve as a result of Obama's election compared with just one out of ten who professed the opposite. A mere 3 percent of respondents foresaw that things would get "a lot worse" in the future.

Sifting through the reams of sunny op-eds and editorials from 2008, like this emblematic example from the *Pittsburgh Post-Gazette,* can make for heartbreaking reading. "Americans woke up to a different nation yesterday," announced the editorial board. "In place of old victories built upon the politics of bitterness and division, in place of the old scourge of racial enmity, a new maturity and responsibility had found its majority. Real change is now not so audacious a hope." At *The New York Times,* under the headline "Obama Elected President as Racial Barrier Falls," Adam Nagourney wrote on the news side of the paper, "Barack Hussein Obama was elected the 44th president of the United States on Tuesday, sweeping away the last racial barrier in American politics with ease as the country chose him as its first black chief executive." He continued, "The election of Mr. Obama amounted to a national catharsis." In the opinion pages the tone was far less cautious. The columnist Tom Friedman went so far as to proclaim, "And so it came to pass that on Nov. 4, 2008, shortly after 11 p.m. Eastern time, *the American Civil War ended*" (emphasis mine).

Some political analysts have always cautioned that the upliftingly racialized narrative of the Obama election obscures a much more banal reality. In this telling, such moments of broad national cohesion "involve the American people rallying around the flag, or the president, or an ideal (among other things)," with the near-unanimous support for George W. Bush in the wake of the September 11 attacks being the starkest modern example of the phenomenon.* All rally events sooner or later fade away, and the patriotism and positive effects they engender inevitably recede. Seen this way, the typical honeymoon phase virtually all new presidents enjoy was no exception for the first black head of state. Its predictable devolution, however, was fatefully entangled with a larger disillusionment after *seeming* to have made such giant steps toward a common project of racial reconciliation.

Which is why, from a certain angle, Obama's reelection in 2012 could be said to represent an even *greater* test of racial feeling than was present in the previous contest. By the fall of 2010, Rasmussen polling already showed that only 36 percent of Americans maintained that race relations were improving. Yet four years into the Obama era, there was still in the mainstream imagination the most powerful desire to see our politics as a cohesive story of transcendence and redemption. "It could be argued that Barack Obama's

* Monika L. McDermott and Cornell Belcher, "Barack Obama and Americans' Racial Attitudes: Rallying and Polarization," *Polity* 46, no. 3 (July 2014).

first term will be regarded as disastrous for U.S. race relations," Keli Goff wrote in *The Washington Post*. "This is precisely why a second term could be seen as one of the most important steps forward in this country's race relations since the height of the civil rights movement in the 1960s." In a special winter 2011 issue of the journal *Daedalus* devoted to the question of "the Negro American," Gerald Early identified a major turning point in the Obama era: Sergeant James Crowley's arrest of the distinguished Harvard professor Henry Louis Gates Jr. on the front porch of his own home in Cambridge, Massachusetts, in 2009.

Speaking at a news conference, when asked about the arrest, Obama acknowledged the provisional nature of his answer, "not having been there and not seeing the facts," before venturing that the policeman "acted stupidly." He then situated the incident in a larger social context, noting that "there's a long history in this country of African Americans and Latinos being stopped by law enforcement disproportionately. That's just a fact." As Early wrote (and it's worth quoting at length),

> Obama's response here may have been the beginning of a fracture along racial lines about precisely what Obama represents in "postracial America." For the man who, as Joe Klein put it for *Time* magazine in 2006, "transcends the racial divide so effortlessly," there was nothing postracial in the president's analysis of the Gates affair. For blacks, Obama spoke the pure and simple truth: blacks and Latinos are stopped—harassed, really—much more by the police than whites. Young black and Latino males in particular live in a virtual police and penal state, where they are under constant suspicion. . . . And to think that a black professor at Harvard would be arrested on the grounds of his own home! That he

would be asked to produce identification and prove that he lived there! For blacks, Obama was right to side with "the brother," despite not knowing the facts of the case. He was right to be skeptical of cops and the so-called justice bureaucracy they represent.

Many whites, on the other hand—conservatives in many instances, but not exclusively or even mainly so—were appalled. How could the president adopt a stance on a case whose details were largely unknown to him? Why, indeed, was he even commenting on a case that involved local law enforcement? It was in no way a federal matter, and therefore the president, rightly, should have made no comment. To these white Americans, Obama's response seemed as crazy as if Bill Clinton had commented on O. J. Simpson's arrest in 1995 for the murder of his wife. . . . Moreover, many whites were uncomfortable about the president's rush to judgment of the Cambridge police. After all, it is true that blacks and Latinos are stopped disproportionately by the police, but it is also true that they commit a hugely disproportionate share of violent crime in America—the other half of the fact that Obama's initial response seemed to elide. . . .

Blacks are generally proud that Obama openly took their side in this matter, that he understood, articulated, and, more important, legitimated their position. Many whites, however, were surprised that the president took any side at all, that he did not see the necessity as president to transcend such a matter. This was not Little Rock or Selma. The Cambridge police officer was not Bull Connor. (Indeed, the Cambridge Police Department is highly diverse, and its officers are given sensitivity training.) Henry Louis Gates is not an uneducated, unemployed black victim of the inner city but rather a man of considerable intellectual, financial, and institutional resources who can well take care of himself in his disputes with the city of Cambridge. The problem with African Americans (and their liberal left enablers and comrades), as many whites see it, is that they are constantly seeking to relive the days of grand martyrdom from the civil rights movement, recasting every racial disparity and every racial incident as a sign that nothing has changed. Blacks feel that they must be forever vigilant lest things, in fact, do change for the worse. Yes, the Gates arrest and Obama's reaction may have marked the beginning of the end of the fragile racial unity and hope that Obama's presidency had inspired in many Americans.

The subsequent controversy over Obama's remarks so besieged his administration, overshadowing and coloring even his landmark health-care reform, that he went so far as to invite both Officer Crowley and Professor Gates to the White House to hash it out in person, in an awkward and in retrospect inevitably counterproductive attempt to quash the matter over drinks.* This meeting, which became known as the beer summit, put the police officer and the professor on more than civil terms but could not assuage the larger suspicion Obama's intervention aroused. As Ta-Nehisi Coates observed in *The Atlantic,* the president's popularity had yet to recover one year later. "It seems that a lot of people voted for Obama on what they thought was the understanding that he would never take the part of a black person against a white person." This period marked a shift not only in some white people's sense of trust in Obama's ostensible post-racialism but perhaps more pro-

* Inexplicably, Joe Biden joined in, too.

nouncedly, as Coates's comment shows, in an increasingly visible and influential black commentariat's pessimism toward the prospect of racial equality in America—with or without a black head of state. There is of course a long and distinguished tradition of black intellectuals and leaders, from Marcus Garvey through early Malcolm X, who have rejected out of hand the possibility of racial progress, arguing instead that white supremacy is a feature, not a bug, of American life. The law professor Derrick Bell, one of the pioneering intellectual forces behind the critical race theory movement, published *Faces at the Bottom of the Well* in 1992, in which he maintained that "racism is not a passing phase, not just a fleeting thing. It is a fundamental, deeply rooted and deeply felt constant in our society." This view never went away, not entirely, and would be familiar to even the most casual fan of rap music. But it was by no means the dominant lens. Despite Bell's claims—"fully 25 years after the beginning of the civil rights movement, blacks are still at the bottom. Blacks are still the country's symbol of poverty. We are still the group whose victimization cries out for vengeance"—the seismic, indisputable victories of that globally unprecedented movement led to the explosive success of black Americans across the fields of sports, music, and other dominant forms of popular culture in the 1980s and 1990s, and to the establishment of a highly credentialed and educated corporate and academic elite, which culminated in the first term of the Obama administration, amounting to the most potent symbol not just of equality but of mainstream inclusion and normalcy. This long and gradual but inexorable ascent up King's mountaintop was hard won, a point of pride, and not to be gainsaid. Yet all of that had changed, dramatically so, by the beginning of the second decade of the twenty-first century.

As Early remarked in his *Daedalus* essay, "What race relations so profoundly reflect in America is the complex nature of our social dynamic: how in this country, as Ralph Ellison brilliantly encapsulated in *Invisible Man,* one can move without moving. Many African American cynics ask, what has changed, except the façade that masks the great American racial leviathan, whose belly still contains the two worlds of race?" Indeed, to answer that rhetorical question seriously, what has *changed* most noticeably since the peak of racial optimism in 2008 are not, strictly speaking, the material conditions or even symbolic degrees of oppression experienced by black Americans. On the contrary, the most notable difference in an institutional world and mass culture profoundly oriented around the intrinsic value of diversity, "antiracism," and inclusiveness is the paradoxical fact that today it is the *cynics* alone who have taken narrative, imaginative, and therefore philosophical and political control. How did that come to pass? No other writer, or indeed voice of any kind capable of articulating a sense of reality from within black America, so epitomized—or perhaps it's equally fair to say, so galvanized—the pivot from post-racialism to its polar opposite as Ta-Nehisi Coates in the 2010s.

"Obama was born into a country where laws barring his very conception—let alone his ascendancy to the presidency—had long stood in force," Coates wrote in "My President Was Black," his 2017 epilogue to the Obama era. "A black president would always be a contradiction for a government that, throughout most of its history, had oppressed black people. The attempt to resolve this contradiction through Obama—a black man with deep roots in the white world—was remarkable. The price it exacted, incredible. The world it gave way to, unthinkable." By this point Coates had become as influential on the American cultural and political conversation as any writer I have ever observed. Though he has come and gone from the public eye in recent years, it is necessary to reflect on the extent to which for the better part of a decade, all left-leaning and a considerable amount of center-right thinking on race in America—*especially* in non-black quarters—was directed by the scholarship, reporting, and polemic, indeed the *mood,* of a single writer from Baltimore.

In 2014, when Coates explained on his wildly popular blog the "origins" of his assiduously followed "blue period"—a decisive and widely imitated turn in outlook away from progressivism toward Afro-pessimism—he traced it to a single source, a video clip in which the Princeton historian Nell Irvin Painter discusses her 2010 book, *The History of White People.* "On the one hand, the idea of blackness, that is poor dark-skinned people, I think we will have that with us always," Painter explained:

> We have a great inequality of wealth and income. This group of people who are scraping by, there will be a lot of them, but they will probably be largely black and brown and that will tend to reinforce racial ideas. So on the upper strata, among these few people up here who are doing very well there will be people of various colors and from various backgrounds, but they will probably not be so racialized as the people who are not doing well.

Coates confesses to having been "horrified" when he first encountered that simple statement (which could, in fairness, also lead to a far more optimistic interpretation) during Obama's first term. "Watching my own son interact with the world, in a way that I did not, I've often felt that there really could be—at some distant point—a postracial moment, minus the requisite irony," he wrote at the time. "At that point I was a progressive in every sense of the word. I believed that you could sketch a narrative of progress in this country from enslavement to civil rights. It seemed logical, to me, that this progress would end—some day—with the complete vanquishing of white supremacy." No more.

The pivotal death of the social media era took place within the confines of a gated community in Sanford, Florida, half an hour from Orlando.* Though the atrocity was not videotaped in the way that some previous encounters had been, and virtually all subsequent, highly consequential killings would come to be, its inescapable discussion marked the moment I was first aware of the full power and immediacy of activist messaging and organizing on social media, particularly Twitter. Soft-edged personalities ensconced in mainstream establishments, such as Touré Neblett, of MSNBC at

---

* It was not, however, the *first* murder of the social media era: "One of the first and most visible instances of the shift to digital- and social media–based racial justice organizing followed the 2009 murder of Oscar Grant by Bay Area Rapid Transit (BART) police officer Johannes Mehserle. Grant, a twenty-two-year-old Black father on his way home from celebrating New Year's Eve with friends, was shot in the back by Mehserle in the early morning hours of January 1, 2009, after BART police responded to calls of a fight on the train. Grant had no weapon and was already subdued when Mehserle pulled his service weapon and fired. Grant died of his injuries seven hours later.

"A number of bystanders recorded the killing on their cell phones. One person anonymously submitted footage to local television station KTVU, which broadcast the unedited video and later posted it to YouTube. The videos shot by bystanders would prove important to the case, particularly because of the discrepancies between the officers' accounts of what happened and that of other witnesses." Sarah J. Jackson, Moya Bailey, and Brooke Foucault Welles, *#HashtagActivism: Networks of Race and Gender Justice* (Cambridge, Mass.: MIT Press, 2020).

the time and the personification of 1990s and early 2000s media access and success, who had never displayed a radical feather—indeed who spent his childhood within the upper echelons of white America* —suddenly began tweeting incessantly about the scourge of white supremacy from his leafy, multihued, and fully gentrified corner of New York City. Neblett, specifically, was a local writer from my neighborhood in Brooklyn, someone I had followed since his days at *Rolling Stone* and MTV and viewed as a reliable measure of discursive incentives—a relentless barometer of the shifting pressures bearing down on black thought and personal branding. He had astutely ridden the wave of Obamamania only one year prior with his bestseller, *Who's Afraid of Post-blackness? What It Means to Be Black Now*. Those emergent pressures seemed now to coalesce around and emanate from a simple, two-word hashtag appended to tweets, #TrayvonMartin, which would ultimately evolve into a three-word phrase that would prove far more influential: #BlackLivesMatter. As Sarah J. Jackson, Moya Bailey, and Brooke Foucault Welles argue in their 2020 book, *#HashtagActivism: Networks of Race and Gender Justice,* "Over time, #TrayvonMartin transformed from a signifier of Martin himself to a symbol of the broader condition of racial bias and injustice in America." In addition to the galvanizing death of Oscar Grant in Oakland in 2009 and others thereafter, they continue, "it was the 2012 murder of Trayvon Mar-

---

* Touré is a writer, television personality, and podcaster who goes by one name, like Sinbad or Colette. *The New York Times Book Review once* described him as follows: "A graduate of the prestigious prep school Milton Academy in Massachusetts, and a formerly top-ranked amateur tennis player, Touré thinks blacks have too often embraced a hard-edged, ghettoized idea of what it means to be black in America." "Up Front: Touré," *New York Times Book Review,* May 1, 2009.

tin that solidified Twitter hashtags as a crucial organizing tool for racial justice activists."

More than a month passed before the clownish twenty-eight-year-old assailant, George Zimmerman, faced any legal repercussions for the killing at all. The online activism that blossomed organically and then was amplified by a broad and multiracial assortment of celebrities, from LeBron James to Rihanna, Anderson Cooper, and Bill Maher, was instrumental in forcing reluctant prosecutors finally to bring charges against Martin's killer in the court of law. This was deeply impressive, and the outrage was admirably "trans-partisan," as Ta-Nehisi Coates pointed out at the time: *"National Review,* a magazine that once opposed integration, ran a column proclaiming 'Al Sharpton Is Right.' The belief that a young man should be able to go to the store for Skittles and an iced tea and not be killed by a neighborhood-watch patroller seemed uncontroversial."

What was striking, however, even then, was the flatness of the emerging narrative, and the presentism and hyperbole of its historical connections. For example, the hashtag #EmmettTill was also appended in conjunction with tweets about Trayvon Martin, thus raising the stakes of the Martin tragedy from the specific to the eternal, placing it on the level of one of the most gruesome and reprehensible lynchings in American history. "The linking of these cases, which span nearly sixty years, also indicates the role that collective memory plays in contemporary digital racial justice spaces," write the authors of *#Hashtag Activism.* Activists were keen to "argue that the fate that befell Martin, Till, and those in between reflects the glaring continuation of anti-Black violence and [white] supremacy."

This was a decisive rhetorical flourish. Even though, at the time and even more so now, it was far from clear that the lamentable killing of a single teenager in Florida at the hands of a crazed and pathetic Latino* man was any more indicative of the state of national racial progress for some 44 million black Americans than was the fact of a handsomely compensated and culturally privileged professional like Touré using his outsized platform to discuss it. The racially inflected violence that befell Martin is unbearable, yet, thankfully, it is also exceedingly rare. According to FBI statistics for 2019, broken down by race,[†] a total of 2,906 black deaths resulted from homicide on the year. Of that number, 246 were at the hands of "white" offenders, another 23 were committed by racial "others," and 63 were committed by racial "unknowns." The overwhelming majority of murders, some 2,574, were the result of black offenders. (Most victims of violence, of any race, are harmed by members of their same group. Between 1980 and 2008, 93 percent of black victims were killed by black offenders and 84 percent of white victims by white offenders, according to data compiled by the Department of Justice. Black-on-black crime stats are not always useful or morally relevant, as activists rightfully point out. Yet they are not without *any* analytical meaning or force, either, as those

---

* This was also the moment mainstream audiences were introduced to a very strange and novel mental contortion that would become increasingly common going forward. George Zimmerman, the momentary poster boy for white supremacy, was inconveniently *not white,* certainly not by any standard the genuine white supremacists of Till's day would be able to imagine. In fact, Zimmerman himself, as a tan-skinned Latino man, was technically also a racial minority. And so *The New York Times* squared the circle: Zimmerman was henceforth to be described as a "white Hispanic," emphasis on the "white." See: Erik Wemple, "Why Did New York Times Call George Zimmerman 'White Hispanic'?," *Washington Post,* March 28, 2012.

[†] Admittedly an unscientific and imprecise marker that I would prefer to abandon. Eugene Volokh, "Homicide Rates by Race, and the Mehdi Hasan Controversy," *Reason,* May 1, 2023.

activists sometimes not entirely persuasively suggest.) Whites, by contrast, who make up a population roughly five times the size of black America, accounted for 3,299 total homicides, of which 2,594 were at the hands of fellow whites, and some 566 were at the hands of blacks. This is not the space to contemplate the many direct and subtle consequences of historical oppression and the intergenerational residues of dehumanization and exploitation on present-day populations. Here, I simply wish to emphasize the paucity—both comparative and in aggregate—of white-on-black killings in the twenty-first-century United States, a nation of more than 335 million citizens.

In the context of the first black president, however, there was simply no way that Obama—who had, to the dismay of many, assiduously avoided talking about race in the wake of the beer summit—was not going to have to weigh in. Talking to reporters, he said,

> When I think about this boy, I think about my own kids, and I think every parent in America should be able to understand why it is absolutely imperative that we investigate every aspect of this, and that everybody pulls together—federal, state, and local—to figure out exactly how this tragedy happened. . . .
>
> But my main message is to the parents of Trayvon Martin. If I had a son, he'd look like Trayvon. I think they are right to expect that all of us as Americans are going to take this with the seriousness it deserves, and that we're going to get to the bottom of exactly what happened.

As with the arrest of Henry Louis Gates Jr. previously, Obama's intervention proved catastrophic. "Before President Obama spoke, the death of Trayvon Martin was generally regarded as a national tragedy," Coates observed. "After Obama spoke, Martin became material for an Internet vendor flogging paper gun-range targets that mimicked his hoodie and his bag of Skittles." Coates continues:

> The election of an African American to our highest political office was alleged to demonstrate a triumph of integration. But when President Obama addressed the tragedy of Trayvon Martin, he demonstrated integration's great limitation—that acceptance depends not just on being twice as good but on being half as black. And even then, full acceptance is still withheld. The larger effects of this withholding constrict Obama's presidential potential in areas affected tangentially—or seemingly not at all—by race. Meanwhile, across the country, the community in which Obama is rooted sees this fraudulent equality, and quietly seethes.

Obama would be reelected later that same year, but the honeymoon was decidedly over. "Polarization," not change you can believe in, was the term you couldn't escape now. The online racial derision directed at the Obamas was appalling,* dim-witted, and childish, though not entirely surprising.† The country had not every-

---

* In 2015, netizens noticed if one were to search "n— house" on Google Maps, they would be redirected to the White House. That same year, when President Obama launched the @POTUS Twitter account, his replies and mentions were flooded with images of monkeys, racial slurs, and a picture of the president in a noose. His iconic "HOPE" poster was replaced with the word "ROPE." One user responded to his inaugural tweet: "Get back in your cage, monkey."

† The journalist George Packer told me that in 2009 and 2010 he was researching his National Book Award–winning *The Unwinding* "in North Carolina and southern Virginia, and it was clear that the Tea Party movement tapped into a powerful white reaction against Obama—even, though not often, among people who voted for him." In other words, before the high-profile incidents of

where and all at once become post-racial. It is unclear whether at that time it even could have. Nonetheless, with the benefit of hindsight, I am convinced a genuine opportunity was squandered. We make our nation collectively, daily. We change our values, norms, customs, and linguistic habits and significations together. It is not the racists alone who get to determine our state of transcendence. It certainly should not have been a deal-breaker, and too many Americans were too eager to receive Obama's comments with zero generosity, but it was a mistake for the president to personalize the killing and hypothesize about what his son might look like. It was also pointless—depending on the physical characteristics of this hypothetical son's mother, he could easily have presented as a beige-skinned "white Hispanic," not unlike George Zimmerman. Some of Obama's critics had a point: the purpose of a post-racial presidency was to help move the country beyond the injection of race into every consideration. The killing of Trayvon Martin was abominable and gratuitous, no matter how one's progeny might appear. The universal principle—that people should not be profiled, stalked, and confronted by homicidal vigilantes—was something the overwhelming majority of Americans could—and did—buy into. This was not always the case in a society that enforced "sundown laws" throughout the twentieth century and should therefore be interpreted as a sign not of perfection but of progress, unambiguously so.

It was not seen that way. As Coates concluded, any sense of improvement was illusory; in fact, come to think of it, there was

---

miscommunication, Packer continued, "something changed when he entered the White House." There are undeniably feelings that are not just complicated or ignoble but ineffable and unable to be accurately captured in polling. Perhaps there were any number of people who were open to and even desiring of the idea of a black president but could not tolerate the reality.

no such thing as progress to begin with. "Barack Obama governs a nation enlightened enough to send an African American to the White House," is how he put it, "but not enlightened enough to accept a black man as its president." This may have been true. It was also, however inadvertently, as clear a distillation of the fundamental flaw in our historical and current political and cultural thinking as can be presented. The genuine post-racial project did not fail because the country could not accept a *black* man as president. The post-racial project will only have been attempted when categories such as "black" and above all "white" are emptied once and for all of their historical, visceral, unscientific salience.

This is the American future Barack Obama's candidacy had initially shown us, but that my young students could no longer find remotely plausible. Coates's sense of futility was both derivative and utterly infectious, and the example of his stratospheric rise as the gloomy foil to Obama's uplift taught a generation how to think publicly about race on liberal and mainstream platforms. The ideas were not his own and were not novel. Rather, he was an extraordinarily capable vector, the first blue-chip black writer so thoroughly ensconced within the establishment—with bylines in *The New Yorker,* recurrent guest columns in *The New York Times,* a staff position at *The Atlantic,* book contracts with Random House, and frequent appearances on top cable news and public radio programs—to espouse what he himself described as a worldview devoid of belief in the possibility of meaningful or transformative progress. Like the cliché about terrorism, the forces for order, good, justice, and progress must always be perfect—and we interpret this as normalcy, the bare minimum—whereas the agents of destruction need to succeed just one time, and we feel our entire condition to be precarious. The second term of the Obama presidency coincided precisely with the dawn of the social media era and the sudden ubiquity of the smartphone, that earth-shattering new reality that transformed all of us into amateur videographers, equipped with the equivalent of George Holliday's video camera, as well as what he did not have—a global publishing network at the ready in our pockets. Any and all abuses and aberrations could henceforth go viral. There was another Rodney King—or worse—trending all the time now. When Dylann Roof massacred nine churchgoers in South Carolina, in the summer of 2015, Ta-Nehisi Coates's editor rushed his bleak memoir *Between the World and Me* to bookstores months ahead of schedule, to coincide with the barbarity of the news cycle. It became one of the most impactful and transformative publications of the century. Addressing his own black son, who was not hypothetical, Coates's message put to rest the heroic idealism of Obama's grand vision. His message was brutal, irresponsible, and decisively victorious. "We are captured, brother, surrounded by the majoritarian bandits of America," he addressed his son:

> The terrible truth is that we cannot will ourselves to an escape on our own. . . . You have been cast into a race in which the wind is always at your face and the hounds are always at your heels. . . . The plunder of black life was drilled into this country in its infancy and reinforced across its history, so that plunder has become an heirloom, an intelligence, a sentience, a default setting to which, likely to the end of our days, we must invariably return. . . . We are, as Derrick Bell once wrote, the "faces at the bottom of the well."

Nearly a decade after Obama's vacating office and Coates's having largely abandoned the discursive arena after having thrust open the doors for a new, less tortured, less equivocal, less modest, less literarily inclined, more powerful class of racial gurus, experts, thought leaders, indulgence sellers, and doomsayers, identity has become the single most potent prism through which all matters of discussion and dispute—certainly political and cultural, but even scientific—are now unceasingly filtered. In a perverse joke, to our national shame, our inability to make good on the genuine promise of post-racialism has corresponded—in a straight line leading from the Tea Party movement to Donald Trump, MAGA, and the QAnon conspiracy—to the sustained and immensely self-destructive, and, at times, frankly evil, yet increasingly multiethnic, backlash that we are still scrambling to contain.*

* In the 2024 presidential election, Donald Trump won 46 percent of the Latino vote, up from 32 percent in 2020. He doubled his support among black voters from 8 percent to 16 percent—winning a quarter of black men. His support among Asians shot up by 11 percent to 39 percent. These were the strongest numbers with nonwhite voters that a Republican has received since Richard Nixon. In other words, this was the least racially polarized election since 1972.

CHAPTER TWO

Donald Trump and the State of Exception

S ome revelations or events are so unprecedented, they so violate our sense of reality and so defy our usual heuristics and laws of experience, that they cannot immediately be integrated either emotionally or intellectually into our broader sense of how the world operates. We can see now that for a significant portion of the American population this was clearly what the Obama victory had amounted to—a flat-out debasement of the narrative fortifications their self-conceptions had always depended on. For the part of the country of which I happen to be a native—by no means a racial or geographic monolith, though strictly speaking a clear numerical majority—it was a later date, Tuesday, November 8, into the morning of Wednesday, November 9, 2016, that was a total assault on our shared epistemological framework. It hit with the nineteenth-century force of "God is dead" and, sure as the night follows the day, the subsequent, inevitable realization that now "everything is permitted." The norms, rules, and behavioral guardrails, those informal structures that had been put to stress in the past but, in holding up, had also been mistaken for formal truths, came crashing down around us with the swiftness of a new Copernican revolution, decimating an entire political, cultural, social, and intellectual cosmos in the process.

That particular Tuesday morning lingers in my memory with an eerie, almost dreamlike simplicity—a crisp, invigorating autumn day in New York City, the last one, it would turn out, in a prelapsarian innocence. I met old friends from college and more recent neighbors lining up to vote at the technical high school on South Elliott Avenue in Fort Greene, Brooklyn. There was a sense of shared civic purpose and goodwill even—perhaps especially—among perfect strangers. The collective positive energy snaking around the block was infectious, as voters of a large assortment of complexions, age-groups, and income brackets made small talk and sipped their coffee from paper cups and thermoses, I VOTED and I'M WITH HER stickers freshly plastered on their iPhone cases. Just three weeks prior, on the eve of the third and final presidential debate, *The New York Times* published a typical forecast granting Hillary Clinton a seemingly invincible 91 percent chance of victory. "At this point, even a large polling miss would not be enough for Mr. Trump to win," the *Times* assured us. "It will take a sudden and striking change in the fundamentals of the presidential race."

It was a calm and happy morning, and like everyone I interacted with, I felt certain that the bizarreness, vulgarity, and mendacity, the utter shamefulness of the interminable campaign season, would finally be put behind us. Every adult in eyesight had emerged to fulfill her civic duty and protect our democracy in a moment of unusual but—so it seemed to us—manageable vulnerability. I took in the scene, went to lunch, and did some last-minute shopping before driving to the airport that evening to fly back to my family in Paris. I was happy to have been in America at that decisive juncture and had spent the previous day on assignment in Manhattan, admiring the stunning, virtuosic brushstrokes of the painter Kerry James Marshall, whose retrospective *Mastry* was showing at the Met Breuer.

As I took in the immersive, phantasmagoric Marshall retrospective, I was struck continuously by the formal beauty of the artwork as well as the contextual banishment of not just whiteness but even mixedness or dark brownness in the canvases (though certainly not in the museum-going audiences). I thought of Albert Murray, who had once observed, "Any fool can see that the white people are not really white, and that black people are not black." As if to emphasize the literal truth of that statement, and to articulate the sheer and willful inaccuracy of the everyday language we rely on to sort others and ourselves into constricting abstract color categories that carry real social consequences, Marshall's subjects are rendered not as brown, nor even dark brown, but inhumanly black. His is a parallel world of bodies sheathed in licorice skin, as if to underscore the degree to which the projection of the idea of "race" onto living flesh destabilizes everything, above all our ability even to see what is objectively right in front of us.

The oddness of the subject's appearances aside, I thought, it is their intrinsic *Americanness*—these are not interlopers, upstarts, or new arrivals—that manifests itself in so many subtle and thought-provoking moments throughout the exhibition. One of the most arresting canvases, *Bang,* depicts a trio of jet-black children, one girl and two boys, standing in a spacious and pristine backyard replete with barbecue grill and white picket fence. The girl, with braided hair and a pink skirt, regards the boys while holding an American flag; the boys, dressed identically in white T-shirts and black-and-white Converse All Star sneakers, solemnly regard the flag, their right hands on their chests in salute. "WE ARE ONE," reads a banner curling beneath the children's feet, and down there too are four pink clouds. Marshall has painted the words "HAPPY JULY 4TH" on the first three, and the last says "BANG," an ambiguous onomatopoeia that could signify fireworks or something grimmer. This is their country, too, the painting would like to remind the viewer; whether that country wishes to reciprocate their pledge of allegiance or not is another question. It was a subtle and provocative, though not at all melancholy or despairing, statement.

From my perspective, I had seen the country reciprocate, not always, not perfectly, but many times over, more than I would ever be able to keep track of. Marshall's rich imagery still streaming in front of my mind's eye when I boarded the airplane, I recorded some thoughts about the show in my notebook:

"All Black Everything" was a phrase that became popular, briefly, around the release of Jay-Z and Kanye West's 2011 album, Watch the Throne. *A rallying cry as well as a sentiment tapping into the larger jubilation and sense of pride that the glamorous Obama presidency had sparked three years prior, it was also a tacit acknowledgment of the historical exclusion that black people had faced, especially at the higher levels of American culture. It was an exuberantly aspirational response to what the Chicago-based Marshall has described— via Ralph Ellison's* Invisible Man—*as "the simultaneity of presence and absence" specific to the African American plight.* Watch the Throne, *as Zadie Smith observed, "paints the world black: black bar mitzvahs, black cars, paintings of black girls in the MoMA, all black everything, as if it might be possible in a single album to peel back thousands of years of negative connotation. Black no longer the shadow or the reverse or the opposite of something but now the thing itself." Black, in other*

words, as just another kind of normal, but also at times a form of excellence.

I dozed off in my seat once the lights had dimmed. Last I'd checked before losing cellular connection, the *Times*'s continuously updated metric still displayed, as of 10:20 p.m. eastern time on November 8, an 85 percent to 15 percent probability of a Clinton victory. "Mrs. Clinton's chance of losing is about the same as the probability that an N.F.L. kicker misses a 37-yard field goal," the accompanying text explained in (what reads with hindsight) far too didactic and satisfied a fashion. The needle of the accompanying graphic dial on the *Times*'s home page angled leftward, almost horizontal in her direction.

The overnight trip between Kennedy Airport and Charles de Gaulle is one I've made scores of times. The lights come on, a black cup of coffee, muffin, yogurt, and plastic container of orange juice materialize on your tray as the captain addresses you in French and English alike. *Bonjour,* welcome to Paris, the local time is 9:00 a.m., temperature on the ground is sixteen degrees Celsius. It's a pleasant and forgettable routine, less a source of information than a bridge between sleeping and waking to guide you into the day when your body knows it is still night. The aircraft's slow descent through the thick and low northern European sky brings with it the first bars of cellular reception for those who don't abide by the strictures of airplane mode. I will never forget, on this particular morning, after the weather conditions had been announced, the pilot jogged us into memory of the political drama we'd left behind on another continent. "We do not have results yet," he said in a solemn tone, "votes are still being counted in several western states." That provoked murmurs around me and sounds of confusion and surprise. Like everyone else, I began to check my phone, and I loaded *The New York Times*. On that familiar graph was the smiling Hillary Clinton, the needle still decisively directed leftward, and then that first and then second bar of signal stuck, and I watched in real time the needle swing across the corner of my screen toward Trump, who had nearly a 90 percent chance of winning seemingly out of nowhere. This is when I suddenly became aware of several women in my cabin who were audibly crying. In at least one instance it would not be inappropriate to use the word "sobbing." It was an inconceivable turn of events I had never seriously envisioned despite the unprecedented length of campaigning that had preceded it. I felt as if I were still stranded in the nighttime, had not come to, had not yet awoken from my dreams, which had now become nightmares. The photos in the *Times* and elsewhere depicted half-shocked, fully emboldened young men in navy blazers and scarlet MAGA hats shaking clenched fists with crazed expressions of defiance, as they too drew unexpected conclusions from the most improbable news from Florida.

That entire week after Election Day is now lost to me. It felt—and I am not at all the only one to describe my feelings this way—as if someone close to me had died and I were sleepwalking away from the disaster. When a journalist friend admitted she was finding it difficult to work in those early days, I realized that I had not been able to accomplish much of anything either. I don't think it would be too much of an exaggeration to say that I had slipped into a mild, temporary state of depression; a particular image of my country had been sullied, and I understood no matter what else might happen in the future that stain, like blood or grease under a hot iron, would be permanent. It would be something that I would always have to see now. Living in a foreign country brings with it a jumble of bittersweet emotions, excitement tinged with nostalgia and regret, but at that moment all I felt was undiluted gratitude to be abroad, to walk into the street and go and pick up my three-year-old daughter from her day care, to stop on the way home for dry cleaning and groceries, and to share a meal with family and friends, not a single one of whom could be implicated in the summoning of this wild American debacle. France in particular and continental* Europe in general, despite the not insignificant problems they also faced, from paroxysms of terror, a staggering migrant crisis, and an ascendant xenophobic right-wing politics, felt like a stable, mature, and sober alternate reality I could seek tangible refuge in when I pulled myself from the dystopia that was my homeland whenever I ventured onto the internet.

If the election of a polished, highly intelligent, and meritocratic—indeed, an *excellent*—man of both European and African ancestry to the highest office in the United States, not to mention his conduct while president, rent the social fabric of a mongrel country that had over the centuries explicitly and implicitly organized itself in terms of the perceived inferiority of non-white people, especially those deemed "black," then the transition from a once-in-a-generation political talent to a pathologically dissembling and race-baiting con man lacking basic curiosity and qualifications ripped the cloth in two and soiled it.

The right-wing pejorative "Trump Derangement Syndrome" (TDS), reflexively deployed to dismiss any and all criticism of the president no matter how legitimate, was nonetheless rooted in something genuine and worth taking seriously—especially since it continued to plague us even in his absence. I suffered from TDS, and I don't think it's in any way an irrational autoimmune response to the scale of assault the scoundrel unleashed on our body politic.

* The fiasco of Brexit makes this unwieldy qualifier necessary.

Still, even perfectly understandable autoimmune reactions can spell unintended disaster when the system becomes so hypervigilant and alert to foreign threats it attacks healthy and normal cells, causing even greater damage. President Trump's election was worse than a contagion; it was more like that surreal crash against a pristine sky of a jumbo jet into the gleaming upper levels of the skyscraper of American society. His tenure, in ways both trivial and profound, would ignite the ensuing fire and extreme heat that has warped and snapped our psychological steel—weakening the democratic structure until all integrity had been exhausted and it collapsed onto itself, releasing dust clouds of lingering toxins as large as whole states. Trump by no means created all or even most of contemporary America's problems—indeed, it seems undeniable that no small part of his unusual and lasting appeal is the result of his very willingness to name and then complain about problems no one else within elite American life was even talking about* —but

---

* During the first GOP debate in 2015, in a blistering and hilarious appraisal of the bipartisan corruption everyday Americans know infests Washington, when the interviewer attempted to back Trump into a corner by pointing out his copious donations to liberal candidates, Trump's response was not to deny the charge but to attest to the pervasiveness of transactional politics:

> **Q:** You've also supported a host of other liberal policies, you've also donated to several Democratic candidates, Hillary Clinton included, Nancy Pelosi. You explained away those donations saying you did that to get business related favors. And you said recently, quote, when you give, they do whatever the hell you want them to do.
> **TRUMP:** You better believe it. . . . I will tell you that our system is broken. I gave to many people. Before this, before two months ago, I was a businessman. I give to everybody. When they call, I give. And you know what? When I need something from them, two years later, three years later, I call them. They are there for me. And that's a broken system.

his surpassing unprofessionalism, his meanness and mendacity, his consistent refusal to rise to the station, his ignorance and petty vindictiveness, exacerbated every single one of them, and we have not yet identified the cleanup crew who can deal with this magnitude of fallout.

"Bitter struggles deform their participants in subtle, complicated ways," Zadie Smith wrote. Trump's very presence forced the nation into a self-sabotaging bind. On the one hand, a reality TV charlatan with authoritarian and nepotistic tendencies, a deranged and belligerent temperament, and an ironclad, cultlike hold over millions of alienated, vulnerable, and polarized adherents increasingly divorced from a fact-based public square had captured the Republican Party and pursued a patently illiberal agenda. This was certainly bad enough. Yet, on the other hand, the very cultural, media, and academic institutions that were meant to safeguard the best of our birthright, our consistently improving liberal democracy, from precisely such threats, and to fortify bedrock norms of tolerance—freedom of expression, search for objective truth, and the open exchange of ideas—were rapidly, even happily, caving to another form of extremism coming from the energized left to oppose him. Some of the most influential voices in the country now professed to believe that the basic framework and baked-in assumptions of American liberalism itself were part of the problem.*

Q: So what did you get from Hillary Clinton and Nancy Pelosi?
TRUMP: I'll tell you what. With Hillary Clinton, I said, be at my wedding and she came to my wedding. You know why? She had no choice! Because I gave.

* See: Nikole Hannah-Jones, "Our Democracy's Founding Ideals Were False When They Were Written. Black Americans Have Fought to Make Them True," *New York Times Magazine,* Aug. 14, 2019.

Trump's election therefore ballooned into a veritable crisis of legitimacy far outstripping even what had occurred at the turn of the century when George W. Bush assumed the presidency under extremely contestable circumstances in Florida, and on the self-anointed and debatable authority of the Supreme Court. Trump's Electoral College victory—and like Bush's, his consequential loss in the popular vote—were not met with the magnanimous country-first stewardship personified by Al Gore. By contrast, they ushered in an unprecedented and often wholly irrational *state of exception* that has justified opposition to his person as well as his larger populist agenda on any terrain, by any means necessary or expedient. This mutual antagonism began before the inauguration* with the widespread suspension of disbelief around the discredited "Steele dossier" and its motivated accusations of Russian collusion,† worsened after the overtly racist tiki-torch march on Charlottesville, Virginia, as well as Trump's awkward commentary about it that was nonetheless willfully distorted, and during the slow-rolling drama of COVID-19. It culminated in a season of toxic mayhem four years later, after the 2020 election, reaching its nadir on January 6, 2021, during the spectacular insurrection at the Capitol.

Two Januarys prior to that singular, appallingly un-American day of rebellion, in 2019, a group of high school students from Covington Catholic, in Park Hills, Kentucky, had traveled all the way to Washington, D.C., for the annual March for Life demonstration, one of the largest pro-life events in the country. That manifestation was in no way commensurate with the events of January 6, 2021,

---

* The turnout for which—orders of magnitude smaller than Obama's—Trump brazenly exaggerated, trolling his critics.

† Note: this is not to make the logical mistake that an absence of evidence equals evidence of absence.

but some of these teenagers did wear scarlet-red Make America Great Again caps that in and of themselves had become in broad swaths of the mainstream imagination unambiguous signifiers of overt white supremacy along the lines of the Confederate flag or Nazi insignia. On the Mall, the students encountered a smattering of Black Hebrew Israelites, a purely outlandish religious cult whose adherents—American descendants of African slaves—delusionally claim to be the true living link to the Israelites of the Old Testament, the storied "chosen people" of Yahweh. Like most other outlets reporting on this gathering, CNN would gullibly describe these cultists as "four African American young men preaching about the Bible and oppression."*

It was a stroke of all-American coincidence that the Indigenous Peoples March also happened to be held in that space on that day. Video emerged and quickly went viral depicting an elderly Native American man, Nathan Phillips, beating a tribal drum while a boy in MAGA paraphernalia stares him down smiling. The boy's classmates are horsing around like young, innocuous fools in the background as he and the man "are locked into something, but what is it?" Caitlin Flanagan wrote in *The Atlantic*. "Twenty seconds pass, then 30—and still the boy is smiling in that peculiar way. What has brought them to this strange, charged moment?"

The New York Times soon weighed in decisively under the headline "Viral Video Shows Boys in 'Make America Great Again' Hats Surrounding Native Elder." Celebrities, activists, and millions of random accounts also flocked to social media to register their dismay, fear, and alarm at what American society had ostensibly become under the instigation of Donald Trump—a country where racists

---

* This is not so different from describing a fifth-floor window simply as an exit from a building.

were now emboldened to roam freely and prey upon any non-white person they encountered. They wore their bigotry proudly. "This is Trump's America. And it brought me to tears," the actress Alyssa Milano tweeted. "What are we teaching our young people? Why is this ok? How is this ok? Please help me understand. Because right now I feel like my heart is living outside of my body." Yet another video soon began to be shared, and in this one Phillips, with tears in his eyes, weighs in: "As I was singing, I heard them saying, 'Build that wall, build that wall.' This is indigenous land; we're not supposed to have walls here. We never did. . . . We never had a wall. We never had a prison. We always took care of our elders." A Vietnam veteran, Phillips became an instant online hero, an emblem of wizened integrity in the face of clear and looming danger.

And yet, as Flanagan continues, *another, fuller* video of the encounter would subsequently emerge; this one, some two whole hours in length, was shot by the Black Hebrew Israelites themselves:

> The full video reveals that there was indeed a Native American gathering at the Lincoln Memorial, that it took place shortly before the events of the viral video, and that during it the indigenous people had been the subject of a hideous tirade of racist insults and fantasies. *But the white students weren't the people hurling this garbage at them—the young "African American men preaching about the Bible and oppression" were doing it.* (Emphasis mine.)

At one point, an Israelite preacher addresses a Native American in costume, "You're not supposed to worship eagles, buffalos, rams, all types of animals," he taunts him. In the back-and-forth that ensues—precisely the kind of antagonistic opposition that increasingly arises in a multiethnic society of the sheer scale of the United

States, which has become far too complex for the historical black-white* binary to adequately capture—many more ridiculous things are said to a Native woman, and more offense is taken, until, suddenly, the Israelite spots the teenagers and draws them in: "It's because of these . . . bastards over there, wearing 'Make America Great Again' hats." Here is Flanagan again:

> The camera turns to capture five white teenage boys, one of whom is wearing a MAGA hat. They are standing at a respectful distance, with their hands in their pockets, listening to this exchange with expressions of curiosity. They are there to meet their bus home.
>
> "Why you not angry at them?" the Black Hebrew Israelite asks the Native American woman angrily.
>
> "That's right," says one of his coreligionists, "little corny-ass Billy Bob."
>
> The boys don't respond to this provocation, although one of them smiles at being called a corny-ass Billy Bob. They seem interested in what is going on, in the way that it's interesting to listen to Hyde Park speakers.
>
> The Native woman isn't interested in attacking the white boys. She keeps up her argument with the Black Hebrew Israelites, and her line of reasoning is so powerful that it throws the preacher off track.
>
> "She trying to be distracting," one of the men says. "She trying to stop the flow."

* Or even the more sophisticated but woefully insufficient "POC"-white binary that wishes to replace it. This dynamic would be on much more flagrant display as the spate of brazen, unprovoked physical attacks and even killings of Asian Americans by black Americans during the pandemic became a subject the mainstream media could not find the language to make sense of.

"You're out of order," the preacher tells the woman. "Where's your husband? Let me speak to him."

By now the gathering of Covington Catholic boys watching the scene has grown to 10 or 12, some of them in MAGA hats. They are about 15 feet away, and while the conflict is surely beyond their range of experience, it also includes biblical explication, something with which they are familiar.

"Don't stand to the side and mock," the speaker orders the boys, who do not appear to be mocking him. "Bring y'all cracker ass up here and make a statement." The boys turn away and begin walking back to the larger group.

"You little dirty-ass crackers. Your day coming. Your day coming . . . 'cause your little dusty asses wouldn't walk down a street in a black neighborhood, and go walk up on nobody playing no games like that," he calls after them, but they take no notice. "Yeah, 'cause I will stick my foot in your little ass."

By now the Native American ceremony has begun, and the attendees have linked arms and begun dancing. "They just don't know who they are," one of the Black Hebrew Israelites says remorsefully to another. Earlier he had called them "Uncle Tomahawks."

The boys have given up on him. They have joined the larger group, and together they all begin doing some school-spirit cheers; they hum the stadium-staple opening bars of "Seven Nation Army" and jump up and down, dancing to it. Later they would say that their chaperones had allowed them to sing school-spirit songs instead of engaging with the slurs hurled by the Black Hebrew Israelites.

And then you hear the sound of drumming, and Phillips appears with several other drummers, all of them headed to the large group of boys. "Here come Gad!" says the Black

Hebrew Israelite excitedly. His religion teaches that Native Americans are one of the 12 tribes of Israel, Gad. Apparently he thinks that his relentless attack on the Native Americans has led some of them to confront the white people. "Here come Gad!" he says again, but he is soon disappointed. "Gad not playing! He came to the rescue!" [. . .]

The drummers head to the boys, and keep playing. The boys, who had been jumping to "Seven Nation Army," start jumping in time to the drumming. Phillips takes a step toward the group, and then—as it parts to admit him—he walks into it. Here the Black Hebrew Israelites' footage is of no help, as Phillips has moved into the crowd.

Now we may look at the viral video—or, as a CNN chyron called it, the "heartbreaking viral video"—as well as the many others that have since emerged, none of which has so far revealed the boys to be chanting anything about a wall or about making America great again. Phillips keeps walking into the group, they make room for him, and then—the smiling boy. One of the videos shows him doing something unusual. At one point he turns away from Phillips, stops smiling, and locks eyes with another kid, shaking his head, seeming to say the word *no*. This is consistent with the long, harrowing statement that the smiling boy would release at the end of the weekend, in which he offered an explanation for his actions that is consistent with the video footage that has so far emerged, and revealed what happened to him in the 48 hours after Americans set to work doxing him and threatening his family with violence. As of this writing, it seems that the smiling boy, Nick Sandmann, is the one person who tried to be respectful of Phillips and who encouraged the other boys to do the same.

The Covington Catholic story is significant not because the teen-age boys from Kentucky are some victims or paragons of upright behavior, or because MAGA paraphernalia is *always* misunderstood and Trump supporters always or even usually occupy the moral high ground. None of that need be true. It is important and worth remembering because it is an instance of a critical mass of legacy media, left-of-center celebrities, public figures, influencers, and activists collectively jerry-rigging events and news stories to neatly fit their biases and prior assumptions. In so doing, they empower and help legitimize the very populist and reactionary forces in society they ostensibly want to eradicate. Days after it became clear that there was zero evidence of a racist mobbing, at least not by anyone who could be plausibly described as white, and that Nathan Phillips for that matter was not even a Vietnam vet, another, even more harrowing instance of predatory, pervasive white supremacy transfixed social and traditional media.

In the frigid early morning hours of January 29, a thirty-six-year-old actor named Jussie Smollett, who identifies as black and gay, and who had been a cast member of the hit Fox soap opera *Empire,* was brutally attacked by two men who screamed racial and sexual epithets in the name of Donald Trump's political movement, according to the celebrity news website TMZ, which broke the story. The incendiary tale shot around the internet, generating as much outrage and condemnation as you would imagine. Smollett had claimed to have arrived in Chicago from New York late on Monday, January 28. Then, around two in the morning, overcome by hunger, he ventured to a Subway franchise to procure a sandwich in the middle of the freezing midwestern night. "Aren't you that faggot *Empire* nigger?" someone allegedly screamed when he left the shop. And then, all of a sudden, "the 2 men—both white and wearing ski masks—viciously attacked Jussie as he fought back, but they beat him badly and fractured a rib," TMZ reported. "They put a rope around his neck, poured bleach on him and as they left they yelled, 'This is MAGA country.'"

The Chicago police noted that Smollett oddly sported his noose, like a prize or an ornament, when he made contact with them nearly forty-five minutes after the assault. He then took himself to Northwestern Memorial, where he was treated and discharged later that morning. It was also reported that eight days prior, around the same time the Covington Catholic boys were thought to be terrorizing the Mall in Washington, a not at all subtle anonymous letter was delivered to Fox Studios in Chicago with cutout letters that spelled, "You will die black fag."

None of these outrageous claims raised suspicions as the story was credulously repeated throughout the press and further amplified across social media. When *Vanity Fair* wrote about Ellen Page's *Late Show* appearance two days later, the publication noted in a you-go-girl tone that it had "turned emotional as the actress addressed the racist, homophobic attack on Jussie Smollett that occurred in Chicago earlier this week. Page condemned not only the attack, but also a government that she said has at least tacitly encouraged this violence." Indeed, Page (now Elliot Page) seized the bully pulpit, confidently calling out the Trump administration for fostering a climate of hate in the United States, specifically against the queer community. "It's absurd," Page said. "The [expletive] isn't a debate." Page, who is white, added that they were "fired up," because it was "impossible to not to [sic] feel this way right now with the president and the vice president, Mike Pence, who, like, wishes I couldn't be married, let's just be clear." Page then told the audience to "connect the dots," explicitly linking a rise in crimes against marginalized people in the United States to the views often espoused by the current administration. "If you are in a position of power and you hate people and you want to cause suffering to them, you go through the trouble, you spend your career trying to cause suffering, what do you think is going to happen?" Page triumphantly concluded.

The organizations GLAAD and Color of Change also released a special video featuring Hollywood luminaries and activists including Ava DuVernay, Lena Waithe, Keiynan Lonsdale, and Wilson Cruz "to expose the harsh reality of being a black LGBTQ person in America," according to *Billboard* magazine. "The actors, directors, and activists all vow to never allow the horrific experiences black LGBTQ people have faced 'to be erased.'"

An impromptu, A-list chorus of reprimand scrambled to weigh in on Twitter. The star of *Scandal,* Kerry Washington, tweeted, "DEAR GOD! Prayers and justice for Jussie Smollett." Cynthia Nixon, the former New York gubernatorial candidate and *Sex and the City* actress, posted her gratitude to Smollett for being "an out and proud artist and activist, and a hero to so many of us—no small feat in the face of racism and homophobia." The writer Roxane Gay tweeted, "I am so sorry to hear what happened to @JussieSmollett," and added that she was "committed to holding this administration and its ilk accountable for this hothouse of hate being fostered." The pop star Katy Perry wrote, "Standing with and sending love to @JussieSmollett today . . . this is a racist hate crime and is disgusting and shameful to our country."

Not to be outdone, politicians chimed in, too. Nancy Pelosi, then Speaker of the House, tweeted, "The racist, homophobic attack on @JussieSmollett is an affront to our humanity. No one should be attacked for who they are or whom they love. I pray that Jussie has a speedy recovery & that justice is served. May we all commit to ending this hate once & for all."

Senator Cory Booker, a former and likely future presidential candidate, wrote, "The vicious attack on actor Jussie Smollett was an attempted modern-day lynching. I'm glad he's safe. To those in Congress who don't feel the urgency to pass our Anti-Lynching bill designating lynching as a federal hate crime—I urge you to pay attention."

Then senator and later vice president Kamala Harris tweeted, "@JussieSmollett is one of the kindest, most gentle human beings I know. I'm praying for his quick recovery. This was an attempted modern-day lynching. No one should have to fear for their life because of their sexuality or color of their skin. We must confront this hate."

And Alexandria Ocasio-Cortez, the icon of the millennial left, tweeted, "There is no such thing as 'racially charged.' This attack was not 'possibly' homophobic. It was a racist and homophobic attack. . . . It is no one's job to water down or sugar-coat the rise of hate crimes."

Perhaps more noteworthy than even the total homogeneity of thought and locution is that no one of any stature in the cultural and political mainstream counterbalanced it; no figure of significance or influence so much as acknowledged the *possibility* that there could be more to the story than the dubious and self-aggrandizing claims being levied. Nor could many notable progressives simply remain neutral on the matter until an investigation had been completed and the facts had been established. On the contrary, countless thought leaders, influencers, and Democratic power brokers felt *compelled* to use their individually and collectively enormous platforms to boost one damaged and narcissistic man's fantastical cry for attention, considering themselves courageously outspoken in so doing.

The inevitable effect was to further discredit and water down in the minds of millions of Americans the very real and necessary criticisms of the Trump administration that more serious people were making. The Smollett hate-crime hoax hemorrhaged moral authority and credibility on the left. It isn't hard to see why. The collective rush to judgment, the total lack of skepticism, and the mimetic, copycat language silenced more ambivalent onlookers and preemptively shut down critical thinking in public. In his 1961 book, *Thought Reform and the Psychology of Totalism: A Study of "Brainwashing" in China,* Robert Jay Lifton described emotionally charged phrases and slogans that are used to dismiss or prevent complex analysis or examination of ambiguous events and ideas as "thought-terminating clichés." In all of the Smollett hate-crime-hoax commentary, the copied-and-pasted use of hypercharged terminology, most disturbingly and repeatedly "modern-day lynching," a phrase that would come back with force in 2020,* exemplifies precisely the kind of manipulative rhetorical tactic that is a common feature of authoritarian ideological systems and movements. And it wasn't coming from Trump; it was coming from his so-called left-liberal opponents who were open to *any* story, no matter how ludicrous on its face, that could affirm what they had already decided to believe.

In late 2021, a jury unanimously found Smollett guilty of falsely reporting that he had been the victim of a racist and homophobic assault. Prosecutors successfully argued in court, with ample text message and surveillance video evidence, that the actor had in fact *hired* two Nigerian brothers, Abimbola Osundairo and Olabinjo Osundairo, to punch him "only hard enough to create a bruise, pour bleach on his clothing and place a rope around his neck like a noose," according to *The New York Times*.

Chicago officials, rightfully incensed about the resources Smollett's farce had caused them to squander in a hyper-violent city where there were 567 murders in 2018, sued the actor to recoup

---

* And again in 2023 with the death on the New York City subway of Jordan Neely at the hands of Daniel Penny.

some of the city's losses. After potentially perjuring himself on the witness stand, Smollett testified, "I am a black man in America. I do not trust police. Sorry, that is the truth." None of the celebrities and politicians who had voluntarily hyped the well-connected performer's stunt—which the *New York Post* accurately described as a social-justice-inflected "21st-century version of a 1980s abducted-by-aliens story"—issued public apologies or corrections. "Nancy Pelosi quietly deleted a supportive tweet," *Vanity Fair* reported. "Cory Booker . . . declined to comment on new developments, as did Kamala Harris. 'I think the facts are still unfolding, and I'm very concerned,' Harris told a reporter at a New Hampshire town hall, after taking several painfully long seconds to formulate a response."

The Covington Catholic and Jussie Smollett debacles are perhaps fleeting culture war flash points, but they are not at all a distraction from the more important challenges facing the country, and it is not an indulgence to dwell on them. They are, on the contrary, the embodiment and natural culmination of larger and deeper dynamics that have made possible the subtle and blunt ways that basic liberal norms came to be jettisoned, first by the right and then—in reaction—increasingly by the left. The country is not a graduate program and never has been. Academics and activists have made postmodern, identity-inflected arguments for decades now, but the *singular* threat and perceived evil of Donald Trump and the voters he excites allowed what most Americans—white, black, and everything in between—would consider niche extremism and identitarian solipsism to find fresh and far more receptive hearings. His specter exposed a schizophrenia within "whiteness" itself and fostered a union of far left, educated cultural elites and a (sometimes imaginary) black and brown client class whose rage and plight have been fruitfully engaged but also frequently co-opted and manipulated for ends that do not necessarily address their own needs.

Quite simply, the racial reckoning, or "revolution" against white supremacy and racism,* immediately became a professional-class affair, existing on another plane entirely from working-class reality. This in turn produced the initially counterintuitive yet demonstrably growing demographic of so-called POC Trump supporters, for whom a slew of dismissive neologisms have had to be invented, most tellingly the oxymoronic "multiracial whiteness."[†]

To what extent, then, must we all bear degrees of responsibility for the social and political morass in which we find ourselves? The obsession with identity and valorous narratives of marginalization and oppression, which we have not only clung to but also nurtured and strengthened, might have actually cultivated the very divisions and tensions it purported to combat. In some cases, this fixation even conjured racism and oppression out of thin air when organic reality could not provide an adequate supply. Any assessment of the recurring Trump nightmare that fails to take these reservations seriously is not only woefully incomplete but also actively contributes to our long-term political insecurity.

---

* As well as patriarchy, Islamophobia, homophobia, transphobia, fatphobia, xenophobia, ableism, neurotypicality, and more.

[†] This is the idea that whiteness extends beyond individuals who are designated racially white to involve cultural norms and social practices thought to uphold white dominance and value systems more generally—even among racially and ethnically non-white people. In other words, in this framework, certain ideas, politics, attitudes, and behaviors are able to *deracinate* so-called people of color, strip them of agency, and reduce them to vehicles of white supremacy with or without their consent in the matter.

CHAPTER THREE

The Plague

O n March 16 my family and I took whatever clothes, books, and toys we could think to grab, ordered a taxi across a vacant Paris and joined a throng of masked travelers at the Gare Montparnasse. As we idled under the LCD monitors, waiting anxiously for the arrival of the trains that would shoot out of the station to various destinations along the country's western reaches, I was aware that we were all of us reenacting a scene that has played out repeatedly over this city's dramatic past.

The day we left, after a week of growing alarm over the spread of the novel coronavirus and decreasing freedom in the attempt to limit the contagion, starting with the closure of schools and swiftly followed by the shuttering of "nonessential" businesses, President Emmanuel Macron was scheduled to address the nation in the evening. He would, as many anticipated, order total home confinement. The only question for anyone with options was where to go to endure it. We barely had a chance to contemplate our decision.

The day before we ended up leaving, by sheer chance we were having lunch with our friends Jordan and Sophie, who had their own young children and an acquaintance in government kind enough to give them advance warning. These friends patiently impressed upon us the severity of what was about to happen. We were going to be housebound for at least the next fifteen days, but in truth, they said, it would be much longer. Our friends would be leaving in a few hours for Sophie's family home in a small village near the Atlantic Ocean. Would we like to hunker down with them? At least this way the kids would have a yard to expand into. Once the order was made official, it would be much more difficult to move around the country.

I had been particularly slow to grasp or take seriously the scale of the debacle that was enveloping the globe from its epicenter of incompetence, opacity, and deceit in China. Just a few weeks prior, I'd been in New York, feeling sorry for myself when I'd had a long-scheduled appearance to promote my new book on a television show in Los Angeles canceled to make room for coverage of the virus. (A preposterous reaction in retrospect, but such is the myopia of self-concern in the moment.) At the time, I thought everyone was overreacting and stubbornly traveled to London to do a reading when I returned to Europe. Even the hacking cough and blinding fever I brought home with me to Paris didn't properly register, so conditioned was I to overlook or misperceive the new reality. But that afternoon, something about Jordan's serenity mixed with certainty got through to me, and I took his laptop and reserved what appeared to be four of the last tickets available to La Baule-Escoublac before confinement, departing the following morning. None of us realized it then or even many months later, but this would be the last normal day in the old, pre-COVID-19 paradigm that any of us would experience.

· · ·

Still, that strangely beautiful and temperate season—one of the loveliest, most sun-drenched springs I can remember in Europe—and those slow, repetitive nights and days under self-administered quarantine and communal living were by no means miserable or primarily defined by deprivation. They were oddly kinetic and inspiring. These were full days, restorative, contemplative, and highly productive. I missed my parents and friends and family profoundly, but the miracle of social media and magic of WhatsApp and FaceTime provided genuine and powerful consolation. The need and opportunity to be directly present and involved in my children's daily routines was a tremendous and unexpected bonus. Deprived of, or freed from, the outside world's enticements, I shared in the simple necessity of household cooking, cleaning, and shopping; in my free time, I wrote and published essays, reread the works of Camus and Baldwin, played sports regularly with Jordan, and adopted—with the ample knowledge available on YouTube and Instagram—a calisthenics regimen that left my body stronger than I had ever known it. I was by no means an outlier. Everyone around me or with whom I corresponded also seemed to be embarking on ambitious and sometimes radical projects of self-improvement. Like so many high-achieving professionals suddenly grounded, Sophie had taken up baking our daily bread and diligently working her way most evenings through the Ottolenghi cookbook, to everyone's benefit. After dinner, once the kids were down, Jordan, a film critic with an encyclopedic knowledge of the format, systematically guided us through an enthralling program of 1970s American cinema.

So common was the impulse to squeeze lemons into lemonade, and channel the adversity of lockdown into some tangible form of personal growth, there inevitably followed a whole cottage industry of *anti*-productivity resentment and backlash. "Shakespeare, as people reminded each other, wrote *King Lear* when he was quarantined during a plague,"* Constance Grady noted in an article on *Vox* from April 2020. "And then, inevitably, came the whispered implication: Shouldn't you yourself be using this time at home— dare we say this *gift*—because you are at home and not working in an essential field? Shouldn't you be using this time to become more productive? Shouldn't you be buckling down and writing a masterpiece or inventing a genre or discovering fundamental laws of the universe? At the very least, shouldn't you be taking up a new hobby, mastering a skill, or perhaps be reaching your fully fledged form as what *Forbes* termed a 'coronapreneur?'" Early on, this Weber-esque mood of accomplishment was linked with disturbing racial implications. In the first place, even the very circumstance of sheltering in place was predicated on the ability—or the *privilege*—to earn one's livelihood at a distance. So-called essential jobs—making deliveries, stocking shelves, nursing the sick, cashiering groceries—that required venturing out into the pandemic and risking one's health and well-being were disproportionately distributed among black and other non-white populations, or, at the very least, the white working classes.

"Time-oriented productivity was invented by industrial capitalism," the *Vox* article continued, which is also a way of implying, to a certain kind of progressive (and receptive) reader, that it is ineluctably a form of what we would increasingly be taught to think of as "white supremacy culture." This was a gesture toward a critique that would become much more common and pronounced

---

* Johnny Cash's daughter Rosanne received 214,000 likes for this tweet on March 14, 2020: "Just a reminder that when Shakespeare was quarantined because of the plague, he wrote King Lear."

in America and elsewhere as the pandemic wore on. But in those early months a great many people retained their positivity and optimism, and sincerely attempted to use the imposition of solitude and interrupted workflow to improve their own well-being and that of the people around them. These were still the heady, quixotic days when New Yorkers gathered at their windowsills and on rooftops and balconies every evening to give earnest public thanks to the city's medical personnel and other frontline workers.

Not everyone was able or inclined to make the best of a messy and complicated—and above all profoundly confusing—situation. In France, we dutifully strapped on our surgical masks and executed our electronic permission slips before driving in twos to the supermarket and wiping down our bananas and other victuals with disinfectant, mostly suffering in silence. Those of us who stayed at home did our best to educate and discipline our children and help them connect to school videoconferences if they were old enough. The government had been firm, in a nationally unified way that would be far stricter and even more authoritarian, and for longer, than happened in most Western societies, with the exception of Australia. And yet there were no meaningful or violent protests or political and social divisions over the epidemiology that I was aware of. Wearing a mask—effective or ineffective as it might have proven to be—was simply a means of trying to stave off contagion, not a proxy for progressive or conservative tribal alignment. The gesture, in France, never implied a larger totemic status or statement of one's political orientation. Which is not to say I knew anyone who was especially *delighted* to have her freedoms curtailed or her ambit drawn smaller. As the months wore on, some of us would bend and flout the rules, grow less conscientious about those ridiculous permission slips or distancing measures—and no one really felt like wiping down the provisions—but actually lashing out and rebelling against the pandemic or the government and medical establishment that was trying, ineptly as it might have seemed but trying nonetheless, to combat the disease felt pointless, undignified even. It made about as much sense as punching at the shoreline in retribution for flooding.

And yet I watched the images on my computer screen in amazement as videos spread around the world of riled-up Americans in places like Florida and Texas and Michigan massed in open and often childlike rebellion. These odd freedom fighters shamelessly confronted, attacked, and even coughed and spat on cashiers and other low-wage workers for daring to enforce their companies' hygienic policies. Such furious behaviors soon took on a bizarre and extraordinarily antagonistic partisan inflection that was decidedly American. Most disturbingly, they were encouraged and to an important degree legitimized by the singularly unpresidential president tasked with guiding the country through this intensely felt time of confusion. Reactively, many to the left of Trump embraced a kind of pandemic orthodoxy and ideological counter-allegiance to lockdowns, masking, and distancing that could itself be extremely irrational and contradictory to the swiftly evolving science. With devastating results, across the board Americans' response to the unprecedented challenge of the coronavirus became dangerously and competitively entangled with one's very sense of personal and group *identity*—the very opposite of what was needed.

When I reflect on that outrageous year of 2020, one of the two defining images in my mind is the surreal figure of the Grim Reaper stalking the blazing Florida coast, scythe in hand, warning the sunbathing hordes of imminent death, and granting interviews to reporters.* There couldn't be a more apt distillation of the squalid condition of ignorance and impotence—mixed with proselytizing self-righteousness—we'd all been thrust in. The other, of course, is a prostrate George Floyd, whose excruciating Memorial Day execution at the sudden conjunction of burgeoning summer restlessness and soul-crushing vigilance sparked a global protest movement against racism and police violence.

Less than two weeks after Floyd's killing, the American death toll from COVID-19 had surpassed 100,000. Rates of infection, domestically and worldwide, were rising. But one of the few things it is possible to say without qualification of that moment is that the country had finally reopened. For thirteen days straight, in cities across the nation, tens of thousands of men and women gathered in tight-knit proximity, with and without personal protective equipment, often clashing with armed forces, chanting, singing, and inevitably increasing the chances of the spread of contagion.

Scenes of outright pandemonium began unfolding daily. Anyone who claimed to have a precise understanding of what exactly was happening, and what the likely risks and consequences could have been, ought to have been regarded with the utmost skepticism. We were living in a techno-dystopian fantasy, the internet-connected portals we'd come to rely on rendered the world in all its granular detail and absurdity, like Borges's Aleph, yet we scarcely knew a thing about what it was we were viewing.

---

* "Daniel Uhlfelder dons a raggedy black robe, conceals his face with a black cloth and wields his scythe," CNN reported. "Uhlfelder, an attorney, is haunting Florida beaches dressed as the Grim Reaper to protest their reopening, which he believes is premature. . . . 'We aren't at the point now where we have enough testing, enough data, enough preparation for what's going to be coming to our state from all over the world from this pandemic,' the lawyer told CNN."

I remember opening my laptop and glimpsing a rider on horse-back galloping through the Chicago streets like Ras the Destroyer in Ralph Ellison's *Invisible Man;* I scrolled down farther and found myself suddenly in Los Angeles, as the professional basketball star J. R. Smith pummeled a scrawny white anarchist who'd just smashed his car window. I kept going and encountered an ethni-cally mixed group of business owners in Van Nuys risking their lives to defend their businesses from rampaging looters; the black com-munity members trying to assist them were swiftly and appallingly rounded up by police officers who'd mistaken them for criminals. Over in Buffalo, a seventy-five-year-old white man approached a police phalanx and was brutally thrown to the pavement; ribbons of blood looped from his ear as the police continued to march right over him. Looming behind all of this chaos was a reality TV lunatic giddily tweeting exhortations to mass murder, only venturing out of his bunker to tear-gas peaceful protesters and stage propaganda pictures in front of St. John's Church, across from his perch in the White House.

But the virus knew and respected none of this overarching socio-political context. Its killing trajectory was not rational, emotional, or ethical; it was strictly mathematical. And just as two plus two is four, when a flood comes, low-lying areas are hit hardest. Relatively poor, densely clustered populations with underlying conditions suf-fered disproportionately in any environment in which COVID-19 flourished. Even though they are a mere 13 percent of the popula-tion, already one-fifth of those 100,000 deaths belonged to black Americans.

After two and a half months of death, confinement, and unem-ployment figures dwarfing even the Great Depression, we had entered the stage of competing urgencies where there could be no perfect options, only trade-offs. One could grasp how police brutality might plausibly be described as a different if metaphorical epidemic in an America slouching toward authoritarianism. And in light of the spectacle of Floyd's reprehensible death, it was clear that the emergency in Minneapolis surpassed my own and many other people's threshold for justifying the risk of contagion in leaving their homes to peacefully demand accountability and justice.

But so long as we are speaking analogically, poverty is certainly another kind of public health crisis. It cannot be overstated: George Floyd was not simply or even necessarily killed on account of race—a point very few Americans of any stripe were willing to admit—his death was very much a function of his being *impoverished*. He died over a counterfeit banknote the vast majority of black people would never come to possess. Poverty destroys Americans of all colors every day by means of lopsided confrontations with the law, exposure to all manner of sickness and disease, substance abuse, environmental degradation, and pollution, neighborhood and domestic violence, and above all existential despair. Yet even as the coronavirus lockdown threw forty million Americans out of work—including, it must be stressed, Floyd himself—many progressives nonetheless accepted this calamity, sometimes with stunning blitheness, as the necessary cost of guarding against COVID-19.

The accepted "correct" narrative about public health—that one kind of crisis had suddenly superseded the other—grew shakier as it spanned out from Minnesota, across the country and overseas, as far away as London, Amsterdam, and Paris, foreign cities that also saw extraordinary manifestations of public solidarity against both distinctly American and local racism, with protesters in the many thousands flooding public spaces.

France began reopening after two solid months of severe national quarantine and in the face of the fifth-highest coronavirus body count. As late as May 11, state-administered permission slips were still a necessary precondition for exercising or shopping. The country had only just begun to flatten its steep death curve— nearly thirty thousand at the time*—which brought its economy to a standstill. Yet even there, in the time it took to upload a black square to an Instagram profile, those of us who moved in progressive circles found ourselves under significant moral pressure to understand that social distancing was now an issue of merely secondary importance.

How could this not feel like gaslighting or something far more devious? Less than two weeks before the death of George Floyd, the enlightened position in both Europe and America was to exercise nothing less than extreme caution and restraint. Many of us went further still, voluntarily taking to social media to castigate others for insufficient social distancing or neglecting to wear masks or daring to believe they could maintain some semblance of a normal life during the outbreak. This was part of what it meant to be a good and responsible citizen in a moment of extraordinary ignorance, selfishness, and race- and class-based inequality and unequal exposure to risk. It was those selfish MAGA cultists who had zero empathy for their fellow citizens—specifically the ones who were not white—or investment in the collective good. They lacked the simple decency just to stay inside. This is the story we told. At the end of April, when the State of Georgia moved to end its lockdown, one major magazine ran an article with the headline "Georgia's Experiment in Human Sacrifice." In the space of two weeks and without really thinking it through, we went from shaming people for being in the street to shaming them for *not* being in the street.

* At one point, the world's fourth-highest death toll.

It is a statement of basic fact that as the direct consequence of lockdowns and quarantines many millions of people around the world lost their income, depleted their savings, missed farewells and funerals of loved ones, postponed cancer screenings, never experienced graduations and proms, at times went without human touch entirely, and generally put their lives on pause for the indefinite future. They accepted these sacrifices as awful but necessary when confronted by an otherwise unstoppable virus. And then, from one day to the next, they were told with a straight face that this had all been done in vain. "The risks of congregating during a global pandemic shouldn't keep people from protesting racism," NPR announced with eyebrow-raising certitude, citing a letter signed by dozens of American public health officials and disease experts. "White supremacy is a lethal public health issue that predates and contributes to COVID-19," the letter further explained. One prominent epidemiologist went still further, arguing that the public health risks of *not* protesting for an end to systemic racism "greatly exceed the harms of the virus."

What was a serious person to make of such whiplash-inducing messaging? At the time, merely pointing out the inconsistency in such a polarized landscape felt tantamount to heresy. And yet "'Your gatherings are a threat, but mine aren't' is fundamentally illogical, no matter who says it or for what reason," as the author of *The Death of Expertise,* Tom Nichols, wrote. "We've been told for months to stay as isolated as humanely possible," Suzy Khimm, an NBC reporter covering COVID-19, noted, but "some of the same public officials and epidemiologists are [now] saying it's OK to go to mass gatherings—but only certain ones."

Public health experts—as well as many mainstream commentators, plenty of whom in the beginning of the pandemic were already incoherent about the importance of face masks* and stay-at-home orders—hemorrhaged their credibility and authority here. It turns out, this wasn't merely a short-term problem either. It has constituted nothing less than a crisis of trust in a country already lacking a shared sense of reality or mutual responsibility in the years following the early halcyon days of the Obama era.† As it became

---

* In 2021, Deborah Netburn, staff writer at the *Los Angeles Times* published a comprehensive timeline of the CDC's advice on face masks. In the earliest days of the pandemic, before mass lockdowns, the U.S. surgeon general assured the public that face masks would not protect the public against the virus, going as far as tweeting, "Seriously people- STOP BUYING MASKS!" This tweet was later deleted. Even after mass lockdowns were implemented, the CDC held the line that healthy individuals not in close contact with the infected did not need to wear masks. However, in April 2020, the CDC recommended everyone over the age of two mask up in public, a sharp pivot from the previously held position. By July 2020, the director of the CDC stated, "Now's the time to wear a mask." Executive orders mandated masking in public spaces. Things changed once again when vaccines became widely available; in late April 2021, the CDC determined that fully vaccinated individuals no longer needed to mask. A few months later, the CDC reversed its position again; new variants called for new mask mandates.

† It is true that earlier still, during the George W. Bush administration, the journalist Ron Suskind published this extraordinary account:

> In the summer of 2002, after I had written an article in *Esquire* that the White House didn't like about Bush's former communications director, Karen Hughes, I had a meeting with a senior adviser to Bush. He expressed the White House's displeasure, and then he told me something that at the time I didn't fully comprehend—but which I now believe gets to the very heart of the Bush presidency.
>
> The aide said that guys like me were "in what we call the reality-based community," which he defined as people who "believe that solutions emerge from your judicious study of discernible reality." I nodded and murmured something about enlightenment principles and empiricism. He cut me off. "That's not the way the world really

even more urgent to persuade skeptical masses to submit to an unproven vaccine or to another round of crushing stay-at-home orders, experts and authorities were surprised to find that fewer and fewer people were eager or willing to obey them. We are still dealing with the manifold repercussions of this self-inflicted moral and intellectual incoherence.

Seventy years ago, Albert Camus showed readers that the human condition itself amounts to a permanent plague-like emergency; we are only ever managing our losses, striving for dignity in the process. Risk and safety are relative notions, and they can never be strictly objective. At the same time, no matter how much interpretations may vary, numbers do not dissimulate. By the summer of 2020, there was one highly inconvenient truth that could not be disputed: drastically more black Americans were killed by three months of coronavirus than the number to have died at the hands of police or vigilantes since the turn of the millennium.

In *The Identity Trap,* the German American political scientist Yascha Mounk observes that there has been for some years now a number of influential doctors, activists, and public health experts advocating for triage decisions to be made *not* on the basis of the long-standing and obvious principle of saving the greatest number of lives but rather in vaguer terms of "racial equity." These ideas were not invented during the pandemic, but they suddenly gained real purchase then, as considerations about who could and could

---

works anymore," he continued. "We're an empire now, and when we act, we create our own reality. And while you're studying that reality— judiciously, as you will—we'll act again, creating other new realities, which you can study too, and that's how things will sort out. We're history's actors . . . and you, all of you, will be left to just study what we do." Ron Suskind, "Faith, Certainty and the Presidency of George W. Bush," *New York Times Magazine,* Oct. 17, 2004.

not access limited vaccines and novel treatments like Paxlovid were being weighed in the aftermath of the death of George Floyd and the protests, riots, and ongoing reckoning that followed his killing. In Mounk's telling:

> As Lori Bruce, the associate director of the Center for Bioethics at Yale University, recently argued in the *Journal of Medical Ethics,* protocols for whom to prioritize when medical goods are scarce *"should be assessed by a broader lens than merely the simplistic measure of the number of lives saved."* Instead, physicians should try to lessen disparities between different demographic groups by implementing "a racially equitable triage protocol," paying special attention to such questions as whether "families will remember being denied treatment or being included."
>
> These ideas and practices help to explain how officials approached key decisions during the pandemic. When public health authorities in the United States were tasked with figuring out whom to prioritize for scarce COVID treatments, they too rejected "race-neutral" frameworks that would only take risk factors like age or preexisting conditions into account. The State of New York, for example, committed itself to adopting medical policies that would advance "racial equity and social justice" in 2021, explicitly noting that this would *"not mean simply treating everyone equally."* Guided by these goals, the New York State Department of Health suggested that doctors could prescribe scarce drugs like Paxlovid to members of ethnic minority groups even if they were under the age of sixty-five and did not suffer from preexisting conditions. Otherwise identical New Yorkers who are white, the guidelines made clear, should not be considered a priority.

The guidelines adopted by the State of New York are part of a wider trend. Earlier in 2021, when vaccines were first being rolled out, Vermont encouraged young, nonwhite patients without preexisting conditions to get shots before allowing otherwise identical white patients to do so. *And even though its own models showed that such a course of action would likely result in a higher number of deaths, the Centers for Disease Control (CDC) urged states to give essential workers access to the vaccine ahead of the elderly on the grounds that older Americans are disproportionately white.* When a lawsuit tried to put an end to such practices, two dozen prominent institutions, including the American Public Health Association, the American College of Physicians, and the American Medical Association, filed an amicus brief defending them. (All emphases mine.)

At the same time that the left and the ostensible liberal mainstream were squandering authority and credibility as a result of a self-sabotaging and ultimately malicious allegiance to facile notions of redistributive justice and abstract identity concerns, the man presiding over the nation's pandemic response was broadcasting alarming daily briefings from the White House that further destabilized the national psyche. These consistently ludicrous and disorienting performances provided a morbid dose of comic relief, it must be conceded, but also served to underscore the degree to which we were bereft of serious and capable leadership anywhere we might turn to look for it.

Throughout the spring, Trump repeatedly promoted the use

---

* That is to say, a greater number of *total* deaths, which would also imply a higher number of gross black and non-white deaths, was deemed *preferable* to a lower total death count that was split inequitably along abstract racial lines.

of the antimalarial medicine hydroxychloroquine, going so far as to call it a "game-changer," despite accumulating studies finding zero health benefits and multiple potential risks associated with the treatment. During one especially memorable press briefing on April 23, 2020, President Trump floated the potentially lethal idea of *injecting* disinfectants directly into people's bodies. "And then I see the disinfectant, where it knocks it out in a minute," he told reporters. "One minute. And is there a way we can do something like that, by injection inside or almost a cleaning?" A minimum of five states, from New York to Kansas, immediately reported an increase in calls to poison control after these remarks were delivered.* Earlier in that same press conference, after the presentation

---

* Trump later tried to claim his comments were "sarcastic." Yet in the days that followed, according to the Michigan Poison and Drug Information Center, the governor of Maryland, Larry Hogan, said his state received "hundreds of calls" from residents about the effectiveness of using disinfectants to treat the coronavirus. "We have seen an increase in numbers of people calling poison control," Michigan's governor, Gretchen Whitmer, also told reporters. "I want to say, unequivocally no one should be using disinfectant—to digest it to fight COVID-19," she added. "Please don't do it. Just don't do it." In addition, New York City's Department of Health and Mental Hygiene reported an increase in calls within the eighteen-hour period after Trump's briefing. The poison control center recorded thirty cases by Friday, including nine "specifically about exposure to Lysol, 10 cases specifically about bleach and 11 cases about exposures to other household cleaners," the department spokesperson Pedro F. Frisneda told NPR. On the other side of the country, Kansas Poison Control saw an increase of 40 percent in cleaning chemical cases, according to Lee Norman, secretary of the Kansas Department of Health and Environment. There was one case of a man "who drank a product because of the advice he received," Norman said. The State of Illinois's public health director, Ngozi Ezike, described receiving calls "in which residents reported dangerous acts, such as using a detergent solution for a sinus rinse or gargling with bleach as a substitute for mouthwash to kill germs." Finally, in response to the president's comments, the Centers for Disease Control and Prevention had to issue a state-

of a Department of Homeland Security study that investigated the effect of sunlight and heat on coronavirus, Trump also freestyled about the possibility of light-based remedies: "Supposing we hit the body with a tremendous—whether it's ultraviolet or just very powerful light—and I think you said that hasn't been checked, but you're going to test it. And then I said, supposing you brought the light inside the body, which you can do either through the skin or in some other way, and I think you said you're going to test that too. It sounds interesting."

The four-year circus of his first presidency notwithstanding, there still existed a narrow yet real pathway to reelection for Donald Trump throughout 2020. It is entirely conceivable, if not downright likely, that without the accident of COVID-19 and its manifold consequences, the kleptocracy, corruption, constant scandal, and general unseriousness* of the Trump era would not have been enough to unseat him. Here, the pandemic functioned as a kind of deus ex machina in the larger American political drama, introducing a grave economic crisis to help cripple the first Republican candidate since Richard Nixon to consistently grow support among non-white populations.[†] "Operating in a context of deep partisan and

---

ment that "household cleaners and disinfectants can cause health problems when not used properly." Aysha Qamar, "States Report an Increase in Calls to Poison Control After Trump's 'Disinfectant' COVID-19 Remarks," Daily Kos, April 28, 2020.

* In June 2018, for one particularly shocking example, in a widely shared clip, Trump was shown meeting various North Korean officials at a summit in Singapore, including a North Korean military general. The general first salutes Trump, to which the president salutes back, before shaking his hand. The North Korean dictator, Kim Jong Un, whom Trump had referred to on previous occasions as "Rocket Man," is seen smiling in the background.

[†] A feat he continued to build on ahead of the 2024 election. As *The New York Times* reported in November 2023, "New polls by The New York Times and

ideological polarization, inflamed racial tensions, and widespread civil unrest, voters' perceptions of the president's efforts to combat the pandemic were highly negative and electorally consequential," writes Harold Clarke of the University of Texas at Dallas. According to his meta-analysis of voter reactions,

> Going into the 2020 election Trump was relying heavily on a traditional political recipe of "peace and prosperity" to make his case for re-election. The economy was the lynchpin of this strategy. During Trump's term in office, corporate taxes had been reduced, the stock market had soared to record highs, and unemployment had continued the downward trend established in the Obama years. In December 2019, shortly before the pandemic struck, the unemployment rate had fallen to 3.9 percent. . . . Peace also had broken out across much of the globe. The ISIS caliphate had been largely eliminated, troop reductions were occurring or had been planned for Afghanistan, Iraq, and Syria; although Trump had engaged in an abundance of bellicose rhetoric with North Korea and Iran, wars had not occurred. Peace accords between Israel and Mideast states including the United Arab Emirates and Bahrain were in the works and would be announced in the run-up to the election.
>
> Covid-19 overturned the president's strategy. In addition

Siena College found that 22 percent of Black voters in six of the most important battleground states said they would support former President Donald J. Trump in next year's election, and 71 percent would back Mr. Biden.

"The drift in support is striking, given that Mr. Trump won just 8 percent of Black voters nationally in 2020 and 6 percent in 2016, according to the Pew Research Center. A Republican presidential candidate has not won more than 12 percent of the Black vote in nearly half a century."

to the mounting death toll caused by the virus, government efforts to combat the pandemic with lockdowns that closed restaurants, retail businesses, schools, sporting events, and many other public gatherings and severely curtailed travel combined to crash the American economy. The negative effects were swift and profound. . . . Unemployment soared to 14.7 percent in April 2020, a much higher figure than at any point during the "Great Recession" of a decade earlier. Although joblessness subsequently declined, when voters went to the polls on November 3, unemployment remained nearly twice as high as it had been before the pandemic began.*

As France and Europe returned in the long summer of 2020 to an interstice of normalcy between waves of raging infection and severe national lockdown,† my family and I mostly stayed away from Paris, moving on to Brittany. I rented, at a steep discount, the holiday home of an American family that couldn't find the usual tenants from the United States that year. From a peak of 7,581 new cases across the country on March 31, there were just 526 new cases on June 13, the day we'd masked ourselves and took the train back out of La Baule. The caseload continued to be small and manageable.

Meanwhile, America was spiraling. Texas, Florida, and Ari-

---

* Harold Clarke, Marianne C. Stewart, and Karl Ho, "Did Covid-19 Kill Trump Politically? The Pandemic and Voting in the 2020 Presidential Election," *Social Science Quarterly* 102, no. 5 (2021): 2194–209, doi:10.1111/ssqu.12992.
† By November, a 6:00 p.m. curfew was put in place, with even grocery stores shutting down. Crucially, however, there were no significant further disruptions to the schools.

zona had become the newest hubs of contagion, having apparently learned nothing from the other countries and states that previously experienced similar surges in cases. The tribal politics of identity could not be assuaged. One particularly memorable viral tweet recounted how Johnny Cash's own granddaughter was heckled and disparaged as a "liberal pussy!" in a Nashville grocery store on the basis of wearing a mask.

That insult succinctly conveyed the American dilemma, which has only intensified since the summer of 2020. From the outset, the pandemic had been so thoroughly politicized we rendered ourselves effectively unable to manage a unified response to it. Instead of preparedness and national coordination, there was only empty posturing, the sad spectacle of the president refusing to wear a mask, just to own the libs, and death threats from his supporters directed at his chief medical adviser, Anthony Fauci. At the same time, even obvious and commonsensical speculations and responses—such as the likelihood of a lab leak or the very serious need to prohibit travel from China—were dismissed as incorrect and even "xenophobic," as the Speaker of the House, Nancy Pelosi, put it, when articulated by the president. The Trump administration's Operation Warp Speed initiative was that rare instance of generally effective leadership capable of harnessing an extraordinary scientific breakthrough in the form of the new mRNA vaccines. In response, top Democrats sought to undermine that effort. In an interview with CNN ahead of the election, when asked whether she planned to get the jab, Kamala Harris replied, simply, "I will say that I would not trust Donald Trump." In a speech that September, Joe Biden insisted, "Let me be clear: I trust vaccines, I trust scientists. But I don't trust Donald Trump, and at this moment, the American people can't either." In such an atmosphere, is it any wonder that the percentage of Americans willing to vaccinate themselves plummeted by September 2020, to just 51 percent, according to research conducted by Pew?*

As Americans spent the summer and fall of 2020 coming apart spectacularly, and queuing up the debacle that would be the election and subsequent insurrection at the Capitol, the view from France was revelatory. Back on June 26, a day when the United States notched some forty-five thousand new cases, the European Union announced that while it would loosen some travel restrictions, its ban on visitors from America and other hot-spot nations would be extended. That was a remarkable and deeply humiliating decision, an unambiguous message that in terms of pandemic management the EU believed that the United States was no better than Russia or Brazil—autocrat-run public health disasters—and that American tourists would pose a dire threat to the hard-won stability the discipline of national lockdowns had earned western Europeans. So much for the myth that the American political system and way of life could serve as models for the world to follow.

Or so it would seem. There endured throughout the summer of 2020 and beyond one very potent way in which the debates, power struggles, and stark ideological divides along the perimeters of group identity functioned as a template for much of western Europe and the rest of the English-speaking world. This was the moment at which the theory-laden jargon, biases, preferences, and, it could be argued, *provincialism* of corporate- and campus-inflected American social justice discourse became, through the amplifier of the internet and social media, a phenomenon of global magnitude.

---

* It had been 72 percent as recently as May. Alec Tyson, Courtney Johnson, and Cary Funk, "U.S. Public Now Divided over Whether to Get COVID-19 Vaccine," Pew Research Center, Sept. 17, 2020.

CHAPTER FOUR

The Death of George Floyd
and the Cult of "Antiracism"

hen all are guilty, no one is," Hannah Arendt argued in *Eichmann in Jerusalem*. It's an obvious truth, but one worth dwelling on all the same: moral judgment requires the discipline of making distinctions. The year 2020 was when a shift toward mass, undiscerning—and in some fields, obligatory—exhibitions of collective (and selective) atonement became contagious. One of the most striking displays was filmed on June 3, in the upper-middle-class suburb of Bethesda, Maryland. Outside the Connie Morella Library, a camera pans over hundreds if not thousands of masked men and women of all ages. Some are seated on the pavement and others stand solemnly behind them. With hands stretched above their heads and banners adorned with "Black Lives Matter" as well as George Floyd's bleak final statement—"I can't breathe"—prominently displayed in the background, they recite in unison that they will renounce their "white privilege." It is every bit a religious tent revival; individual voices, personalities, circumstances, and trajectories meld into the monolith.

These are striving people gathered on the hot pavement that day, people who are struggling with themselves for the betterment of their psyches (or souls, perhaps). Out of this rippling sea of humanity I make out—at best—two objectively brown faces. The ceremony is an act of ostensible solidarity that can be tricky to differentiate from the choreography of self-help or therapy. Or, more generously, was it more politically salient than that, a visceral attempt to counteract the ongoing theater of vitriol in Donald Trump's America? If the president's equal-opportunity chauvinism was all display, no substance, as many of his supporters would contend when downplaying its severity, then it is nonetheless true that he had elevated the category of performative allegiance in all our lives. This cannot be denied. On the spectrum of post–George Floyd ritualistic repentance, the scene in Maryland amounts to an act of significantly more commitment than merely making a post on social media, but less so than kneeling—as several prominent members of Congress draped in kente cloth would do in the Capitol's Emancipation Hall, or as several dozen white people, two days earlier and also in Bethesda, had filmed themselves doing in a downpour, this time in front of fellow black citizens whom they implored to forgive them. Or, to take things further still, not only kneeling but also washing black people's feet, as a group of white parishioners would do several weeks later in Raleigh, North Carolina.

Still, who can deny that these were moving and likely heartfelt moments? In that second clip from Bethesda, men and women on both sides of the color line are visibly crying. Mawkishness is an improvement over hostility or indifference. Glimpsed from a certain angle, what we could witness were masses of people yearning to overcome complicated and burdensome inherited prejudices in public and with one another's approval and guidance. Perhaps there is no entirely elegant way to do this; perhaps any such effort to will into existence a shared social realm that may break free from past degradations is simply destined to appear clumsy.

And yet there was something altogether unsettling in these displays as well, something that cannot be ignored or downplayed. Such rituals of repentance seemed to materialize everywhere all at once and without warning. Though ideas of collective responsibility had certainly been in circulation, if far less conspicuously, for decades or more, this was the season in which Robin DiAngelo's viral assertion that *all* white people participate in racism and white supremacy merely by dint of membership in a vast and often arbitrary racial agglomeration—and irrespective of individual beliefs, actions, or even specific non-white people's perceptions of them— became a matter of conventional wisdom, repeated without pushback or skepticism on virtually every major platform the country had to offer. "White people raised in Western society are conditioned into a white supremacist worldview because it is the bedrock of our society and its institutions," she writes in her 2018 book, *White Fragility,* which became a runaway bestseller for the second time after Minneapolis. "Regardless of whether a parent told you that everyone was equal, or the poster in the hall of your white suburban school proclaimed the value of diversity, or you have traveled abroad, or you have people of color in your workplace or family, *the ubiquitous socializing power of white supremacy cannot be avoided.* The messages circulate 24-7 and have little or nothing to do with intentions, awareness, or agreement. Entering the conversation with this understanding is freeing because *it allows us to focus on how—rather than if—our racism is manifest"* (emphases mine).

"The movement that calls itself 'antiracism' is complete in its pessimism about race relations," the independent journalist Matt

Taibbi pointed out in an early and blistering review of *White Fragility*. "It sees the human being as locked into one of three categories: members of oppressed groups, allies, and white oppressors." The practice of assuaging white consciousness,* as often as not without even requiring the presence of others, could not help but carry with it the distinct side effect of infantilizing black people (and,

---

* A highly lucrative segment of the publishing and consulting markets that often closely resembles the wellness industry. For instance, one can register for a multitiered workshop through the organization White People Confronting Racism. The registration fees for the first-tier workshop range from $100 to $750, in relation to the applicant's income; costs then double for the second-tier workshop, available only upon completion of the first. From the organization's website:

> *In a non-judgmental, supportive setting, participants will* . . . Build confidence in their ability to address racism through action; increase their understanding of how racism functions and what their role in it is; explore their internal racism and barriers to working on it; develop a personal vision for racial justice; build their skills in being accountable allies to people of color and working in coalitions; develop strategies for interrupting racist situations; increase their ability to support other white people doing racial justice work; and build an action plan of concrete next steps." Testimonials include:

- "What a breath of fresh air."
- "Great progression from feelings to history to internal/self to group to system level to fears to real actions."
- "I learned that I don't need to let white guilt keep me from addressing racism or utilizing my white privilege for the good."
- "Good balance of serious focus and lightheartedness and fun."
- "I finally saw the importance/value of taking small, tangible steps."
- "I found a ready, willing, and friendly group of people representing a fairly diverse set of backgrounds."
- "I came in without knowing what I didn't know, and am leaving with awareness and humility, and coming to terms with my upbringing."

as always follows, various other homogenized groups perceived to be separated from whites* on the twin scales of privilege and disadvantage), reinforcing the assumption that they are, en masse, unequal and generically aggrieved, props in the greater national psychodrama of white-progressive moral absolution.

Whether or not DiAngelo's argument was fully convincing, even among its adherents, it was one that a significant number of educated white Americans were at least eager to be *seen* to be endorsing. In an interview for the podcast of Gwyneth Paltrow's luxury lifestyle brand, Goop, in January 2020, DiAngelo was able to claim with zero objection—in fact, with audible approval—from her white-identifying interlocutor, "In many ways we're in the '60s in terms of the permission that's been given to explicitly express racism." That is, on its face, a provably false statement. But to take the claim literally would be to miss the point entirely. The lengths that many prominent self-identified white people and majority-white organizations were now prepared to venture in signaling their antiracist epiphanies and bona fides became ever more conspicuous and extensive, almost a form, in its own right, of meritocratic hyper-competition.

At the launch of *National Geographic*'s special Race Card Project, a reaction to the moment in the form of a collection of slice-of-life vignettes in which more than half a million Americans contributed personal reflections on race to be published as a series of articles and multimedia presentations on the magazine's website, Susan Goldberg signed off on her editor's letter: "Susan Goldberg, Editor-in-Chief, National Geographic, Race Card: White, privileged, with much to learn." On September 2, 2020, the president of Princeton

* And then, even within the field of whiteness, further distinguishing between the ne plus ultra of straight cisgender Christian white males and women, Jews, "white Hispanics," and so on.

University,* Christopher Eisgruber, went further than simply acknowledging his privilege and issued a letter voluntarily declaring that, despite recent efforts, "racism and the damage it does to people of color nevertheless persist at Princeton." That damage is done, he argued, "sometimes by conscious intention." Above all, "racist assumptions from the past also remain embedded in structures of the University itself." It was an extraordinary admission, not least of all because Princeton, like virtually all institutions of American higher education, receives substantial federal research funding and federal student financial aid amounting to hundreds of millions of dollars annually. Were the university genuinely systematically racist, it would be an extremely serious breach of federal law. To onlookers' disbelief—since, again, as with DiAngelo's assertion, such declarations are *not* intended to be read literally—the U.S. Department of Education under Betsy DeVos decided to take President Eisgruber's letter not as mere rhetorical gambit but as legitimate assertion of fact. Within weeks it opened an investigation into civil rights violations at the school—violations that Princeton immediately and formally denied having perpetrated.

Ironically, such acts of do-goodism, in DiAngelo's framework, nevertheless amount to little more than *further* evidence of latent racism. "I believe that white progressives cause the most daily damage to people of color," she writes in her book and has argued at top corporate seminars and keynotes across the country, from Facebook, Amazon, and Goldman Sachs to Nike, CVS, American Express, and Netflix. "I define a white progressive as any white per-

---

* Some 61 percent of Princeton's class of 2024 and 68 percent of its class of 2025 self-identified as "POC." "Diversity Distinguishes Princeton's Class of 2024," *Princeton Alumni Weekly,* April 22, 2020; Office of Communications, "In an Extraordinary Year, Princeton Offers Admission to 1,498 Students for the Class of 2025," Princeton University, April 6, 2021.

son who thinks he or she is not racist, or is less racist, or in the 'choir,' or already 'gets it,'" she continues. "White progressives can be the most difficult for people of color because, to the degree that we think we have arrived, we will put our energy into making sure that others see us as having arrived."*

DiAngelo is without doubt incisive about the very real desire for performative display, and the spring of 2020 provided opportunities to see and be seen the like and scale of which none of us had previously experienced. Isolated in our homes as we found ourselves, we nonetheless were able to easily observe and register each other's public and even private efforts online through the ubiquity of social media, office Slack channels, and ever more user-friendly videoconferencing technology.† One of the most striking, widely adopted, and costless examples of participation in the racial

---

* In what can now appear like a very shrewd meta-commentary, DiAngelo's highly visible books and public persona have increasingly become targets for just this kind of criticism.

† In this medium, specifically, novel modes of signaling that amounted to entirely new forms of coerced and ritualistic behavior gained sudden prominence, such as land acknowledgments, in which the convener of a conversation would begin by name-checking the Native American tribe(s) that once populated the geography from which he or she was speaking. This was particularly bizarre in a moment in which the pandemic had made it necessary for people to disperse to different corners of the country and even the planet. I was booked for a virtual lecture with a major Fortune 100 company in the Pacific Northwest when, before I was given the floor, a local land acknowledgment was solemnly recited even though I was speaking from Paris.

The practice of speakers identifying themselves by race, gender, and style of dress was also adopted, ostensibly to assist visually impaired participants. This led some blind participants to complain, noting that one of the things they appreciated about their condition was *not* being forced to racialize every interaction and simply developing their opinion of a given speaker based on the content of the message.

awakening happening all around us was the sudden mass display of the simple, monochromatic black square that countless Instagram users began posting to their profiles in seemingly self-directed but ultimately highly imitative tandem.* The effect while scrolling her feed for a viewer privy to certain artistic and knowledge-producing industries—beginning with music and entertainment and spreading quickly from there throughout the larger culture—was tantamount to the moment in the board game Othello when entire rows of chips flip black simultaneously. All told, millions of people mimicked the gesture, which was frequently accompanied by the copied-and-pasted hashtags #BlackoutTuesday and #BlackLivesMatter. Some took the additional step of pausing, for a day, all of their social media activity.†

"On 2 June 2020, the movement to support Black folks in music

---

* We have since seen this empty, mass gesture return to Instagram Stories and other social media, with the "All Eyes on Rafah" AI-generated meme, which was shared nearly fifty million times in two days during the spring of 2024. The image depicted an endless grid of tent encampments stretching along a desert plain to the horizon between improbable snowcapped mountains that seem to have been imported to the Middle East from Switzerland. What made it so exquisitely shareable, experts told the BBC, was the AI-generated unreality of the image itself. "The image . . . does not show a real place or the city of Rafah. Notably absent are pictures of dead bodies, blood, shots of real people, names or distressing scenes." In other words, the act of reposting it cost nothing at all.

† On the first Tuesday in June, Instagram users were encouraged to take a break from posting content and instead participate in #TheShowMustBePaused, a mission started by two black women in the music industry, Jamila Thomas and Brianna Agyemang. The idea was to hold the music industry accountable for benefiting from the "effort, struggles and successes of Black people." Mariah L. Wellman, "Black Squares for Black Lives? Performative Allyship as Credibility Maintenance for Social Media Influencers on Instagram," *Social Media and Society* 8, no. 1 (2022).

shifted, involving not only other industries within the United States, but other races and ethnicities as well," writes Mariah L. Wellman, of the University of Utah. "Rules circulated on Twitter for white allies interested in participating in the movement, but confusion ensued, and the guidelines for participating became disconnected from the original mission." Even the profiles of some major brands joined in. The official Twitter account of the wildly popular British children's cartoon *Peppa Pig,* which has been carried on Nickelodeon in the United States, shared an image of a black square in a post for #BlackoutTuesday. So did a verified account linked to Garfield the Cat. This inundation of monochrome pixels adorned with hashtags that had originally been conceived as tools for organizing—what Wellman terms "the memeification of social justice activism"—was not just superficial; it was even counterproductive. The sheer volume of these performative posts "ultimately pushed down valuable information for Black Lives Matter (BLM) protestors and suppressed images of those in the streets protesting police violence," Wellman continues. "Users' feeds were full of black squares for hours, and . . . by mid-day most of the useful information was lost to the algorithm and a discussion began of how white Instagram users co-opted this movement and perpetuated harm. White allies were called out for their lack of contextual knowledge surrounding the hashtags and the performative aspects of the black squares which did little for Black folks and other protestors."

Elsewhere, however, the desire for change was significantly more substantive. A decisive and more durable corollary to DiAngelo's systems-level thinking, which implies impersonal structural bias not only at the level of law enforcement but as a permanent stain that bleeds into every fiber of the American social fabric, from resource-deprived urban enclaves to the recently Obama-inhabited White House, was the historian Ibram X. Kendi's analysis, which holds that *any* disparity between so-called racial groups is necessarily evidence of racial bias. Consider this typical passage from his 2019 *How to Be an Antiracist,* which along with *White Fragility* (and to a lesser extent a handful of other "antiracist" instruction manuals) became mandatory in the days and weeks and months following George Floyd's death in police custody:

> The use of standardized tests to measure aptitude and intelligence is one of the most effective racist policies ever devised to degrade Black minds and legally exclude Black bodies. We degrade Black minds every time we speak of an "academic-achievement gap" based on these numbers. The acceptance of an academic-achievement gap is just the latest method of reinforcing the oldest racist idea: Black intellectual inferiority. The idea of an achievement gap means there is a disparity in academic performance between groups of students; implicit in this idea is that academic achievement as measured by statistical instruments like test scores and dropout rates is the only form of academic "achievement."*

* The very notion of "black minds" as opposed to "white" or other kinds of minds is a classic form of racism (or racialism). Yet it has been highly influential in transforming not just school admissions criteria but even the very nature of math and science pedagogy. In the summer of 2020, the Smithsonian published (and rescinded after much uproar) a graphic in an online portal about race and racism in America that identified rational thought, politeness, objectivity, and the Protestant work ethic as harmful "white" characteristics that perpetuate systemic racism. In February 2021, a consortium of two dozen education organizations funded by the Bill and Melinda Gates Foundation published "A Pathway to Equitable Math Instruction," which argued, amazingly, that a "focus on getting the right answer," requiring students to "show their work," and operating under the assumption that "expectations are [to be] met" were also facets of "white supremacy culture."

Rarely in the history of ideas has an intellectual been so able to witness his own theories be mandated into practice through the immediate buy-in of the decision-making upper levels of his society. But by August 2020, for just one conspicuous example, Jack Dorsey, one of the billionaire founders of Twitter, announced via the platform that he had given Kendi a $10 million "no-strings" gift to launch the Center for Antiracist Research at Boston Univer-

---

Such perspectives, as insulting as they are puzzling, have formed an entire latticework of interlocking and self-reinforcing language and assumptions that obtains throughout the nation's education system. At New York's Fieldston School—where families pay in excess of $50,000 annually in tuition per child, and where an eleventh grader can study neuroscience—even physics class can be reduced to an identity-based power struggle. "We don't call them Newton's laws anymore," an upperclassman confided to *City Journal*. "We call them the three fundamental laws of physics. They say we need to 'decenter whiteness,' and we need to acknowledge that there's more than just Newton in physics."

It is not simply a matter of screening high school and college students, either. Inginia Genao, Yale's graduate medical education director of diversity, equity, and inclusion, proposed in the *Annals of Internal Medicine* replacing the Medical College Admission Test (MCAT) "with alternative measures for evaluating medical school applicants in order to increase diversity," according to the *Yale Daily News*. This once fringe position gained traction during the pandemic as top medical schools removed themselves from the *U.S. News & World Report* rankings on the basis of "anti-racist" protest. A 2023 statement released by the Icahn School of Medicine at Mount Sinai was typical:

> The U.S. News rankings undermine the school's "commitment to anti-racism" and "outreach to diverse communities." "Diversity, equity and inclusion are important factors in our decision," the school's deans, Dennis Charney and David Muller, said. *"We believe that the quality of medical students and future physicians is reflected in their lived experiences, intersecting identities,* research accomplishments, *commitment to social and racial justice,* and a set of core values that are aligned with those of our school." (Emphasis mine.)

sity, a model that would soon be replicated elsewhere.* Companies and institutions around the country began to distribute copies of *How to Be an Antiracist* and require their employees to read them and in some cases—often at universities—to sign binding antiracist pledges.[†] There was something unusually straightforward as well as seductively empowering in this extraordinarily simple binary Kendi had articulated. Unlike in DiAngelo's more damning world of inherently racist white people and their hapless black and brown clients—a soul-crushingly determinist landscape devoid of human agency—here there were no racist or antiracist *people;* rather, there were, in Kendi's framework, merely racist or antiracist ideas, policies, and actions, all of which may pass through and animate any of us depending on a wide variety of time frames and contexts. Yet they do not define us. At any given instant, then, particular men and women and even institutions may fluctuate like elementary particles between the two fundamental states of being, having been influenced by or promoting one or the other regardless of whether they are white or black or something else entirely. What becomes henceforth impossible, however, is occupying a position of mere neutrality. For Kendi, since the status quo itself is not contingently

---

* More broadly, the Black Lives Matter movement and related causes generated astonishing amounts of pledges and contributions from corporations and philanthropists, according to the Claremont Institute's Center for the American Way of Life, which published the most comprehensive database tracking corporate giving to the Black Lives Matter movement and related causes from 2020 to the beginning of 2023. These numbers, including more than $123 million to the BLM parent organizations, directly and likely vastly underrepresent the true magnitude.

[†] Harvard University finally abandoned this practice in the spring of 2024, after the enormous fallout from the Hamas attacks of October 7, 2023, and the subsequent upheaval that pro-Palestinian protests brought to campus, the effects of which will be explored at some length in the afterword.

but *necessarily* "racist," it is not realistic to be simply "not racist"—which is to say, doing nothing can only perpetuate preexisting race-based injustices and damage. One must therefore commit oneself to positive antiracist action in his highly specific understanding of the idea.

In the real world, of course, life is frequently far more complex than such a bare-bones polarity would suggest. While it is true, for one important example, that black men and women are statistically overrepresented in the nation's penitentiary system—and let's be clear, it is also true that at least *some* of this disparity can quite demonstrably be linked to both present-day and residual racism within the workings of the criminal justice system as well as the sheer continuing fact of the black ghetto—it is also inescapably true that the victims of their crimes also overwhelmingly tend to be black. The very communities most affected by this violence and social dysfunction have, as a logical consequence, consistently advocated for "tough on crime" measures to protect themselves from harm.* As it happens, then, two groups of people both designated "black," like all sufficiently large collectives of human individuals, turn out to have competing claims and interests. What is the straightforward, unequivocally "antiracist" policy solution for such a conflicted situation? we might ask. One of Kendi's most cited arguments, constructed in his signature declarative mode of repetition with incremental variation, does not address the issue at hand: "The only remedy to racist discrimination is antiracist discrimination. The only remedy to past discrimination is present discrimination. The only remedy to present discrimination is future discrimination."

---

* See James Forman Jr., *Locking Up Our Own: Crime and Punishment in Black America* (New York: Farrar, Straus & Giroux, 2017).

This thinking, too, which more closely resembles tautology than syllogism, became—at least in some of the most competitive and selective spaces—another kind of conventional wisdom.* By 2020 several highly prestigious magnet-school systems had already taken seriously Kendi's injunction to abandon neutrality and aspire to uncomplicated antiracist praxis. In so doing, they abolished their long-standing merit-based admissions processes entirely on the grounds of racial justice.

Several months prior to the killing of George Floyd, and before his name became household familiar, Ibram X. Kendi had contributed a short, eyebrow-raising proposal to a *Politico* magazine special feature about inequality, which deserves some consideration, too, in this discussion. Though it can read like a satire of idealistic overreach, the passage gives one of the clearest indications I have yet encountered of the naked scope and ambition of the antiracist movement that broke free from rhetorical constraint in the summer of 2020, as well as the sheer confidence its leaders and most ardent adherents hold in their own moral rectitude and managerial capabilities.[†] "To fix the original sin of racism," Kendi pro-

---

* Sometimes the slippage into tautological argumentation is complete: asked how he would define the term "racism" during an Aspen Ideas Festival panel in 2021, Kendi replied, "Racism: I would define it as a collection of racist policies that lead to racial inequity that are substantiated by racist ideas." To which the Columbia linguist and *New York Times* opinion columnist John McWhorter (@JohnHMcWhorter) replied: "In which academic discipline is this circular, naive, deer-caught-in-the-headlights response to a basic and urgent question considered insightful or excellent?" Twitter, June 1, 2021, 6:15 a.m., twitter.com/JohnHMcWhorter/status/1399670923221946372 ?lang=en.

[†] An unearned confidence, as it would become clear:

By now, just about everyone in philanthropy has heard about the implosion at Kendi's Center for Antiracist Research at Boston University. The center,

claimed, "Americans should pass an anti-racist amendment to the U.S. Constitution that enshrines two guiding anti-racist principals [*sic*]: Racial inequity is evidence of racist policy and the different racial groups are equals." To "monitor those policies, investigate private racist policies when racial inequity surfaces, and monitor public officials for expressions of racist ideas," this unelected body would also be "empowered with disciplinary tools to wield over and against policymakers and public officials who do not voluntarily change their racist policy and ideas."

To paraphrase Raymond Aron, the French postwar thinker whose work feels so eerily appropriate again, utopian programs "are refuted not so much by their failure as by the successes they have achieved." By the summer of 2020, such fanaticism (of which Kendi's proposal was but the superlative) could not be dismissed as

---

known as CAR, raised "a whopping $55 million" in philanthropy, much of it right after the murder of George Floyd in the summer of 2020.

But CAR's output wasn't nearly as impressive as its fundraising: "The degree programs that CAR was supposed to launch haven't materialized. *The Boston Globe* is no longer partnering with the group's news site, *The Emancipator*. Much of the research CAR promised never got done. In other words, an appreciable portion of that $55 million appears to have been squandered."

The depth of the problems became widely known when CAR laid off more than half of its thirty-six-person staff. But trouble was gathering.

The Boston University student newspaper, *The Daily Free Press,* reported that in 2021, the associate professor Saida Grundy, who was employed by CAR and left disillusioned, wrote a highly critical letter about the center to the school's provost, Jean Morrison. Grundy accused the center of having a "pattern of amassing grants without any commitment to producing research obligated to them." She noted that the practice "continues to be the standard operating procedure at CAR" and that there is "no good-faith effort to fulfilling funded research projects." Eboo Patel, "Ibram X. Kendi's Antiracism Center Is Struggling. Donors Share Some of the Blame," *Chronicle of Philanthropy,* Sept. 27, 2023.

mere hyperbole or held outside the realm of actionable possibility. Back in Minneapolis, for one eye-catching example, less than two weeks after the death of George Floyd, a veto-proof nine-member majority of the city council stood before a crowd of hundreds gathered in sunny Powderhorn Park and pledged to "dismantle" their police department and create a new system of public safety for the community. "We're safer without armed, unaccountable patrols supported by the state hunting black people," Kandace Montgomery, the director of Black Visions Collective, declared at the rally. "This is the first time we are seeing, in our country's history, a conversation about defunding, and some people having a conversation about abolishing the police and prison state," Patrisse Cullors, one of the founders of Black Lives Matter,* told *The New York Times*. "This must be what it felt like when people were talking about abolishing slavery."

The dream was prematurely interrupted. By November of that same year, *The Washington Post* reported that homicides in Minneapolis had skyrocketed 50 percent, with nearly seventy-five people killed across the city. More than five hundred people had been shot, "the highest number in more than a decade and twice as many as in 2019. And there have been more than 4,600 violent crimes—

---

* According to reporting in *New York* magazine, one of the multiple luxury properties Cullors purchased either personally or through LLCs attached to the Black Lives Matter Global Network Foundation she founded was described as having "more than 6,500 square feet, more than half a dozen bedrooms and bathrooms, several fireplaces, a soundstage, a pool and bungalow, and parking for more than 20 cars, according to real-estate listings. The California property was purchased for nearly $6 million in cash in October 2020 with money that had been donated to BLMGNF. . . . Two mothers who lost their sons to police violence demanded the organization stop using their names to raise funds." Sean Campbell, "Black Lives Matter Secretly Bought a $6 Million House," *New York,* April 4, 2022.

including hundreds of carjackings and robberies—a five-year high."
The majority of that violence occurred after the killing of Floyd and
the subsequent push to "end policing as we know it"—a rhetorical gambit that led, according to the city's Latino chief of police,
Medaria Arradondo, to more than a hundred officers vacating the
force, a figure more than twice the annual rate. By 2021, when
the initiative was finally put to a vote, residents of Minneapolis—
including many of those non-white constituents directly impacted
by rising crime, whose safety is somehow never considered an
antiracist priority—roundly rejected (56–44 percent) the plan to
remove the Minneapolis Police Department from the city charter
and replace it with a "public-health oriented" Department of Public
Safety. Though the initiative had been viewed as a test of the viabil-
ity of broader calls to defund or abolish police departments across
the nation, its resounding failure and the palpable instability caused
by months of growing demoralization and public uncertainty did
little to blunt the fervor and confidence of its proponents, who
would counter that their ideas simply had not been properly implemented. For the predominantly black citizens bearing the brunt of
this sociological experiment—"the seven-year-old boy wounded in
a drive-by shooting; a woman who took a bullet that came through
her living room wall while she was watching television with her
family; and a 17-year-old girl shot in the head and killed," as the
Post recounted—such rationalization could scarcely be more com-
forting than telling a ravaged subject of the Soviet Union that genuine Marxism simply had never been tried.

And while the new antiracist activism galvanizing the progressive left has no equivalent central organizing authority, there were
other striking parallels to previous era's debates around communist
ideology. In *The Opium of the Intellectuals,* Raymond Aron makes

the careful distinction between "subtle" or "esoteric" and "literal" or "common" understandings of key terminology in idealistic movements. Because the basic tenets of the dogma *by definition* can never be wrong, there was a second, ready-at-hand response from the true-believing advocates of police abolition: they did not mean "abolish the police" *literally*—a move that would *of course* wreak havoc. "Councilor Andrew Johnson, one of the nine [city council] members who supported the pledge in June, said in an interview that he meant the words 'in spirit,' not by the letter," *The New York Times* reported. "Another councilor, Phillipe Cunningham, said that the language in the pledge was 'up for interpretation' and that even among council members soon after the promise was made, 'it was very clear that most of us had interpreted that language differently.' Lisa Bender, the council president, paused for 16 seconds when asked if the council's statement had led to uncertainty at a pivotal moment for the city. 'I think our pledge created confusion in the community and in our wards,' she said."

For the truest of the true believers, such as the mostly white anti-police activists who attempted to prevent police and emergency personnel from accessing George Floyd Square—a chaotic pilgrimage site that retains a pseudo-religious ambience to this day—to deliver aid to a woman who had been shot there in December 2020, the very meaning of basic words, such as "harm" and "safety," could be reengineered so that their esoteric understandings eclipsed all common sense. In this way, since black and other non-white people were *by definition* subject to racist violence with regard to the institution of policing, even allowing a fellow protester to *bleed to death* on the street in the absence of law enforcement personnel was a vision of comparable security.

This alarming incident had scarcely been reported. When I interviewed Jeanelle Austin, the charismatic young executive director of the George Floyd Global Memorial,* at a Minneapolis coffee shop in 2021, she explained to me that the area in those days was essentially lawless and impenetrable, regulated by motivated neighbors and activist members of the local community on their own terms but also in constant negotiation with other outside agitators, many of whom were not even black and seemed to, as Austin put it, "hate cops more than they loved black people."

The only way a journalist could even physically access the square without being forcibly evicted in those days "was that they had to be vouched for by a community member," Austin explained. "For the most part, the people we allowed in were mostly international press, because they were the most respectful. International BIPOC†

---

* According to the George Floyd Global Memorial website,

> On May 25, 2020, George Perry Floyd was lynched by the Minneapolis Police Department just steps away from the intersection of 38th Street East and Chicago Avenue South. In response to this atrocity, people came from across the world to pay their respects, lay expressions of pain and hope as offerings, and grieve the ongoing violence against black bodies.
>
> The memorial started out simple, with circles of flowers and a few distinct locations to lay offerings. It has now expanded to encompass offerings in every direction, both large and small. It would take a museum several years to build a collection of the magnitude to which the memorial has grown. Since the 2020 uprising, caretakers have built a greenhouse for the plants and delicate offerings and developed a temporary conservation room kindly provided by the Pillsbury House & Theater and supported by the Midwest Arts Conservation Center. They continue to tend to the offerings at the intersection of 38th & Chicago laid in memory of George Floyd and other black lives lost in this community and across the nation." "About," Rise and Remember, georgefloydglobalmemorial.org.

† "Black, indigenous, people of color."

press were the most respectful." Within this information silo, "a black woman was shot," Austin conceded:

> I got a message on my phone. It was late at night. And there was a shooting that happened in George Floyd Square, the police are here, protesters are not letting the police in, there's no black people here. And so, I was like, "Okay, I'm coming." And so, I first stopped and I talked to the medic on-site and I said, "Brief me, what's happening?" And she briefed me on everything and said the patient refused treatment, but they were bleeding severely and "I'm afraid that she might bleed out." And [she added], "If those protesters are not letting the police in to investigate, they can get charged with aiding and abetting." So I'm like, "Okay, what's happening?" And the protesters didn't know any of that. They're just anti-police in this moment.
>
> So then, I show up, and then a couple other black neighbors show up and we started talking to say, "Okay, here's the situation." And I briefed them on what the medic told me. And I'm like, "We have to be able to figure out how are we going to get justice for that young black woman who got shot." That's how I framed it. We have to be able to center her life first. But then we were also dealing with a community that had real police trouble, because the police militarized themselves and marched in our communities. But based off of the information that we had, trying to say, "Okay, what do we do?" And one of the neighbors, who was actually a black neighbor, she said, "Well, let's pray for her." And so I said, "Okay," because I'm a person of faith. And I said, "Okay, that's fine." So we had to pray now.
>
> So, you have community members, who are also protest-

ers. I say protesters, but these are not outside folks, literally people who live here, this is why people can get there so quickly, because they were residents. So, you have people who are there, you have police officers, and then you have everybody, we're pausing to pray. We get done praying, and then I look up and I said, "Okay, and now what? Now what do you all want to do? How are we going to get justice for this black woman?" And nobody had a solution. And so, I suggested, and in consultation with some of the other black community members there, said, "Well, can we come to a compromise? Will we walk the police in, allow them to do whatever information gathering that they need to do, and then we walk them out? So that way we ensure that they are not abusing their authorities and power."

I talked to the lieutenant, talked to the community, and made sure that everybody was in agreement, that this is what we'll do, and then invited community members to be a part of that. So, every officer had a buddy officer, and then every community member had an officer. It's just like, "All right, if we're going to go in, we're going to go in together. Community members can do cop watch. Cops can do whatever investigation they do. And then we walk you in, and then at any point, if community members feel uncomfortable, then we walk you out." That's what we did. There is a group of leftists, activists, community members, and protesters who were upset that we did that because they're extremely anti-cop.

It had become an intensely subjective proposition, then, what was to be regarded as justice or a threat. Likewise, protests that engulfed entire city blocks in flames and razed black-owned businesses to the ground could be described on national television as "fiery but mostly peaceful" because "violence" in the subtle context is first and foremost a product of white supremacy and the agents of the state—whatever color they happen to be—who alone are empowered to dispense it.

The demands to ignore the evidence of one's own faculties, though powerful and contagious, were ultimately not quite enduringly persuasive for most community members. In many ways, however, reform of policing was only ever a tangential issue within the larger antiracist project. The reality is that most non-white people's experiences at any income level do not adequately resemble George Floyd's—a genuine member of the American subaltern, bereft of voice, representation, and, to a significant degree, agency or what psychologists call "internal locus of control" by dint of forces far more complicated and multidimensional than sheer ancestry or pigmentation alone. Let us be painstakingly clear: What happened to Floyd outside the Cup Foods convenience store was an atrocity; it was murder without qualification.* The difficult circumstances of his life that preceded the encounter, however—most notably severe poverty, lack of education, and chronic hard drug use—are by no means universal facets of the black experience, not in the twenty-first century and not in previous eras, either. For most black Americans, particularly those in the politicized middle classes who possess the means and inclination to make their voices heard, the real significance of this horrific and statistically quite rare instance of white-on-black violence lay in the broader and more tangible reckoning it prompted. *That* reckoning centered on the evolving

---

* The talking point, at first notably put forth by the right-wing influencer Candace Owens and parroted by Kanye West—and later echoed in the sham film *The Fall of Minneapolis*—that it was in fact the drugs in his system that killed George Floyd, and not the knee on his back for almost ten minutes, is as lacking in basic human decency as it is in logic.

understanding of "diversity, equity, and inclusion" within admissions and human resources departments.

As Slavoj Žižek wrote at the time, "In this case, as in most other cases, those who appropriate the role of the leaders of the revolt are precisely not the brutalized victims of the racist oppression." Or, as Camus observed before him, "rebellion does not arise only, and necessarily, among the oppressed, but that it can also be caused by the mere spectacle of oppression of which someone else is the victim." In that vein, one of the first and most ambitious responses to the killing of George Floyd—again, an impoverished black man without an education or vocational training—took place, *of all places,* four hundred miles away at the Poetry Foundation, in Chicago. There, in that not particularly representative American institution, a $257 million endowment set the stage for an extraordinary power struggle—a dramatic melding of *Mau-Mauing the Flak Catchers* and *Barbarians at the Gate*—that would be indicative of the new and loftier planes of social justice upon which the bounties of "antiracism" could best be tallied.

On June 3, 2020, a week after the killing of Floyd, the Poetry Foundation, which publishes *Poetry* magazine, released a statement of unambiguous support for what it referred to as "the Black community":

> The Poetry Foundation and *Poetry* magazine stand in solidarity with the Black community and denounce injustice and systemic racism.
>
> As an organization we recognize that there is much work to be done, and we are committed to engaging in this work to eradicate institutional racism. We acknowledge that real change takes time and dedication, and we are committed to making this a priority.

We believe in the strength and power of poetry to uplift in times of despair, and to empower and amplify the voices of this time, this moment.

In response to this not just anodyne but laudable four-sentence pledge of solidarity, twenty-nine high-profile activist-poets led by Eve Ewing—a tenured professor of sociology in her mid-thirties at the University of Chicago and the author of the *Ironheart* series for Marvel Comics, as well as the co-author of Colin Kaepernick's memoir—formally responded to the Poetry Foundation with an extraordinary declaration of their own. Their letter, which was significantly longer than four sentences and eventually signed by some eighteen hundred allies, called the foundation's communication "worse than the bare minimum," "an insult," and "given the stakes, which equate to *no less than genocide against Black people,* a violence" (emphasis mine). The signatories demanded the "immediate" resignations of the foundation's president, Henry Bienen, as well as the chair of the board of trustees, Willard Bunn III, both of whom swiftly complied.

That June, as I followed reports of this incident trickling through the press and social media, I could not help but return to the extreme distortion of language, which felt oddly Trumpian in scope and far removed from observable reality. A "genocide"?* Even granting the

---

* Around 250 black Americans are killed each year in police custody—only a fraction of whom are unarmed—out of somewhere between 1,000 and 1,500 such deaths annually, with a black population of approximately 44 million in a nation of 335 million. These numbers are disturbing in relation to comparable Western societies, and they do not capture myriad nonlethal abusive encounters. Still, they are *nothing* like a genocide.

By way of comparison, as the conservative black political scientist Wilfred Reilly pointed out rather bluntly, but with receipts to back up his claims:

most generous application of poetic license, that remains an impossible stretch. The activists' letter then called for a reallocation of "every cent" of that $257 million endowment, a gift from the Eli Lilly pharmaceutical fortune, "to those whose labor amassed those funds," as if Prozac and insulin were manufactured by the enslaved.* The letter's other demands included a "tangible plan to eradicate institutional racism"; increased investment in the Community and Foundation Relations Department; and the vaguely worded requirement to dedicate funds to "protect and enrich Black lives."

A very small group of highly motivated activists, then, had called for leadership of a more-than-quarter-billion-dollar purse to be replaced by agents of their own choosing with "a demonstrated commitment to both the world of poetry and the project of creating a world that is just and affirming for people of color, disabled people, trans people, queer people, and immigrants." The signatories vowed to withdraw or withhold their contributions until the foundation made a "significantly greater allocation of financial

---

"Wokeness got a lot of people killed. When the cops actually pulled back, per BLM, the Black murder rate jumped 50+%—glad to share data/info—inside three years." Wilfred Reilly (@wil_da_beast630), X, Feb. 6, 2023, 12:44 a.m., twitter.com/wil_da_beast630/status/1622471285346381824?s=20. As he expanded via email, "Murder has risen dramatically in recent years. If you just track murders using any standard resource like FBI or Disaster Center, there were about 14,000 per year around the 2014 start of Black Lives Matter. In contrast, by 2021, the total had risen to 22,900." He continued, "The black homicide surge is really just a matter of math. I've attached the most recent FBI data showing blacks as 60.4% of murder perps, in graphic form. If we go from [blacks representing] 40–50% of those responsible for 14K murders annually to 60% of those responsible for 23K, the surge is at least in the 50% range."
* In fact, the company's founder, Eli Lilly, fought for the Union army during the Civil War. He was even captured in September 1864 and held by the Confederate army as a prisoner of war until January 1865.

resources toward work which is explicitly anti-racist in nature"—a pedantic imperative that is on its face in serious tension with, if not antithetical to, the ethos of experimentation and the aesthetic concerns of artistic production. In other words, as an immediate consequence of what had happened in Minneapolis one week prior, a wholly unrelated cultural arts institution in Chicago would now be *forced* to become activist in the Kendian mold in mission. The connection was never more than tenuous, yet this audacious bluff amounted to a genuine hostile takeover of a rich but exhausted target institution whose wealth could now be redistributed in a variety of ways an ascendant raider class desired. "If the Poetry Foundation acquiesces to all the letter's demands, it would do more than shake up the existing leadership and culture," *Chicago* magazine reported. "It would represent a radical form of wealth distribution not typically seen in the multimillion-dollar nonprofit world"—and this happened not because of any transgression or evidence of wrongdoing on the part of the foundation's leadership but because of the perception of a "too-mild" statement of pure advocacy.*

---

* Weeks later, on June 26, the publication was sent into further upheaval when the editors issued an apology letter for having published "Scholls Ferry Rd.," a poem by Michael Dickman, of Princeton University, which the editors now claimed contained "racist language." The letter itself is a stunning document and reads like a written confession in Stalinist Russia. During the great terror in that society, "many of the accused sealed their fates by agreeing to confessions after torture or interrogation," as Igal Halfin's study of the phenomenon, *Stalinist Confessions: Messianism and Terror at the Leningrad Communist University,* maintains. "Some, however, gave up without a fight." Certainly, no one had to torture the editors of *Poetry,* but the zest for self-purging was reminiscent of the "rooting out evil (opposition) wherever it hid. . . . Confessing to trumped-up charges, comrades made willing sacrifices to their belief in socialism and the necessity of finding and making examples of its enemies." From the editors' note to readers:

. . .

The residues of the normative revolution of 2020 have lingered, marking the country in numerous, often counterintuitive

> *Poetry* subscribers recently received their July/August print editions and members of our communities have expressed outrage due to racist language used in this poem.
>
> We acknowledge that this poem contains racist language and that such language is insidious, and in this case is particularly oppressive to Black, Pacific Islander, and Asian people, and we are deeply sorry. We are grateful to readers who have reached out with their questions and criticisms of the decision to publish this poem.
>
> This poem centers whiteness and employs racist language, which is hurtful and wrong. We published this poem because we read it as an indictment of racism within white families; this was a mistake. We clearly have more work to do in considering how poems center certain voices and affect our readers. We regret not taking serious action sooner to interrogate the editorial process, and we apologize. Our commitment to this work is ongoing, and changes in the magazine's structure and process are imminent.

And from the editor Don Share's far longer and more enthusiastic resignation letter that followed:

> My poor judgment demonstrates that *Poetry* has much work to do in considering how poems center certain voices at the expense of others, and the impact this has upon our readers. The magazine is committed to doing this work, and readers will see that great changes in the magazine's structure and process are immediately forthcoming. The first of many is my departure, and this, along with a restructuring of the editorial masthead and process, will create a better space to empower marginalized voices, and result in a magazine that serves as a far more equitable and inclusive place. I'm sorry that in addition to other burdens they bear, many of our readers have had to do the work of demonstrating what ought to have been obvious: that such changes are urgently necessary, and overdue.

places and ways. The summer was a turning point that extended and midwifed latent tendencies that had not yet come to fruition and that might never have done so in the absence of certain interconnected preconditions. In a sense it allowed them moral cover. Portland, Oregon, for instance, is by a long shot the whitest, least multiethnic urban center of the thirty-five cities with a population of more than half a million in the United States.* Nonetheless, it was the only city in the country to see a streak of a hundred nights and days of frequently violent, sometimes deadly protests and rioting following the death of George Floyd. White activists, often cosplaying as antifa militants, besieged and ransacked the city's downtown area around the Multnomah County Justice Center. The pandemic exacerbated problems by further emptying out public spaces and encouraging mass outdoor camping, the scale and scope of which really must be seen to be fully appreciated.

When I visited Portland in the winter of 2022, I stayed in the Hoxton on NW Fourth Avenue, near Chinatown, a boutique hotel chain with thriving properties in Brooklyn, London, and Paris, popular for its expansive lobby spaces where "knowledge economy" types not staying in rooms could purchase beverages and plug in laptops to work remotely. Here that same template remained eerily abandoned. I took my coffees in solitude, except for a single

---

* On July 24, 2020, *The New York Times* ran an article titled "How One of America's Whitest Cities Became the Center of B.L.M. Protests." It begins, "Seyi Fasoranti, a chemist who moved to Oregon from the East Coast six months ago, has watched the Black Lives Matter protests in Portland with fascination. A sea of white faces in one of the whitest major American cities has cried out for racial justice every night for nearly two months. 'It's something I joke about with my friends,' Mr. Fasoranti, who is Black, said over the din of protest chants this week. 'There are more Black Lives Matter signs in Portland than Black people.'"

silent young man dressed in black, ensconced in a corner each of the four days I was present. He had several suitcases and his own snacks and was constantly charging his cell phone, by all appearances having moved into the lobby. The all-white staff told me they were powerless to intervene and preferred to ignore him.

A fifteen-minute walk down SW Third Street through a vast downtown of open-air drug use, tent encampments of a magnitude equivalent to the Roma settlements of western Europe, and Black Lives Matter signs and murals posted on countless surfaces served as preparation for the state of disrepair that had become the Justice Center—a large looming government structure that, a year and a half after the riots of 2020, remained boarded up and reinforced at street level like a U.S. embassy in a hostile foreign territory.* I had

---

* In fact, according to local reporting, workers only began "removing the planks reinforcing the three-story glass panes at the front of the new central courthouse" on May 7, 2023. "The grand atrium was boarded up shortly after the $325 million courthouse opened at the westside foot of the Hawthorne Bridge in October 2020—a tumultuous era when protesters routinely besieged the nearby police headquarters and federal courthouse. Police removed the fence around the entrance to the Multnomah County Justice Center, which houses the central precinct and county jail, later in 2020, but did not remove the boards from some of the ground-floor display windows until this February. . . . [T]he wooden perimeter wall surrounding the courthouse block will remain until 'further solutions' can be found." Zane Sparling, "Windows No Longer Boarded Up at Portland Courthouse but Fence Remains," *Oregonian,* May 12, 2023.

On the other hand, fortifications remained in place at the Mark O. Hatfield U.S. Courthouse next to the Justice Center all the way until June 2024: "The fences that have surrounded the perimeter of the Mark O. Hatfield U.S. Courthouse in downtown Portland for the past four years are finally coming down. . . . The decision to remove the fencing follows the installation of massive stainless steel walls that function like hinged airplane hangar doors, which will allow the building to withstand most thrown projectiles." Aimee Plante,

never seen anything equivalent in the United States. Directly across the street, a beloved statue of an elk had been toppled, and the surrounding area had been left vacant. A shantytown had been erected around its footprint. I could make out not a single brown-skinned man or woman in the vicinity; nonetheless, BLM posters adorned even the flapping tarpaulin coverings of the unhoused white people's makeshift lodgings. A few blocks farther on, in what would ordinarily be a prosperous shopping district, several small stores had been looted and abandoned, and the gleaming Apple flagship was now encircled by a multilayered military-grade barricading reminiscent of Checkpoint Charlie in the 1980s. To my amazement, an armed guard paced the entrance as if it were the lone general store in Guatemala City or Luxor.

At the RingSide Steakhouse, I spoke to a physician heading to a Blazers game who confessed his patients now called to inquire if it were safe to visit his downtown office for appointments. At Mary's, an iconic strip club (and formidable taqueria), a white dancer in a surgical mask calling herself Katrina told me she had personally participated in eighty nights of "de-arrest activities," which is to say, "physically confronting cops" throughout 2020. On my last night in town, Chandler Pappas, a furious young Trump supporter who had witnessed his best friend shot dead in the street—a chilling video of which went viral in its own right*—during the protests, told me something I already strongly suspected, "You could discharge a firearm in the city and the cops wouldn't show up."

One morning before I left, I watched from the Hoxton lobby as a workday procession entirely comprising white men and women

---

"Federal Courthouse in Downtown Portland Removes Fence Erected During 2020 Protests," KOIN, June 19, 2024.

* Before his white antifa killer was hunted down days later in a motel and shot to death by federal agents.

chanting, "Black Lives Matter," slowly passed outside the window, obstructing traffic. The permanent tenant did not so much as glance in their direction. Who was their audience? I wondered, to a local white coffee shop owner who told me that since the summer of 2020 there had been enormous pressure from other white people to exhibit a kind of antiracism "solely for each other." That summer, he said by way of illustration, a young white woman had barged into his own shop with a humorless ultimatum: display *her* specific BLM sticker prominently or she and other activists would denounce his business as "racist" on social media—in this town, an unambiguous invitation for vandalism. He complied, but it didn't make his business safer. During the pandemic he'd been stuck up and had a rock tossed through his plate-glass windows. "Those are the things you deal with in Portland," he told me, echoing the sentiment of a cashier at the century-old Portland Outdoor Store on SW Third Avenue, when a friend and I had asked him if they'd also had their windows broken. "Yeah, yeah, like four times in total," he said. "We kept calling [the police] and saying they're breaking our shit, but they wouldn't do anything until someone was assaulted. We've had knives stolen."

I had flown to Portland that winter, specifically, in an attempt to empathize with and understand the kinds of white people who have little to no legitimate interpersonal contact with black people but who had collectively pledged allegiance to a slogan abstractly stating that we "mattered." As recently as the Obama era, the last time I had been there, the town was defined by a well-deserved reputation for comparatively affordable rents, exquisite gastronomy, and the air of optimism that accrues to all spaces that attract, at scale, youthful talent and energy. There was certainly disarray then, but it didn't feel like the city's predominant feature. In the wake of the killing of George Floyd, I had watched videos of the chaos and anarchy that enveloped downtown and gave President Trump an excuse to propose military intervention. A year and a half later, with the desire to see what, if anything, remained palpable from that tumultuous moment, I left feeling, quite honestly, forlorn and despondent about the chasm separating such performative and self-referential (and self-sabotaging) displays of enlightened "antiracism" and anything like comprehension or actionable progress toward mending the national, or even local, social fabric at its split seams.

In a tangible way, Portland seemed to epitomize the cult of antiracism, its geographic capital, replete with all its excesses and contradictions, all of its dizzying incoherence and debility. In a way, this is not at all unreasonable. As ought to be well known but seems to have been willfully forgotten, the state of Oregon "was founded on principles of white supremacy," as the *Times* reminded readers that summer. "A 19th-century lash law called for whipping any Black person found in the state. In the early part of the 20th century Oregon's Legislature was dominated by members of the Ku Klux Klan." Any serious attempt to make sense of the staggering excesses and incongruities of the cult of "antiracism" therefore demands a sober and clear-eyed meditation on just what, precisely, so many white Americans—in Portland and elsewhere—suddenly became so eager to, at the very least, be seen to be breaking away from. This in turn would necessitate an honest acknowledgment of the very real distance we have traveled away from it.

CHAPTER FIVE

The *New* New Journalism:
Media in the Age of "Moral Clarity"

The late French critic and philosopher René Girard's mimetic theory, and his notion of the scapegoat as an enduring mechanism of social control, has found much renewed interest in recent years among writers, scholars, and cultural observers attempting to make sense of the sheer energy and viciousness that have been unleashed on uncountable targets in the era of social media. It is not at all difficult to see why. Though he died in 2015, Girard's ideas continue to provide a durable framework for analyzing the brave new collision of human nature and technology—as well as the ramifications of the unprecedented global psychological experiment we have willfully subjected ourselves to on the major social platforms—which we all must now contend with.

Girard was primarily a literary theorist, and his argument begins with a treatment of desire that is rooted in insights gleaned from the Western tradition's enduring novels and dramas, above all the foundational stories of the Hebrew Old Testament. For Girard, desire is not linear—I want, in a volitional vacuum, a suitcase that just happens to be plastered with Louis Vuitton's initials—but always formed in the context of other people's manners and tastes. That particular luggage is desirable to me *because* it is desired by others.

(This is basic marketing, of course.) Thus, according to a group of scholars of mimetic theory, the Colloquium on Violence and Religion, desire "is not *individual* but collective, or social."* It is only through mediators—or models—that our own desires first disclose themselves to us, and this can and does spur tension and rivalry if left to develop indefinitely.

"Mimetic desire leads to escalation as our shared desire reinforces and inflames our belief in the value of the object." Such escalation is untenable, holding the potential of "a war of all against all." It must therefore be defused somehow, and, for Girard, this happens by means of a shared release, what he calls "the scapegoat mechanism." The community unites against a single, *arbitrarily* chosen target who will absorb its pent-up violence and, as a result, avoids a broader, chaotic conflict. Crucially, a social order achieved in this way is only possible "if the excluding parties unanimously believe that the person or group expelled is *truly* guilty or dangerous." If this sounds religious, it's supposed to.

The scapegoat's guilt is proven *because* of the peace that is won through the group's unity against her. This seemingly virtuous peace is necessarily blinding, as the colloquium explains:

> When a community in the throes of conflict obtains peace through the violent expulsion of a scapegoat, they cannot perceive that it is their own unanimous violence which produced the peace. This blindness on the part of the participants with respect to what they are really doing—killing an innocent victim—is the one essential element required for the scapegoating mechanism to work. Girard points out that *to have a scapegoat is not to know you have one*. In other

* mimetictheory.com

· 123 ·

words, participants in the scapegoating mechanism hold an authentic belief in the guilt of the victim, a guilt seemingly demonstrated by the restoration of peace. (Emphasis mine.)

Perhaps no incident so perfectly encapsulates the atmospheric, and indeed the normative, shift of the summer of 2020—at least within culture- and knowledge-producing, nationally influential institutions—as a single, unexpected employment dispute at the New York Times Company, an internal affair that spilled alarmingly into the public. It was part of a larger and more consequential transformation of mission at the publication, from paper of record to organ of "the resistance" in the era of Donald Trump. This activist pivot—compounded by an ongoing, industry-wide decline in advertising revenue that has decimated the local news ecosystem and turned the surviving regional papers into national and even global businesses—naturally enough altered coverage that aspired (however imperfectly) to objectivity to a form of journalism that began to cater to a self-selecting and increasingly politically motivated subscribership numbering in the eight figures.* When this same dynamic applies to a self-employed writer at Substack, it's called "audience capture"; when it overwhelms the most essential and trusted news-gathering operation in the English-speaking world, it's something like a crisis of democracy.

But it wasn't just audiences whose biases and preferences were reshaping publishing practices. The digital-first nature of the new media landscape also meant that increasing numbers of younger staff writers, editors, producers, and technicians had arrived at the paper with novel and sometimes starkly divergent ideas about its

---

* *"The New York Times* now has more than 10 million subscribers," according to a November 2023 press release, "edging closer to its goal of 15 million by the end of 2027."

core journalistic mission and their own roles inside it. On the same day that the Poetry Foundation released its statement in support of black lives, *The New York Times,* which had spent the previous eight months tethering its brand and editorial reputation to an unprecedented special issue and multimedia spin-off of its Sunday magazine titled the 1619 Project,* published a guest op-ed by Tom Cotton, the junior Republican senator from Arkansas, under the headline "Send in the Troops." In this piece, Senator Cotton argues provocatively and perhaps insensitively, though to many Americans not irrationally,[†] that the federal government ought to apply military force to restore safety and order and protect property during the spasms of rioting and looting that had erupted in U.S. cities since the killing of George Floyd.[‡] He described the widespread disorder as an "orgy of violence" that was being excused by elites "in the spirit of radical chic." He also clearly rejected a false moral equivalence between "rioters and looters" and "peaceful, law-abiding protesters," and explicitly defended the rights of the latter

---

* Before the text was "stealth edited," after considerable backlash to the wording, the landing page for the digital version of the publication read, "The 1619 Project is a major initiative from The New York Times observing the 400th anniversary of the beginning of American slavery. It aims to reframe the country's history, understanding 1619 as our true founding, and placing the consequences of slavery and the contributions of black Americans at the very center of our national narrative."

[†] The article itself cited "a recent poll, [according to which] 58 percent of registered voters, including nearly half of Democrats and 37 percent of African-Americans, would support cities' calling in the military to 'address protests and demonstrations' that are in 'response to the death of George Floyd.'" Tom Cotton, "Send in the Troops," *New York Times,* June 3, 2020.

[‡] The Floyd family forcefully condemned rioting and violence, it should be stressed. "I'm not over here blowing up stuff," George Floyd's brother Terrence said, addressing a crowd in Minneapolis on June 1, 2020. "What are y'all doing? You're doing nothing. That's not going to bring my brother back."

to gather peacefully, a crucial qualification that would be consistently overlooked or willfully forgotten.

The op-ed enumerated a litany of anarchic paroxysms, which the National Guard and state and local police appeared ill-equipped to quell: "In New York State, rioters ran over officers with cars on at least three occasions. In Las Vegas, an officer is in 'grave' condition after being shot in the head by a rioter. In St. Louis, four police officers were shot as they attempted to disperse a mob throwing bricks and dumping gasoline; in a separate incident, a 77-year-old retired police captain was shot to death as he tried to stop looters from ransacking a pawnshop. This is 'somebody's granddaddy,' a bystander screamed at the scene."

Controversial, even unsavory views presented seriously and rigorously are foundational to the mission of *The New York Times* as articulated in 1896 by its current iteration's founder, Adolph Ochs, who insisted his paper's columns would make "a forum for the consideration of all questions of public importance, and to that end to invite intelligent discussion from all shades of opinion."* In other words heterodoxy is not just to be tolerated; it has always been official company policy. As Adam Rubenstein, one of the key editors who worked on the Cotton assignment, would subsequently recall,

> In the years preceding the Cotton op-ed, the *Times* had published op-eds by authoritarians including Muammar Qaddafi, Recep Tayyip Erdoğan, and Vladimir Putin. The year of the Cotton op-ed, it also published the Chinese Communist Party mouthpiece Regina Ip's defense of China's murderous crack-

---

* Adolph S. Ochs, "Business Announcement," *New York Times*, Aug. 19, 1896.

down on prodemocracy protests in Hong Kong, Moustafa Bayoumi's seeming apologia of cultural and ethnic resentments of Jews, and an article by a leader of the Taliban, Sirajuddin Haqqani. None of those caused an uproar. Last year, the page published an essay by the Hamas-appointed mayor of Gaza City, and few seemed to mind.*

Despite that record, what happened next was highly unusual. On Twitter, beginning on June 3, 2020, the day the op-ed ran, a number of high-profile *Times* journalists and staffers began to share a short, eyebrow-raising declarative sentence above a screenshot of the op-ed's headline. "Running this puts Black people, including Black @nytimes staff, in danger," the tweet alleged. The reasoning was as logically unpersuasive as the phrasing was prefabricated and strategically coordinated to initiate a specific response from the company's management. The realm of intellectual, political, and journalistic disagreement had been forsaken; this was now, however implausibly, a matter of *physical safety,* and therefore it was nonnegotiable.

By June 4, a group of *Times* employees performed a virtual walkout (the offices were already shuttered for the pandemic) in protest of the article's publication. Nikole Hannah-Jones, a star reporter at the magazine whose profile, as the creator of the 1619 Project, was attaining the level of genuine celebrity—a development that lent her an unofficial,[†] though highly influential, moral authority within the institution—vocalized her disdain: "As a black woman, as a jour-

---

* Adam Rubenstein, "I Was a Heretic at *The New York Times,*" *Atlantic,* Feb. 26, 2024.

[†] It is important here to stress: Hannah-Jones was never invested with editorial powers.

nalist, as an American, I am deeply ashamed that we ran this."* She further tweeted that the paper "should have done a news story to push back against Cotton's ideas, as opposed to 'simply giv[ing] over our platform to spew dangerous rhetoric.'" Another reporter— which is to say, another *Times* employee who was decidedly not an editor—implicitly rebuked Ochs's own position and tweeted, "If electeds want to make provocative arguments let them withstand the questions and context of a news story, not unvarnished and unchecked."† (He seems not to have realized that the op-ed *was* fact-checked.)

By June 5, the paper's newish publisher, A. G. Sulzberger, Ochs's fourth-generation descendant, who'd inherited his position from his father about two years prior, was forced to respond. At first, he defended the decision to run the op-ed while hedging that the paper had not properly vetted the piece before it went to print—a framing that does not bear scrutiny. Forty-eight hours later, he'd lost his nerve entirely, and James Bennet, the editor of the opinion section, resigned under immense pressure. By June 7, the *Times* had issued a bizarre apology, stating obliquely—and for reasons that contradict its own stated values—that the piece "did not meet our standards."

What happened in the wake of the Cotton op-ed, then, was fundamentally different from any previous newsroom crises, one veteran reporter I spoke to—who had witnessed up close both the Jayson Blair plagiarism scandal in 2003 and the Judith Miller debacle around the invasion of Iraq during that same era—explained. In what has always been an extremely hierarchical institution, the paper's history does not include an equivalent episode of staffers—a

* None of the longtime *Times* staffers I spoke with at the time could think of a single similar instance of a journalist publicly disparaging the paper and its editors this way.

† Erik Wemple, "James Bennet Was Right," *Washington Post,* Oct. 27, 2022.

significant number of whom were not even journalists but rather digital media technicians and producers—mutinying their bosses (at times in openly ad hominem and patently insulting terms) in order to exact punishment on a top figure for doing what had been fully within the purview of his job: publishing a widely held perspective articulated by an important political actor.*

As Bennet wrote in his own highly detailed account of what went wrong at *The New York Times* during the summer of 2020,[†]

> The *Times* had endured many cycles of Twitter outrage for one story or opinion piece or another. It was never fun; it felt like sticking your head in a metal bucket while people were banging it with hammers. The publisher, A. G. Sulzberger, who was about two years into the job, understood why we'd published the op-ed. He had some criticisms about packaging; he said the editors should add links to other op-eds we'd published with a different view. But he'd emailed me that afternoon, saying: "I get and support the reason for including the piece," because, he thought, Cotton's view had the support of the White House as well as a majority of the Senate. As the clamor grew, he asked me to call [Dean] Baquet, the paper's most senior editor.
>
> Like me, Baquet seemed taken aback by the criticism that *Times* readers shouldn't hear what Cotton had to say. Cotton

* Bennet, who had helmed *The Atlantic* from 2006 to 2016 and had been at op-ed for four years, was until June 2020 considered among a small number of credible candidates for the top job at the *Times* as soon as the executive editor, Dean Baquet, retired.

† At seventeen thousand words, the essay, an extraordinary document worth reading in its entirety, was published online in *The Economist*'s magazine, *1843,* in December 2023.

had a lot of influence with the White House, Baquet noted, and he could well be making his argument directly to the president, Donald Trump. Readers should know about it. Cotton was also a possible future contender for the White House himself, Baquet added. And, besides, Cotton was far from alone: lots of Americans agreed with him—most of them, according to some polls. "Are we truly so precious?" Baquet asked again, with a note of wonder and frustration.

The answer, it turned out, was yes. Less than three days later, on Saturday morning, Sulzberger called me at home and, with an icy anger that still puzzles and saddens me, demanded my resignation.

And so Bennet was forced to absorb the accumulated frustrations and pent-up symbolic violence of a multiethnic mob of junior employees, onlookers, and enablers who were unwavering in their sense of self-righteous schadenfreude and fury. Though he might have been arbitrarily selected—or to be more precise, though the infraction that brought him down can only be understood as arbitrary; it could have easily been something else entirely or nothing at all—the order that was restored through his personal destruction was fueled, at least on one level, by a corresponding mimetic desire for prestige and career advancement. It cannot be overstated that one immense side effect of social justice activism is the redistribution at scale of recognition and enrichment. Since "Bennet was widely expected to be a frontrunner for the *Times*' top job, executive editor, . . . [h]is sudden fall from grace open[ed] up unexpected opportunities for others."* Bennet's particular misfortune, the spe-

* Robby Soave, "James Bennet's Resignation Proves the Woke Scolds Are Taking Over *The New York Times*," *Reason,* June 8, 2020.

cific oblation of a single prominent leader, put a name and face on a much greater and more diffuse transfer of influence and authority throughout the mainstream media. Here, then, was a Girardian sacrifice in all its complex cruelty that ultimately *did* win the peace at the nation's most important paper—though it was a victory that could only ever be understood as Pyrrhic.

On another, more enduring level, the Bennet firing was much more than a pressure-releasing communal sacrifice: it was illustrative of a *power struggle* between competing versions of what most fundamentally journalism itself is supposed to be. Later that same month, the *Times*'s op-ed pages, under new leadership, would platform a diametrically opposed framing of the profession: "A Reckoning over Objectivity, Led by Black Journalists," under the byline of the reporter Wesley Lowery, then of *The Washington Post*. "As protesters are taking to the streets of American cities to denounce racism and the unabated police killings of black people across the country," he wrote, "the journalism industry has seemingly reached a breaking point of its own: Black journalists are publicly airing years of accumulated grievances, demanding an overdue reckoning for a profession whose mainstream repeatedly brushes off their concerns; in many newsrooms, writers and editors are now also openly pushing for a paradigm shift in how our outlets define their operations and ideals."

The solution Lowery ventriloquized—also the animating idea behind the campaign to punish Bennet—was to *abandon* the ideal of neutrality, which he dismissed as a "failed experiment." From this angle, it becomes clearer that the scapegoating of Bennet had always been bound up in a larger, multifaceted phenomenon, not merely the end point of a grand and abstract mimetic gesture of release. Rather, quite concretely, what this controversy so potently entailed was the literal embodiment of legacy media capitulating in the face of coordinated mobs of junior staffers, who—though they psychologically and cathartically might have benefited from the social killing of one high-level competitor*—were even more decisively vying to fundamentally reshape journalism's marquee institution according to their newfangled conception of the trade and inevitably biased narrative vision.

In subsequent posts on Twitter, Lowery would expound, deriding that ideal as "American view-from-nowhere, 'objectivity'-obsessed, both-sides journalism," and urging editors instead to "rebuild our industry as one that operates from a place of moral clarity." *Moral clarity?* It sounds enticing. And yet it must be remembered that many Americans—including black and brown business owners and stakeholders in communities being battered—inconveniently agreed, at least provisionally, with Senator Cotton's message about the fundamental need for order and safety. How do we reconcile that discrepancy? It would seem difficult to reduce such a complicated question to a single, unequivocal position—and perhaps more respectful of readers' intelligence not to presume to. Yet here was the radical case for newsrooms to become *more* activist and ideologically blinded in theory as well as in practice.

"I fear that the most self-righteous of Americans nowadays are precisely those who have most to gain from what they preach," Allan Bloom warned in his 1987 cri de coeur, *The Closing of the American Mind.* Suddenly, equipped with the doctrine of "moral clarity," some of the very same voices that had grown so influential *extra muros,* mainly on Twitter, began to view themselves as *mandated* not simply to bring forth news of the world and to

---

* " 'Wow,' Meghan Louttit, who is now a deputy editor in the newsroom, wrote on Slack. 'James's resignation makes me somewhat . . . Hopeful?' " Rubenstein, "I Was a Heretic at *The New York Times.*"

inform their *readers*—nor even simply to argue for a position and then work to persuade them—but rather to instruct their *followers* on the indisputable Truth of what was moral, above all what was "racist," and what would heretofore be considered impermissible. It was an extraordinarily powerful and privileged position from which to practice news gathering. For colleagues and peers observing from the sidelines—many of whom exchanged concerned texts and emails in private but neglected to voice their disapproval publicly—the most salient lesson to be drawn from Bennet's ouster and Lowery's subsequent proclamation could not have been clearer, and it sounded a lot like Ibram X. Kendi: reality itself can be said to skew racist; there can be but one correct response to this; human resources departments will from now on operate collectively and coordinate via social media; sanctions for perceived transgressions will be severe, without recourse, and meted out swiftly.

The truth is that institutions matter gravely. Authority and reputations, while accumulated over successive lifetimes, once squandered, are not remade easily. It should go without saying, then, that key institutions have a primary obligation to prevent themselves from being hijacked or undermined internally. Failing to perform this most basic function adeptly is even more of a breach of stewardship and professionalism than bungling a story or even printing errors. Visibly successful assaults on the organizational hierarchy of an institution leave lasting, sometimes irreparable disfigurations, even when they are ultimately defeated—to say nothing of when there remain remnants of the motivating ideology lying dormant in the system, waiting to be reactivated. That this ascendant view of activistic moral clarity—the full meaning of which is perhaps best captured in the writer Wesley Yang's formulation "successor ideology"*—forced, *even temporarily,* the custodians of *The New York Times* to relinquish their ultimate position as the telos setters of journalism, and their own centuries-old self-described edict to their audience, has done immeasurable harm to the national trust and continues to wreak havoc on our political predicament.

These were the early days of an entirely new season of manners and assumptions in American society, extending far beyond debates in the media. No culturally prestigious fields were left unaffected. Diversity, equity, and inclusion was the coin of the realm now—even when it shrank irreducible questions of individual identity and collective justice to oversimplified and formulaic solutions and prescriptions. Potential new hires at universities in disciplines as far from sociology or critical theory as math and physics were expected to sign pledges and articulate their explicit commitment to antiracist practices.[†] Scapegoating of the kind that had destroyed

* Yang has described this as "the melange of academic radicalism now seeking hegemony throughout American institutions." Further, it is "a bourgeois revolution . . . in which certain foundational liberal values concerning free speech, due process, the presumption of innocence, and so forth, have come to be seen increasingly as obstacles to the path of the attainment of a particular vision of justice that's been articulated and pursued by the activist class whose ideas, that were once confined to obscure pockets of academia, have increasingly become sort of mainstream through the media and through social media as a part of the parlance of everyday life that affects those who are operating within those settings."

[†] By 2024, the *Times* itself would weigh in on how widespread, disastrous, and coercive such activism had become. "Some higher education institutions have required new employees to sign statements supporting their personal commitments to D.E.I. principles, a litmus test that could have the effect of creating a uniform campus culture without a variety of viewpoints," the editorial board wrote. "One 2021 survey found that 19 percent of college jobs required

James Bennet became more rampant. Curators at major art institutions were dismissed for transgressions so tenuous as purchasing and programming work by white artists.* Even Hollywood produc-

---

these statements. Last year, The Times wrote about a noted psychology professor (and affirmative-action supporter) who lost a chance to teach at U.C.L.A. because he disagreed with the usefulness of required diversity statements, calling them 'value signaling.'" "When States Try to Take Away Americans' Freedom of Thought," *New York Times,* Jan. 20, 2024.

* "Gary Garrels, the senior curator of painting and sculpture at the San Francisco Museum of Modern Art, has resigned following an uproar from employees over his comments at a recent staff meeting," a July 2020 article on Artnet reported.

> Earlier this week, Garrels was confronted by an employee at an all-staff Zoom meeting about previous comments he had made regarding the museum's collecting priorities. (In a widely shared Instagram post on the account @changethemuseum, an employee recounted that the senior curator, who is white, ended a presentation about new acquisitions by artists of color by saying, "Don't worry, we will definitely still continue to collect white artists.")
>
> At the meeting, Garrels said that the museum could not avoid collecting the work of white men, which would amount to "reverse discrimination." Soon afterward, a group of former employees who have been advocating for change at the museum created a petition calling for his resignation, which had been signed by 180 people as of publication time.
>
> "Gary's removal from SFMOMA is non-negotiable," the petition's authors wrote. "Considering his lengthy tenure at this institution, we ask just how long have his toxic white supremacist beliefs regarding race and equity directed his position curating the content of the museum?"

In October 2020, Nancy Spector, the chief curator of the Guggenheim, left the museum after thirty-four years. She'd been accused of fostering "an inequitable work environment that enables racism, white supremacy, and other discriminatory practices," according to a letter submitted to management that June. An independent investigation found no evidence of wrongdoing.

tions were mandating themselves to meet *racial quotas* in order to be considered during awards season.*

At the same time, Trump and his movement were monsters, in no small part, of the mainstream media's own making. By every estimate, the most covered human being in all of history, Donald Trump kept the lights on at CNN and MSNBC and to an extent even Fox News while also serving as the most reliable source of click-bait for print publications on both sides of the partisan divide— including the ones that now assumed for themselves the standard of moral clarity. As Dean Baquet of the *Times* himself acknowledged, the main thrust of the newspaper's coverage during a period of record growth "went from being a story about whether the Trump campaign had colluded with Russia and obstruction of justice to being a more head-on story about the president's character." In a town hall meeting in 2019, he explained, "We built our news-room to cover one story, and we did it truly well. Now we have to regroup, and shift resources and emphasis to take on a differ-

---

* These mandates were excruciatingly spelled out according to the Academy of Motion Picture Arts and Sciences' new "representation and inclusion standards." As listed on Oscars.org, for a production to be eligible in the Best Picture category, two of four inclusivity standards would have to be met, such as "at least one of the lead actors or significant supporting actors is from an underrepresented racial or ethnic group in a specific country or territory of production"; "at least 30% of all actors in secondary and more minor roles are from at least two underrepresented groups"; "The main storyline(s), theme or narrative of the film is centered on an underrepresented group(s)"; "At least two of the following creative leadership positions and department heads— Casting Director, Cinematographer, Composer, Costume Designer, Director, Editor, Hairstylist, Makeup Artist, Producer, Production Designer, Set Decorator, Sound, VFX Supervisor, Writer—are from an underrepresented group and at least one of those positions must belong to someone from an underrepresented racial or ethnic group."

ent story."* In other words, once the Pandora's box of monetizable TDS had been cracked open, the crusading new journalism that eschewed the antiquated ideal of objectivity, and explicitly sought to reduce all aspects of American politics and society to questions of social justice, racial injury, and disparity, was a convenient fit for the broader demands of a new business model within an evolving media landscape. "Moral clarity" centered on a sense of permanent racial oppression—and therefore permanent racial rectification—had arrived just in time to exploit that shift in emphasis. That "different story," permeating every facet of American life, became an unending narrative of "racism," the definition of which had simultaneously been expanded so far beyond any layperson's understanding as to be virtually unrecognizable.

What all of these instances and more have amounted to is, of course, a crucial, still unfolding disagreement about liberal ends and even liberalism itself, the central function of which has been for three centuries the balancing of order and equality through commitment to neutral procedure—a function that was already severely sabotaged by the populist right. In the frenzy of ideological conviction and mimetic fury, the progressive institutional mutineers of 2020 and their spokespeople and supporters on the social internet forgot that it is the business of state-run presses and totalitarian governments to dispense moral clarity. A healthy, tolerant, and pluralist democracy, by contrast, safeguards a tense array of attitudes, conventions, and mores. At its best, it channels that tension productively. The proclivity to tip the scales of justice, to *trump,* as it were, disagreement, whether progressive or reactionary, is, at root, fundamentally *illiberal.* In the most basic sense, the norma-

* The full transcript of the *New York Times* town hall is available in the *Slate* magazine archives.

tive insurgents at *The New York Times* and elsewhere could only but aid and empower their most reactionary opponents—also the enemies of liberal democracy—the moment they began agitating to predetermine moral questions and constrict the area of possible disagreement within media, cultural, political, and academic settings.

To frame the complicated and necessarily contested story of unrest that was sparked from the confluence of the pandemic, the racial reckoning, and the presidential campaign that engulfed virtually all of our mainstream and left-leaning knowledge-producing and knowledge-curating institutions in 2020 and beyond as a single story of oppressors and the oppressed was therefore to attempt to eradicate by fiat the natural stress within an open society that arose from the basic reality that enormous numbers of Americans— particularly those outside the institutional and educational elite— understood it first and foremost as a story of order and chaos. *That* story of a breakdown in social order—if not definitive, then broadly compelling outside progressive orthodoxy—was not only suppressed; it was deemed functionally unspeakable to catastrophic and lasting consequence.

CHAPTER SIX

"Fiery but Mostly Peaceful Protests"

Two days before the country went to the polls on November 3, 2020, I flew to America to share a freezing al fresco birthday lunch with my parents for my mother's seventy-fourth and then to travel for work down the Eastern Seaboard from New York to Philadelphia and Washington. An impromptu post-pandemic, post-reckoning tour of urban compromise. I had lived in Europe for a decade by then, and had grown accustomed to viewing the United States, at least in part, through the eyes of a foreigner, yet aspects of this trip still alarmed me. During the summer, I'd watched grainy videos of brazen, racially inclusive bands of looters ransacking boutiques in Manhattan and big-box stores in Philadelphia (and many other locations), stripping clothing racks clean or wheeling heavy appliances through seething parking lots, but I was not prepared for the extent of the capitulation to the threat of lawlessness and mayhem that *still* met me in these streets, half a year after the catalyzing event.

As I wandered through SoHo on Election Day, virtually every single facade in the prime shopping area between West Broadway and Lafayette Street, while open for business, had been heavily fortified with plywood boarding over the plate-glass windows.

Uniformed guards in front of the Nike store lent the streetscape an air of eastern European or Latin American instability. These were measures taken in anticipation of the breakdown of civil order, and they were not excessive or irrational. These same blocks had been pillaged recently, and it was no secret who had done the pillaging. Just as the betting markets would reveal the winner of the contest later that evening and early the next morning, days before the media would confirm it, the decision by Nike, Sephora, and Apple to safeguard their inventories was an unambiguous assessment of where the real-world danger could come from, unbeholden to the Manichaean dictates of a neat and tidy narrative woven from the fabric of moral clarity. These companies were not reinforcing their outposts in downtown Manhattan in anticipation of violence from MAGA-hatted Trump supporters, just as they were not overreacting against "peaceful" progressive demonstrators.* They were calculating probabilities based on what had happened months earlier. "A day of citywide mass protests on May 31, a week after Floyd's death, was followed by chaos in the night," *The Intercept* reported. "Hundreds of people who had no apparent connection to the protests commanded the streets of Manhattan's SoHo district. . . . They looted businesses, and robbed each other, with impunity. Burglar alarms blended with the roaring of getaway engines, the chaotic medley punctuated every few moments by tumbling plywood, crashing plate glass, and grating steel. Then a gunshot went off, as a 21-year-old man was shot. The police were nowhere to be seen."†

One particularly memorable article in the *Times* quoted an off-duty security guard who put an even finer point on it: "'I don't think this has anything to do with Black Lives Matter,' said a 24-year-old

---

* Such cognitive dissonance would not in any way excuse but would certainly help to fuel the sense of grievance behind the January 6 insurrection.
† This, of course, had been the point of the Cotton op-ed.

man at the corner of Houston and Broadway, some time after midnight. 'It's just chaos. People are just using this as an excuse to act crazy, do stuff they never dreamed of doing before.' The man declined to give his name, because he, too, was looting."*

I was reminded of those hours of bedlam, scenes of which mingled in my mind with another clip that had gone viral that summer, after the Wisconsin town of Kenosha had collapsed into violence following the police shooting of a twenty-nine-year-old man named Jacob Blake, on August 23. The details of this altercation were at once far less debatable than those surrounding the confrontation with Floyd and even less amenable to the new reportorial demands of so-called moral clarity. Blake already had an outstanding warrant for his arrest on serious charges of third-degree sexual assault and criminal trespass against the mother of three of his six children when she called the police again to register a new domestic disturbance, telling 911 that "her boyfriend was present and was not supposed to be on the premises." Court documents allege that Blake had previously broken into her home, assaulted her as she slept, then fled with her debit card and automobile.

On this afternoon, when officers moved to arrest Blake outside her home, he refused to comply and physically resisted. They tased him twice without subduing him as he approached the driver's side of his vehicle, in which the couple's three children, aged eight, five, and three, were seated. A neighbor's video then captured the decisive moment, when Blake unlatched the door and leaned inside and Officer Rusten Sheskey fired repeatedly into the back of his torso. In total Blake was shot seven times, left paralyzed from the waist down, and a pocketknife was found on the driver's side floor-

---

* "Shattered Glass in SoHo as Looters Ransack Lower Manhattan," *New York Times,* June 1, 2020.

board of the vehicle he intended to use to flee the scene with three minors trapped inside. Sheskey claimed to have feared Blake would use the knife once the tasers had proved so ineffective. From any angle, it was a sad and wholly gratuitous turn of events with no uplifting aspects. It is not at all difficult to imagine how, in those fateful moments, Blake must have despaired, must have wished for nothing more than to achieve what Ta-Nehisi Coates once called "escape velocity" from all the diminishing constraints of being poor and black and stuck with a record that threatens the next encounter with law enforcement will be life altering, no matter how you comport yourself in that moment. And yet there is no conceivable world in which it would be responsible or merely even fair for police officers to allow a man—of any complexion or ethnic background or mitigating circumstance—worked into such a state of agitation to escape with a weapon and small children from an arrest warrant. To suggest otherwise is either disingenuous or emotionally blinded, even if we simultaneously pause to acknowledge that one, two, three, four, five, six, *seven* bullets to the spine is an exorbitant price to levy for a chain of actions Blake alone was responsible for setting in motion.

In his 1955 essay "Notes of a Native Son," James Baldwin describes a police shooting of a black soldier in the lobby of the Hotel Braddock in Harlem. There was, he says, the complex array of facts of the shooting as well as the *invention* of the narrative that flowed "immediately to the streets outside." People, Baldwin observes, were not interested in the facts of the altercation. "They preferred the invention because this invention expressed and corroborated their hates and fears so perfectly," he writes, before making a much deeper and more essential point. "It is just as well to remember that people are always doing this. Perhaps many of those legends, including Christianity, to which the world clings began their conquest of the world with just some such concerted surrender to distortion." In any event, then like now, the effect was "like . . . a lit match in a tin of gasoline," and the mob began "to swell and to spread." The city exploded.

In the days following the shooting of Jacob Blake, a similar reaction to what Baldwin observed occurred in Kenosha. A powerfully oversimplified narrative took hold and slotted into the discursive space that the case of George Floyd had flung wide open three pandemic months prior. We can understand why certain stories arise and resonate with audiences, and we can empathize with the evident communal pain they serve to address while still refusing to sacrifice the fundamental need for truth and sobriety in a world of tangled and competing moral imperatives. Put more simply, we cannot hope to solve the problems we do not allow ourselves to see in the first place.

The chyron read "Fiery but Mostly Peaceful Protests After Police Shooting," as the CNN correspondent Omar Jimenez held forth in front of a large building blanketed in leaping flames one day after the Jacob Blake shooting. Whole blocks of downtown Kenosha were being incinerated on national television—the previous night almost the entirety of a hundred-car lot on Sheridan Road had been immolated—but this was inconvenient to say, at least without equivocation. "It wasn't until nightfall that things began to get a little bit more contentious," Jimenez hedged in front of an incandescent hellscape of orange blaze and hollowed-out car frames. "Things were thrown back and forth; police started using some of those crowd dispersal tactics like tear gas, even playing very loud sounds to push them out," he continued. "And then, what you're seeing, the common theme that ties all of this together, is an expression of anger and frustration over what people feel like has become an all too familiar story playing out in places from across the country, not just here in Kenosha, Wisconsin." That was the same week that NPR of all venues published a wildly credulous interview with a young white trans author—the child of an MIT research scientist—named Vicky Osterweil, on the subject of her new book, *In Defense of Looting*. "A fresh argument for rioting and looting as our most powerful tools for dismantling white supremacy," is how Hachette, the book's publisher, describes Osterweil's patronizing manifesto of ironic white privilege, using simplistic, "morally clarified," and highly selective terms very few working and marginalized people could afford to entertain:

> Osterweil argues that stealing goods and destroying property are direct, pragmatic strategies of wealth redistribution and improving life for the working class—not to mention the brazen messages these methods send to the police and the state. All our beliefs about the innate righteousness of property and ownership, Osterweil explains, are built on the history of anti-Black, anti-Indigenous oppression.

Or, as the author expanded to her wide-eyed NPR interviewer, as though she were simply discussing the merits of do-it-yourself crafting, "So you get to the heart of that property relation, and demonstrate that without police and without state oppression, we can have things for free." *This* was the discourse being promoted in even our most vanilla of mainstream media outlets at the very moment that small, frequently minority-owned businesses in cities around the country were being reduced to ashes, their proprietors beaten to the brink of death, bodies twisted up like discarded coat hangers, for having the gall to attempt to safeguard their livelihoods, as was caught on an appalling video in Dallas.*

Throughout 2020 as our urban centers convulsed, often, bizarrely,[†] violence and wanton vandalism *in the name* of "black lives" was frequently perpetrated by *white people* on both sides of the political spectrum. This is what I would observe in its purest distillation, even nearly two years later in the desecrated streets of downtown Portland. From the earliest days of the demonstrations in May 2020, there had always been reports of black activists imploring overzealous white participants to refrain from defacing businesses and public property. On one galling compilation on YouTube with more than half a million views, we hear a black activist plead with her cosplaying "allies," "When you do that, they don't come after you. They'll come after us." Another narrates into the camera as a slender girl dressed in black, her sleek locks gathered into a loose ponytail, graffities BLM and other slogans on a pristine storefront: "This is not a black woman who's putting Black Lives Matter, I just want you to know!" The white woman turns, indignantly, to dismiss such concerns through a black N95—an instance of *peak* white privilege if ever there was one. The camerawoman isn't having it: "Listen, don't spray stuff out here when they're gonna blame black people for this, and black people didn't do it!"[‡]

---

* "Man Viciously Beaten for Defending Business," TMZ, May 31, 2020, www .tmz.com.

[†] Or entirely predictably if we take seriously the mimetic, cultlike, pseudo-religious aspect of the "Antiracism"™ that has animated many different kinds of whites and placed their personal and collective quests for self-realization and rebellion at the center of the project.

[‡] "Black Protesters Beg White People to Stop Destroying Public Property," NowThis, YouTube, www.youtube.com/watch?v=iBbPJsNZMPg.

It's a jarring and infuriating exchange. Despite a consistent, confused, and confusing desire in traditional and social media to interpret so many spontaneous, complicated, and heterogeneous uprisings as fundamentally righteous and peaceful if occasionally excessive or misguided—often in defiance of the evidence of one's own senses—such gaslighting and cognitive dissonance fell apart during the orgy of *white-on-white* violence that punctuated the night of August 25 in Kenosha.

On that evening of rebellion, the third straight, the *Kenosha News* reported there were thirty-four active fires and thirty businesses had been razed or damaged by arson. Structures set on fire included "a furniture supply store, an automotive repair business, and a Department of Corrections field office," according to CNN. "A dump truck was also set on fire." Countless cell phone and other videos of this night exist and accumulate to present a hallucinatory vision that does not neatly delineate across racial categories. Footage at Car Source, the used-car lot on Sheridan Road, shows a democratically mixed-race and mixed-class crowd of black and white teens and adults, men and women, at turns milling around, at turns smashing vehicles with crowbars and drizzling accelerant through shattered windows. "Ay, don't set it on fire yet, let me get one of these bitches," a young black man exclaims with a joy so palpable one could almost be excused for mistaking it as innocent. If rioting is the language of the unheard, as Martin Luther King is often cynically invoked to have said—and it certainly can be such a patois, at least in certain situations—it must also be acknowledged that it can easily amount to the gibberish of the debilitatingly bored and disengaged. It is the dialect of the dilettantes and LARPers and nihilists who are not at all oppressed—no more than the rest of us—but simply looking for an activity or a reason to smash things.

It is the idiom that functions as a Band-Aid applied to the existential wound of non-meaning in a society that is frankly more democratic, multiethnic, and egalitarian than any other in recorded history.

As that giddy young man strides into the distance in search of virgin tinder, a masked young white man approaches the videographer. "Hey, man, who are you with?" he asks, not quite timidly but far from authoritatively.

"I'm with Kenosha."

"All right, can you not film that?"

"No, no, I'm filming this, you guys have been burning my town down."

"Are you fucking kidding? You fucking cop!"

The cameraman keeps filming in defiance of the threat as his masked interlocutor raises his voice, attempting to enlist the roving crowd to confront him, which they lazily begin to do. He denies being a cop and does not stop recording. As the mob moves on, one more young white man turns and screams before retreating, "BLM is . . . bro, that's *Black* Lives Matter, not *building* lives matter, bitch!" We are witnessing a circus, an evening of boundless farce and stupidity that would be worthy of little more than mockery were it not to transition to grisly tragedy so swiftly.

By the time a local militia group called the Kenosha Guard created a Facebook event for August 25, 2020, called Armed Citizens to Protect Our Lives and Property, there had already been broadcast around the country the complete failure and total abdication of the state's primary mandate, which is to guarantee safety and order for law-abiding citizens. It was by no means a failure unique to Kenosha; on the contrary, this was the now familiar abdication of the state's fundamental responsibility to monopolize violence in response to which Senator Cotton had penned his infamous and hotly debated op-ed in *The New York Times*. A profound ceding of authority, in response to which it should be recalled the mostly black inhabitants of Minneapolis's crime-impacted communities were still beseeching their elected officials to reassert. The pleas of the latter, of course, still falling on deaf ears.

So tenuous had the situation in Kenosha grown that the *Milwaukee Journal Sentinel* relayed a now-deleted Facebook post signed "Kenosha Guard Commander" that was addressed to the Kenosha chief of police:

> As you know I am the commander of the Kenosha Guard, a local militia. We are mobilizing tonight and have about 3,000 RSVP's. Our effort has made the national media. I ask that you do NOT have your officers tell us to go home under threat of arrest as you have in the past. We are willing to talk to KPD and open a discussion. It is evident that no matter how many Officers, deputies and other law enforcement officers that are here, you will still be outnumbered.

That is an audacious, dangerous, and possibly illegal message. One with which it is difficult for me to sympathize—representing as it does yet another tin of gasoline to be exploded amid an ongoing conflagration—except it is also entirely predictable, and it expresses a principle lying at the very core of Western political theory. "The obligation of subjects to the sovereign is understood to last as long, and no longer, than the power lasteth by which he is able to protect them," Thomas Hobbes wrote in 1651 in *Leviathan*. "For the right men have by Nature to protect themselves when none else can protect them, can by no covenant be relinquished."

. . .

When a doughy seventeen-year-old named Kyle Rittenhouse, too young to purchase the AR-15 assault rifle he'd armed himself with, ventured from his home twenty miles away in Antioch, Illinois, into the flaming streets of Kenosha, he was doing many things simultaneously. First and foremost, he was placing himself in a deranged situation that should not have been unfolding to begin with—a carnivalesque social dilemma that a do-gooder teenager closer to the age of puberty than to legally drinking, with scant life experience, should never have felt compelled to be involved in. His very presence there was provocative; the ostentatious display of a military-grade firearm slung across his chest heightened the level of danger for himself and everyone around him. But it is undeniable that he was also attempting, however misguidedly, to make his community safer,* volunteering for a Hobbesian project, the evident need for which had been broadcast nightly on our television, computer, and smartphone screens and was itself the direct consequence of a conspicuous lack of legitimate and effective authority.†

On the morning of August 25, two drastically divergent white lives inched inexorably closer to conflict. As Rittenhouse, along with his sister and another young family member, took up with a

---

* Rittenhouse had family in Kenosha and worked there as a lifeguard. He also participated in cadet programs offered by the Antioch Fire Department and another nearby police department. On August 25, he was carrying a homemade medical kit, which was for him a routine practice.

† One can easily acknowledge that this lack of legitimate and effective authority *precedes* the spectacular inability to control mass rioting, arson, and looting, and is on stark display in the prior inability to apprehend a man—in this case, Jacob Blake—without resorting to lethal violence. Which is to say, if *three* Kenosha police officers could have simply subdued a single suspect without discharging their firearms, the situation would not have devolved into a Hobbesian state of nature in the first place.

makeshift crew to assist with cleanup* at local businesses, Joseph Rosenbaum was discharged after a short stint at the Aurora psychiatric hospital, outside Milwaukee. A deeply troubled thirty-six-year-old with a history of homelessness and an extensive criminal record—including recent domestic violence against his fiancée and prior sexual assault of minors—whom the hospital had deposited in the middle of Kenosha's pandemonium, Rosenbaum attempted to retrieve his belongings from the police station, only to find it shuttered because of the ongoing melee. As *The Washington Post* reported, he then continued on to Walgreens to procure his medication, but the store had also been closed due to the protests. Meanwhile, Rittenhouse had begun preparing to join another crew that evening to stand guard outside one of Car Source's auto lots.†

As night descended, Rosenbaum left the motel where his fiancée was living, unable to spend the night on pain of being rearrested, and Rittenhouse was filmed standing guard outside the dealership with a gathering group of armed men, people he describes as complete strangers who had also come to protect local businesses. Rittenhouse speaks affably with citizen journalists live streaming the protests on social media. "People are getting injured, and our job is to protect this business, and part of my job is also to help people," he says unaffectedly. "If there's somebody hurt, I'm running into harm's way. That's why I have my rifle, because I need to protect

---

* There is footage of him that day with others, removing graffiti from the facade of Reuther Central High School, which reads "FUCK 12 BITCHES!!!" and "FUCK 12 PIGS."

† Incidentally, Car Source's owner, Anmol Khindri, was an immigrant from India. Rioters had caused some $1.5 million in damages to his property on the night of August 24 and an additional $1 million on August 25, the night that Rittenhouse and others attempted to dissuade them.

myself obviously. But I also have my med kit." Mid-conversation, he looks up and shouts, "Medical, EMS right here, do you need assistance? I am an EMT," and rushes out of frame.

An hour before midnight, in the claustrophobic lot of the Ultimate Convenience Center, a gas station where thick crowds of rioters and protesters, some concealing themselves with medical and makeshift masks, some with bicycle helmets, hoodies, and ball caps pulled low on top of them, jostle against the armed civilians—some of whom are also masked—Rosenbaum emerges for the first time on video. Head shaved to a polish, fluorescent stud jutting from his earlobe, and a look of fury tinged on his troubled countenance, his compact figure berates and even butts into much larger men with long guns.

Rosenbaum looks and sounds not fearless but reckless. "Don't point no motherfucking gun at me, homey!" he screams one moment before quickly changing tacks: "Shoot me, *nigga*! Shoot me, *nigga*! Bust on me, *nigga*! For real!" he taunts the militia members without getting a rise, in the process embodying some of the strangest, most thoroughly American racial alchemy that is as familiar to me as it would be inscrutable to someone foreign born. It is precisely the kind of subtlety the blunt mainstream narrative around blackness, whiteness, and antiracism is so ill-equipped to convey accurately or even to recognize in the first place, and so it is effaced. I have seen no evidence in the hours of footage that exist to indicate the militiamen themselves had treated the protesters they encountered with racial prejudice. While it is possible it has perhaps for many participants always existed as subtext, it is Rosenbaum alone who has deployed the n-word. But he does not do so pejoratively, at least not regarding black people. Many of the black men standing nearby register the epithet yet take no exception to it, even as they protectively move to restrain him—a white man who is ventriloquizing a distinctly African American Vernacular English style of speaking, out of control and in conflict solely with *other white men*. Those black men and women who are present, and they are numerous, are not visibly involved in the same confrontation. They remain circumspect and, it seems, far more aware of the latent capacity for violence.

*Plus royaliste que le roi,** Rosenbaum appears, in the spirit of so much ante-raising allyship on display that risky season. He edges himself closer to the brink now. Soon he is shoulder to the metal, shoving a flaming dumpster toward the idle gas pumps, as scores of bystanders do nothing, filming this act of patent lunacy from a distance. One young man has the sense to douse the flames with a fire extinguisher.

It is important to take a moment to step back and note the feebleness of the professional police forces on the scene. They appear sporadically in armored vehicles and weakly address the combustible crowd through loudspeakers. Whereas Rittenhouse and the other armed civilians are physically present in the streets, inserting their bodies into the commotion, law enforcement officers are just as good as absent. Both Rittenhouse and Rosenbaum, who has now removed his shirt and wrapped it around his head like a desert nomad, are among the hundreds of men and women told to disperse on Sheridan Road, the main artery. "Back away from the business, back away from the business," an officer commands from the safety of his tank's interior. Rosenbaum is seen among the crowd, swinging a metal chain. Officers slow to a crawl and toss Rittenhouse and his colleagues bottled water through the roof hatch of an armored truck. "We appreciate you guys, we really do," the disembodied voice from the loudspeaker intones. There is something shameful,

* "More of a royalist than the king."

darkly comical, and infuriating about this exchange, and not for the reasons many of the critics of the police have sought to claim. The issue is *not* that law enforcement was too cozy with citizens who have a Second Amendment right to bear arms and prevent their property and communities from being ransacked. The real scandal is that they have *outsourced* the task of keeping fuel pumps from exploding to improvising adolescents. These police are *spectators,* watching a seventeen-year-old attempt to save them.

Fifteen minutes later, the streets still buzz, protesters linger, restlessly scrolling their phones. Rittenhouse walks among this multiracial assembly and asks, "Medical, does anybody need medical?" He is rebuffed by a couple of men in masks and continues onward to an intersection. Officers, who have used their vehicles to corral the mob southward, prevent him from resuming his post in front of Car Source. At 11:44 p.m., reports that rioters are trying to set on fire yet more cars at another lot come across the scanners. "We've seen at least four people with handguns running around here," a dispatcher warns.*

Two minutes after that, Rittenhouse is filmed holding a fire extinguisher, running away from the gas station before slowing to a walk. Now Rosenbaum follows in his wake before picking up his pace, closing the distance between them, and throwing a bag of his own belongings at him. Then the night cracks with a nearby gunshot. Our videographer films from a distance as four more shots in quick succession scatter the crowd into a frenzy. The camera shakes, but Rittenhouse, who's been separated from his colleagues, circles around a parked car. Another three-round burst, and as the focus resumes, he is standing upright and Rosenbaum has fallen.

* "How Kyle Rittenhouse and Joseph Rosenbaum's Paths Crossed in a Fatal Encounter | Visual Forensics," *Washington Post,* YouTube, www.youtube.com /watch?v=LBM9Ke_JI1Q @16:16.

The latter's limp body is hoisted into an SUV and shuttled to a nearby hospital. Rittenhouse makes a phone call, then begins to flee before it's finished. The crowd has grown attuned to him in unison, with tragically imperfect information, reacting to the presence of what seems to be an *active* shooter, as rumor pulses through it. "What did he do?" one man shouts, chasing after Rittenhouse, who stumbles onto his back in the middle of the thoroughfare. Four masked white men are soon upon him, one drop-kicking him in the chest before another smashes him over the head with his skateboard. Rittenhouse receives the blows and shoots the skater in the process, killing him. A third approaches, raising a handgun, and Rittenhouse fires another round, blowing apart his forearm. Then he stands up, the remaining bystanders give a wide berth now, and he shuffles down the street back to the gas station, where a cluster of police vehicles, lights flashing, slowly approach the scene—far too late to be of use to anyone. Hands raised, he attempts to turn himself in, but the armored vehicles *drive right past him.*

Even though the shooter and each of his three targets, as well as the immediate, instigating crowd around them, are *white*—as are a significant, if not majority, share of the protesters—as *The Washington Post* reported, "dispatchers initially relayed a description identifying the gunman as a black man." Rittenhouse ultimately leaves the scene and returns home to his mother. At 1:20 a.m. she drives him to the police department in Antioch, where he attempts to turn himself in a second time, vomiting in the precinct lobby and telling officers that he had "shot two white kids." He is arrested and extradited two months later, on October 30, 2020, from Illinois to Wisconsin. He is charged with two felony counts of intentional homicide, two more felony counts of recklessly endangering the safety of others through use of a dangerous weapon, and a single misdemeanor for possession of a dangerous weapon as a minor.

K enosha: Teen Charged with Murder After Two Black Lives Matter Protesters Killed," read one thoroughly misleading, though illustrative, headline in *The Guardian*. It is crucial to understand that in the context of the summer of 2020 what had happened among four white men could never be understood as unfortunate or tragic or even simply illegal; it was necessary to interpret it as fundamentally *racist*. Rosenbaum—with no discernible history of political engagement on his lengthy curriculum vitae—had been elevated posthumously to the status of "a Black Lives Matter activist." The other two men who'd been shot, Anthony Huber, who hit Rittenhouse with his skateboard, and Gaige Grosskreutz, who drew his handgun, both had criminal records that included convictions for offenses such as disorderly conduct, as well as repeat offenses related to domestic violence in the case of Huber and a misdemeanor conviction for "carrying a firearm while intoxicated" in the case of Grosskreutz. In other words, the specific and complicated causes and effects that produced the awful violence of August 25—all of which contradict the notion that these were primarily peaceful demonstrations—much like the particularities of the shooting of Jacob Blake that preceded it, were reconfigured into a tidier story.

The most prominent voices on race and racism in the country were almost aggressively uncurious when it came to making sense of what had happened. "The violence of Chauvin and Rittenhouse bookended the summer of Trumpism," wrote Ibram X. Kendi in early September:

The three long, hot months from May 25 to August 25 compressed 413 years of American history into a cellphone video in which anyone could easily see the history for what it has always been: the violent "self-defense" of white male supremacy. Colonialism, capitalism, slavery and slave trading, Indian removal, manifest destiny, colonization, the Ku Klux Klan, Chinese exclusion, disenfranchisement, Jim Crow, eugenics, massive resistance, "law and order," Islamophobia, family separation—all were done in the name of defending life or civilization or freedom.

Thus took hold an excruciatingly simplistic tale, fueled by a powerful unwillingness and incapacity to grapple with contemporary American racial and social complexity. It would be repeated from institution to institution, ad nauseam. By the time that Rittenhouse was acquitted of all charges one year later—an anticipated outcome for many legal scholars, given the videotaped facts on the ground in Kenosha and the laws on the books in the state of Wisconsin—universities across the country, for example, felt compelled to issue ideologically committed and reductive moralizing statements in the same vein as Kendi. "Certainly, the verdict raises questions about the wide availability of guns in the United States, this nation's broad definitions of 'self-defense,' and vigilantism in the service of racism and white supremacy," wrote Dwight A. McBride, the president of the New School. But it wasn't just "unabashedly progressive" institutions, as the New School bills itself. In an article cataloging the lockstep reaction, Conor Friedersdorf notes, "More than 2,000 miles away [from Kenosha], administrators at UC Santa Cruz . . . issued a statement that began like this: 'We are disheartened and dismayed by this morning's not guilty verdict on all charges in the trial of Kyle

Rittenhouse. . . . We join in solidarity with all who are outraged by this failure of accountability.'"* The fact that UC Santa Cruz is an enormous *public* school, with more than nineteen thousand students—and thus necessarily a diversity of perspectives—did not give its administrators pause before making such a weighted intervention, presenting "arguable positions as certainties," as Friedersdorf paraphrased the Brown economist Glenn Loury. "Why must this university's senior administration declare, on behalf of the institution as a whole and with one voice, that they unanimously—without any subtle differences of emphasis or nuance—interpret contentious current events through a single lens?"

What was only recently a noncontroversial, indeed a thoroughly *liberal,* position—that academic institutions should remain neutral on debatable issues about which reasonable people can, in good faith, disagree—was being seen in the post-Floyd era of moral clarity as a conservative stance or, worse, one that was complicit with oppression.† With the broad expansion of diversity, equity, and inclusion bureaucracy, it was also increasingly a niche one. UC Irvine's vice-chancellor for DEI issued a statement on behalf of

---

* Conor Friedersdorf, "Universities Try to Force a Consensus About Kyle Rittenhouse," *Atlantic,* Nov. 26, 2021.

† The Kalven Report, a 1967 document commissioned by the University of Chicago and officially titled *Report on the University's Role in Political and Social Action,* famously enumerated the key themes and principles surrounding the role of the university, the limits of institutional involvement, freedom of expression, and larger responsibility to the public. The report emphasized that the mission of the university is the pursuit of knowledge and the free exchange of ideas. While there should be maximal tolerance for individual students and scholars to voice unpopular viewpoints, the institution itself ought to prioritize neutrality. "A good university, like Socrates, will be upsetting," the report concluded.

the school claiming the Rittenhouse verdict meant "neither Black lives nor those of their allies' [*sic*] matter," as if it were obvious that the sole or best way to dignify black lives given the circumstances would be to stand by as young men of various racial and ethnic backgrounds obliterate the property and capital of brown-skinned immigrants.

Nonetheless, such statements and interventions were boosted by journalists and thought leaders across social and traditional media, as though conveying uncontested truths that were self-evident.*

* And here again, social media further muddied the discursive waters: Was that *The New York Times, The Nation,* or *The Guardian* speaking, or was it merely the opinion of one of its employees?

1. Elie Mystal: "In a just world, Rittenhouse would go to jail for a double homicide and illegal gun possession. But we do not live in a just world; we live in a white one." Elie Mystal, "I Hope Everyone Is Prepared for Kyle Rittenhouse to Go Free," *Nation,* Oct. 27, 2021.

2. Nikole Hannah-Jones on Twitter: "In this country, you can even kill white people and get away with it if those white people are fighting for Black lives. This is the legacy of 1619." From "1619 Project's Nikole Hannah-Jones on the Rittenhouse Verdict," GZERO, Nov. 23, 2021, www.gzeromedia.com.

3. Al Sharpton: "These continue to be dark days for black people killed at the hands of people that believe our lives do not matter. This verdict was not only outrageous and dangerous, it was also an obvious signal that encourages and notifies 'vigilantes' that they can continue to use violence to assert their power, and more importantly that they are above the criminal justice system when they do." "Reactions to Not Guilty Verdict in Kyle Rittenhouse Trial," Reuters, Nov. 19, 2021.

4. Kathleen Belew (historian): "The other part of it has to do with white power and militant right groups that are essentially opportunistic. They are looking for a window and this is a big window. Because what it does is, it allows them to not only mount similar shootings like the one carried out in Kenosha to see if they could

More than simply betraying core liberal principles of neutrality and openness, this kind of posturing from elites—much like the expert public health messaging around COVID-19—proved counterproductive and highly provocative. Indeed, it has been *crazy making* for millions of Americans, huge swaths of the electorate who are themselves of diverse makeup and will never be invested in the jargon and orthodoxy of social justice activism, though they can plainly see bias and hypocrisy when it is directed at them.

---

do it elsewhere, it also lets them mobilize in a sector of the right-wing mainstream that is sympathetic to the Rittenhouse story." April Glaser, "A Historian of White Power Reacts to the Rittenhouse Verdict: 'A Bonanza for the Far-Right,'" *Guardian*, Nov. 24, 2021.

CHAPTER SEVEN

We Are All Americans Now: "Antiracism" Goes Global in the Age of Social Media

An isolated monument to a previous era of explicit class hierarchy, the sixteenth-century Château de Tocqueville in coastal Normandy could not lie at a further remove from the intricacies of multicultural life in contemporary Western society. I found myself strolling its immaculate parklands in the fall of 2021, one of a few dozen speakers at the annual Tocqueville Conversations, a two-day conference that would become a referendum on the emergent American social justice ideology most commonly and frustratingly referred to as wokeness. The setting felt significant. After all, this fine home had produced one of the world's keenest interpreters of the American experiment and its global implications. Alexis de Tocqueville's 1835 classic, *Democracy in America,* is the first and best exploration of the paradoxical nature of a vibrant new multi-ethnic society founded on the principles of liberty and equality but compromised from the start by the fact of African slave labor and indigenous land theft. Its author was skeptical such powerful divisions could ever be transcended since, unlike in the racially homogeneous European society he'd been reared in, social rank was written into the very physical characteristics of the nation's diverse inhabitants. Which is to say, in the eyes of white Americans, the presumed inferiority of the Indian and even more so of the African was legible on their faces.

In many ways, it is Tocqueville's world, and we are still living in it, still debating not the truth or untruth of his grim appraisal but merely the degree to which America has been able to move beyond it. Self-proclaimed antiracists insist we haven't and that many of the country's most cherished ideals—individualism, freedom of speech, even the Protestant work ethic—are in fact obstacles to equity, illusions spun by those who have power in order to keep it and hold the marginalized in their place. The short-lived color blind vision of the civil rights movement has, in the post-Obama era, given way to an identity politics of irreconcilable group differences. Yet as the saying has it, when America sneezes, Europe catches a cold.

The French, by contrast, have long prided themselves on an idealistic, republican system of government that doesn't officially recognize racial or ethnic designations. Even keeping official statistics on race has, since the Holocaust, been impermissible. In previous eras immigrants also professed allegiance to this Gallic universal humanism. More and more visibly since the racial reckoning of the summer of 2020, however, and to the alarm of many in the traditional intelligentsia and commentariat in France, American-style, antagonistic multiculturalism has proven attractive to a new and suddenly more diverse generation of students, writers, and activists on the other side of the Atlantic—a generation increasingly prone to suspect that, regardless of any official doctrine, their own social position has also been inscribed in their racialized bodies and faces.

It felt appropriate, then, in a tent set up beneath the window of Tocqueville's exquisite private study, to witness a rather extraordinary exchange of a kind no longer feasible in the U.S. mainstream. I was watching from the audience as the last panel, "Media and the Universities: In Need of Reform and Reassessment?" got under way.

Over the course of the conversations, there had been one recurring question regarding the extent to which what the French have termed *le wokeisme* is or is not a matter of grave concern. Most, if not all, of the speakers and audience, myself included, had answered, more or less, in the affirmative. Taking the stage to argue the opposing position was Rokhaya Diallo, a French-Senegalese journalist, activist, and media personality in her early forties—besides myself and one man who briefly Zoomed in from Washington, D.C., the only person of open African descent in attendance, and the sole Muslim.

On the panel with her were Arthur Milikh, of the hard-right Claremont Institute in Los Angeles; Jean-François Braunstein, a professor of philosophy at the Sorbonne; my friend Yascha Mounk, a professor of political science at Johns Hopkins; and finally the moderator, Perrine Simon-Nahum, a professor of philosophy at the École Normale Supérieure. Diallo is a well-known and intensely polarizing figure in France. An author, documentarian, and *Washington Post* columnist, she is a telegenic proponent of straightforward identity politics with a large social media following and a regular presence on national radio and television programs. As *The New York Times* described her in an editorial, she is "a French journalist whose most noted work addresses a concept that doesn't officially exist in France." She draws parallels between the French and the American criminal justice systems (one recent documentary is titled *From Paris to Ferguson*) and makes the case that there also exists "institutional racism" in her country, for example in discriminatory police stop-and-frisk practices. Her views would hardly be considered extreme in a post–Black Lives Matter American setting, but here in France she is scrutinized as a genuinely subversive agent, perhaps less because she is black or Muslim than because she is unabashedly influenced by a distinctly American ideology. In 2017, under pressure from both the left and the right, President Macron ousted—as Diallo put it to me, "canceled"—her from a government advisory council on the grounds that it is illegal to classify people by race. This move scarcely drew criticism in the mainstream. His education minister at the time, Jean-Michel Blanquer, went further and sued a teachers' union for using the words "institutional racism" in a workshop. Diallo refused to stop using the construction and invited Blanquer to sue her as well.

Many of her critics point out that in 2010 she visited the United States and participated in a "Minority Engagement Strategy" seminar administered by the State Department, in their eyes becoming a trained proselytizer of American social justice propaganda, which in the ostensible service of bolstering marginalized voices and strengthening ethnic-group "representation" directly contradicts key principles of secularism, or *laicité*. During the panel, I was struck almost immediately that Diallo was extended none of the customary, at times fawning, deference name-brand minority intellectuals such as Ibram X. Kendi and Ta-Nehisi Coates receive by default in America from white interlocutors on matters of identity and racism. At first this seemed a healthy change of pace to me. There is, after all, something deeply infantilizing and even perverse about the performance of identity that makes our lives ever more incommunicable to one another, arranged along a scale of sometimes real but often merely presumed suffering defined by group membership that we can only ever narrate or absorb, but never fully share or overcome.*

---

* The writer Coleman Hughes terms this "the Myth of Superior Knowledge" and identifies it as one of the fallacies of the new "antiracism," which he redefines as "neoracism." "People of color are not only morally superior, they claim," he writes. "People of color are epistemically superior as well: they have knowledge of race and racism that is superior to the knowledge that white people have." As such, "neoracists use The Myth of Superior Knowledge to

The moderator opened the conversation with the query "How can we shape citizens in a democracy?" and then spoke pointedly about the potential "destruction of democracy from within by growing elements that undermine humanist fundamentals." If the republican ideal is to produce universal citizens, then are proponents of identity politics "the locus of totalitarianism, a new moral order"? she wondered before pivoting: "I'm not sure that passing on knowledge should be done on an egalitarian platform—it's not possible or even desirable in my view."

Diallo's response was firm but hardly radical. "The circulation of knowledge is also the circulation of experiences," she maintained. "Some minority experiences may be more visible now" thanks to the emergence of social media, which poses a challenge to traditional "elite" knowledge production, which had "filtered out" certain perspectives in the past. The assertion of a knowledge filter, of course, is difficult to dispute. A few weeks after this conference, Macron would become the first French president to publicly acknowledge the 1961 massacre of Algerian protesters by police in Paris. Many French people I've met and talked to over the years admit they'd never been taught this matter of historical record.

"The woke have discovered new epistemologies," Jean-François Braunstein retorted, calling Diallo's position "a staunch attack against science and truth, an insurrection against reality." He wished to expand the scope of the discussion beyond racial identity to encompass the dissolution of the gender binary, which was not a subject Diallo had been addressing. For Simon-Nahum, the larger disagreement about "the conception of knowledge" nonethe-

---

preempt any opposition to what they have to say." Coleman Hughes, *The End of Race Politics* (New York: Thesis, 2024).

less formed a key distinction between the United States and France and was the basis of a justified fear of an increasingly Americanized discourse.

Diallo replied that most people in attendance were very likely "privileged"—not an absurd claim in the setting—and, as such, disproportionately fearful of the "emergence of minorities, people that indeed didn't have access to certain clubs and are questioning things that were considered unquestionable."

"Of course we cannot experience what others experience," Simon-Nahum acknowledged, no longer moderating but fully entering the debate and appearing somewhat angered. "It's called empathy in philosophical terms. Philosophy is about entering into contact with the other, developing a critical mind, to extract myself out of myself with a view to sharing my knowledge of the world with others. I deeply disagree with what you say about privilege."

As the conversation continued like this, with Diallo effectively isolated from the rest of the panel, I started to notice scattered hissing in the audience when she spoke. At no other time had this occurred during any other panel. As the moderator herself refused to play the devil's advocate or even to concede the theoretical possibility of *any* knowledge at all that is derived from or influenced by identity, I noticed a subtle shift in Diallo's face. The expression in her eyes began to retreat. Simon-Nahum pressed on, referring to lived experience not simply as a mistaken argument but as a kind of "domination." "We need a new lexicon to deal with a new democratic project," she expanded. "This intellectual war being waged is a threat to democracy. I feel *threatened* as a citizen."

"A Jew can never understand Racine because he's not French!" Braunstein suddenly added, implicitly comparing Diallo to the extravagantly racist twentieth-century writer Charles Maurras, a

Nazi sympathizer who welcomed Hitler's invasion.* "This is the whole idea of literature," Simon-Nahum parried off him without refuting his excess. "You can understand something without living it in the flesh."

When Diallo objected to the use of "warlike language," calling it an exaggeration, and acknowledged the palpable tension in the room, she reiterated a compromise, taking the conversation away from gender, religion, and race and noting that the *gilets jaunes* movement—a grassroots, working-class uprising spanning the nation that had erupted in November 2018 over a proposed fuel tax and severely challenged Macron's presidency until the onset of COVID-19—had simply made "audible" an economic experience that, to her, ensconced in her own economic bubble, had previously been imperceptible.

"You're placing things on a social level," Simon-Nahum said, dismissing the invocation of class, "but I want to speak about the intellectual level. Plato is more interesting than other writers, but I'm told now I need to teach 'excluded' voices."

"I'm not saying you shouldn't teach Plato!" Diallo interjected with exasperation. To this, an audience member positively screamed, "Mais, si!" (Yes, you are!).

By the end of the discussion, I was feeling somewhat shaken. Perrine Simon-Nahum's comments contrasting the social and the intellectual levels echoed a division I also felt within myself at that very moment. On each discrete point, and with my head, I tended to agree with the philosophers. It would be a terrible, perhaps even insurmountable loss in theory to abandon the universalist, color-blind ideal to the fractured incommensurability of tribal identity. If

* Diallo took exception, and Braunstein replied that he was not comparing her to Maurras.

the sudden ascendance of identity-derived "moral clarity" has taught us anything in the American cultural and institutional landscape, it has taught us this. Yet cumulatively, viscerally, with my heart, and on a level not strictly rational, I also sensed that something unfair, perhaps even wrong, had just transpired. France, like America, is a constantly evolving society, not a fossil preserved in amber. In the past, until much more recently than in America, French society was not made up of many people sharing Diallo's perspective. But today that is less true, and even if the borders were to be permanently sealed, it would still be even less the case going forward. Any attempt to make sense of the contemporary reality, then, will increasingly have to take her arguments seriously, not simply dismiss them. She had attempted to share an experience of French life right now that her interlocutors' behavior—that the entire broader interaction—suggested could not or would not be accepted. Yet, isolated as she was, it would be impossible for her to prove this point without a witness. I understood viscerally how this—every bit as much as watching a news anchor mansplain to you that the violent riot you are regarding is "mostly peaceful"—could be maddening.

Prior to that day, I had considered Diallo my opponent, and she had regarded me warily, as a foreign and privileged non-white spokesman for a universalism that only serves to embed and conceal white prerogatives. It is certainly true that her personal credo, *kiffe ta race* (love your race), which is also the title of her most recent book, directly contradicts my own published positions against the continued reproduction of racial identity, which have found sympathy in the French media across the political spectrum. And yet, when she walked off that stage alone, I found myself rushing to catch up with her. As we spoke, to my surprise, my eyes became teary. What I realized was that I simply wanted her to know that I had also seen what she'd experienced. "That happens all the time here," she told me. "It happens all the time."

Before the presidential election in April 2022, in real political terms the French left had appeared to be in tatters, broken by the centrist En Marche movement (now Renaissance) that Macron founded in 2016 after parting from the Socialists and moving his policies rightward. The unexpectedly strong third-place finish of the far-left candidate, Jean-Luc Mélenchon, illustrated a more complicated electoral picture.* But what remained certain was that in institutional terms it is difficult to perceive in France any of the informal but highly coercive power progressives in America exercise throughout the media, academia, and cultural and elite-corporate spaces. There is no French Robin DiAngelo, and a journalist of the stature and integrity of James Bennet could never be scapegoated in France for the crime of publishing an insensitive opinion. Representation is far from a mainstream obsession. Outside a sole prestigious school, Sciences Po, in Paris, affirmative action is scarcely ever practiced. Perhaps because of comparatively muscular labor laws (which Macron has moved to weaken), people do not live in constant fear of cancellation for controversial speech or any other transgression, either in university or in the workplace, and even the #MeToo movement could not gain traction in a country whose major left-leaning newspapers published unequivocal, star-studded defenses of pedophilia as recently as the late 1970s.† When it comes

---

* A picture that has grown far more complicated with the snap parliamentary elections of 2024 that have elevated both the disparate left and the Le Peniste right and enfeebled Macron.
† "In 1977, a petition was addressed to the French parliament calling for the abrogation of several articles of the age of consent law and the decriminal-

to the American culture war staples like newfangled pronouns and genderless bathrooms—which alongside race are definitional to "wokeness"—there is little patience here for the embellishment of personal self-presentation. Even the relatively modest, gender-neutral *iel* was forcefully dismissed by the first lady, Brigitte Macron. "Our language is beautiful. And two pronouns is enough," she has argued.

Yet, since 2020, the reaction to the language and rhetoric of identity politics in the United States and France has overlapped to an ever greater degree, though with at least one critical distinction: in the latter case the controversy over *le wokeisme* is almost always a proxy for a deeper, older, and not completely unjustified concern about Islam and terror on the European continent. Those seen as permissive of wokeness are presumed to be indulging not merely a narcissistic victim complex that would sort the national population along a scale of virtue based on supposedly quantifiable oppressions, but something far more sinister: *islamo-gauchisme,* what the far-right, perennial presidential contender Marine Le Pen has defined as the unhealthy alliance between "Islamist fanatics" and the French left, or what the traditionally liberal philosopher Pascal Bruckner describes as "the fusion between the atheist Far Left and religious radicalism."* Rooted in anti-capitalist perceptions of

---

ization of all consensual relations between adults and minors below the age of fifteen (the age of consent in France). A number of French intellectuals—including such prominent names as Michel Foucault, Jacques Derrida, Roland Barthes, Simone de Beauvoir, and Jean-François Lyotard signed the petition." "The 1977 French Petition to Abolish Age of Consent Laws," Medium, Mar. 1, 2022. See: "1977 French Petition against Age of Consent Laws," Internet Archive, https://archive.org/details/letter-scanned-and-ocr.

* This kind of leftist Islamism has recently become more legible to Americans in the wake of October 7, as an alarming amount of LGBTQ and secular anti-

Islam's potential for fomenting unrest toward the goal of radically remaking bourgeois society, this is understood as a marriage of convenience with reactionary Muslim parties, who in turn pretend to join the left in its opposition to racism, neocolonialism, and globalization as a tactical and temporary means of amassing power. It is the potentially violent Muslim, then, not simply the man with dark skin, who represents the ultimate "other" in France's racial imaginary. But even in the absence of physical violence, the politics of identity that would give cover to any grievance-inflected separatism that diminishes common citizenship is seen in this light as wholly unacceptable—this is what Simon-Nahum really meant when she admitted to feeling "threatened" as a citizen—and so, for some, matters as trivial as halal-themed aisles in the supermarket take on an existential quality that has no pure equivalent in American life in the twenty-first century.

Social-media-driven international "wokeness" tends to trivialize these serious concerns or dismiss them as nothing more than brute racism. This is an error. At the same time, such vigilance over the most severe consequences of tribalism permanently raises the stakes of any debate and makes compromise unlikely. This is counterproductive to addressing the complexity of minority and

---

racist progressives on college campuses and in the media openly celebrated and embraced Hamas. The Rutgers University chapter of Students for Justice in Palestine called the massacre a "justified retaliation." Jeffrey Brown, Sam Weber, and Shoshana Dubnow, "Israel-Hamas War Leads to Heated Debate and Protests on College Campuses," PBS, Oct. 23, 2023.

Most infamously, a coalition of Harvard student groups published a statement just three days after the attacks proclaiming to "hold the Israeli regime entirely responsible for all the unfolding violence." J. Sellers Hill and Nia L. Orakwue, "Harvard Student Groups Face Intense Backlash for Statement Calling Israel 'Entirely Responsible' for Hamas Attack," *Harvard Crimson,* Oct. 10, 2023.

religious life in a traditionally secular society already remade by waves of immigration. Worse, it allows valid concerns about a perceived lack of recognition, dignity, and inclusion to go painfully unaddressed. Though there are no official statistics in France, by some estimates young people perceived to be black or Arab are up to twenty times as likely to be stopped and frisked. In 2020, a video of the savage, unprovoked beating of a black music producer at the hands of armored police in a Paris vestibule went viral, shocking the nation and lending credence to the argument that there are some identity-based experiences the language of universalism has not yet evolved to articulate. And so the activists and those listening to them have looked to America for another vocabulary to express what is happening in their own country, whether or not it fully makes sense here. After George Floyd died, a growing number now felt they'd found it.

"Ideological debates differ from country to country, according to which particular aspect of the situation is emphasized or disregarded, according to the angle of vision or the tradition of thought," Raymond Aron wrote in *The Opium of the Intellectuals*. "Sometimes the debates truly reflect the problems which a nation must seek to resolve, sometimes they distort or transform them in order to fit into would-be universal patterns." Living between these two particular countries, France and America, and studying the same arguments in both of them, I have come to believe the former provides something like a control set—an eerily familiar parallel universe with several crucial variations—through which Americans might contemplate the excesses and limitations, as well as the values and merits, of the social justice ideology that has gripped and transformed our own society so powerfully over the past decade and a half.

· · ·

On September 13, 2001, beside an image of the Statue of Liberty shrouded in heavy clouds of smoke, the cover of *Le Monde* proudly declared, "Nous sommes tous Américains." It was a grand and heartfelt gesture of solidarity in the face of incomprehensible hatred and barbarity, one that was returned in 2015 as a wave of terror swept back across the Atlantic over France. That extraordinary year began in Paris with the massacre by militants affiliated with al-Qaeda of twelve people in the offices of the satirical magazine *Charlie Hebdo,* which had republished blasphemous Danish caricatures of the Prophet. It concluded with a citywide rampage in November, which left hundreds slain in cafés, restaurants, and the iconic Bataclan concert hall, all slaughtered by homegrown radicals declaring allegiance to ISIS. The immediate outpouring of grief in the American press at the sight of this destruction, and the widely adopted initiative on Facebook to filter millions of profile pictures in real time with the tricolor, was as moving as it was justified. The sense of shared struggle and common values was palpable, undeniable.

What a difference just five years can make. By the fall of 2020, America in the age of George Floyd and Donald Trump had fully turned its gaze inward, no longer seeming to have the stamina or the desire to interpret events elsewhere on their own terms. In the United States, there was simmering guilt over the very real legacy of slavery and systemic racism as well as contemporary police brutality. This was combined with an evolving elite consensus—often well meaning but just as often imaginatively impoverished—around a new and totalizing racial binary: at one pole, monolithic, undifferentiated whiteness (peoples of European descent, but, when it is narratively convenient, Arabs and "white" Latinos and Asians, and even wrong-thinking black people); at the other pole, generic non-whiteness, comprising the vast bulk of humanity or so-called

POC. Seemingly overnight, there was a new and pronounced reluctance in the mainstream press and agenda-setting social media to view what was happening in France (namely, a spree of gruesome machete cuttings, full decapitations, and stabbings, from Paris down to the Riviera) through the lens of agency and ideology, radical religion, terrorism, or even simple good and evil. Suddenly it was about identity categories and systems of oppression. In the cold light of the current racial reckoning, fanatically secular and officially color-blind France had, in a sense, brought this grief upon itself.

An eyebrow-raising headline in *The New York Times* encapsulated this new attitude of reproach. Following the monstrous beheading of a high school teacher named Samuel Paty in October 2020—for the transgression of showing the *Charlie Hebdo* cartoons in class for instructional purposes—the first analysis of the attack read simply, "French Police Shoot and Kill Man After a Fatal Knife Attack on the Street." Adam Nossiter, then the paper's Paris bureau chief, described the victim as having "incited anger" among his Muslim students. The implication, echoed throughout the American media in stark contrast to the events of 2015, was unambiguous: it was as if the very act of teaching the universal value of free speech to all students, regardless of ethnic affiliation, were what had *really* led to Paty's murder. (The soft, "antiracist" bigotry here being, of course, the unstated assumption that Muslims could not be expected to understand satire or handle free expression.) This in turn seemed to exculpate Paty's assassin, an eighteen-year-old Chechen asylum recipient with deranged and extremist beliefs who had brutally hunted down his victim only after learning of his existence through a reckless and misinformed outrage mob on Twitter.

The asymmetry here matters. It is a mark of American insularity—and certainly of American power—that it is impossible to imagine Americans having a profound or sustained reaction of any kind to reporting and commentary on the United States in *Le Monde*. Yet it was painful for many French people of all ethnicities and religious affiliations to read such coverage in the American press. For months, the perceived abandonment of an admired and most influential ally became the subject of constant conversation in the French media and in living rooms, too. After all, was it not the Islamists who just five years earlier had left hundreds—including many non-whites and some Muslims—dead in the streets and many thousands more with lifelong trauma? Was it not the individual adherents of a radical ideology, and not some abstract identity group, who had made it necessary for the poor teacher to organize a lesson around the principles of civil liberty in the first place? Why had the world's English-language paper of record framed this act of barbarism in the logic of a simple—and, the insinuation being, possibly excessive—police shooting? Worse, why were journalists at other outlets, most notoriously *The Washington Post** but there were others, suddenly invested in reinforcing a narrative that would reduce complex issues of *laïcité,* republicanism, and immigration into the blunt racial catchall of "whiteness"? (After all, it's not as though significant numbers of African and Arab-descended French citizens were not also vocally appalled by such violence.) Why was this ideological framework being imposed on France?

Out of a deep-seated and reflexive anti-American impulse and regardless of the social reality on the ground, then, many French people began to see—and *wished* to see—France emerge as a pivotal

---

* "Instead of responding with moral clarity and dignity to the international spotlight on France's race relations, discrimination and state violence," wrote Karen Attiah, *The Washington Post*'s global opinions editor, "Macron and the French media establishment have responded with a feverish fragility." Karen Attiah, "Macron's Centrist and Tolerant Facade Is Crumbling," *Washington Post,* Dec. 3, 2020.

theater of resistance to this new orthodoxy, with President Macron himself becoming an energized and vocal opponent, insisting that his country has its own unique culture and way of achieving a multiethnic democracy and would not be well served by mimicking the identity-obsessed American model. "We have left the intellectual debate to . . . Anglo-Saxon traditions based on a different history, which is not ours," he argued in his October 2020 speech against separatism. "There's a battle to wage against an intellectual matrix from American universities," is how Blanquer described the problem.

The unease with *le wokeisme* in France, then, is twofold, stemming from legitimate concerns about homegrown jihadism and the decades-long erosion of distinctly French culture through domineering Yankee influence. And so the highest levels of government were now preemptively confronting this tricky combination of an acute domestic threat blanketed in the nebulous projection of a distinctly foreign situation. As one journalist I spoke to put it, "It is almost like the French are playing an intellectual game, like, '*Imagine* if France were woke, how would we respond?'" And yet there may be real value in such a thought exercise all the same—even if it is a rehashing of similar debates that already played out here in the 1990s, when fears about the imposition of American-style PC culture were all the rage.

Jean-Michel Blanquer, the minister of national education from 2017 to 2022, emerged as one of France's most consistent, controversial, and powerful opponents of wokeness. In January 2022 he spoke at and lent the state's imprimatur to a colloquium at the Sorbonne, titled "After Deconstruction," which brought together an array of critics of the new race- and gender-inflected social justice ideology, from traditional non-identitarian liberals to some genuinely illiberal voices on the far right, such as the Canadian commentator Mathieu Bock-Côté, who replaced the xenophobic presidential candidate Éric Zemmour on the Fox News–esque cable network CNews. As one attendee, the French scholar Bruno Chaouat of the University of Minnesota, wrote, the two-day conference "would have gained in interest if it had included opponents, but it is not the first symposium that has been reduced to an echo chamber." However, as Chaouat emphasized to me over dinner near his home in St. Paul, Minnesota, despite this lack of diverging perspectives, "something is indeed happening to us that threatens the construction of a common world, a construction to which the teaching of the humanities is supposed to contribute. It is indeed faith in a human universal that is shaken." What is of the utmost concern to Chaouat, and what Blanquer is attempting to combat—perhaps prematurely in a French context but with the benefit of hindsight from an American one—is a new reality of social fragmentation, "not at the sociological, economic, and political level but at the ontological level, at the level of [society's] very being."

Critics of the symposium, and of Blanquer, such as the sociologist François Dubet, of the prestigious École des Hautes Études, who published a scathing op-ed in *Le Monde,* warn that a state-sponsored conference against a loose assortment of positions and views smacks of a "soft McCarthyism." "It is no more and no less than the creation of an internal enemy," he argued, a move that itself threatens to undermine the very values of reason and republicanism it claims to uphold, in no small part by forcing "those who value academic freedom to defend the right to exist of ideas, work, and research that they would certainly not support" on purely intellectual grounds. "How can we think that it is up to the State to say which currents of thought are acceptable and which are not? How can we not have enough confidence in the academic and scientific world to let a minister of education lead a prosecution against the ideas and research that disturb him?"

In less alarmist terms, as Mathieu Lefevre of More in Common, an Anglo-French nonprofit working to reunite divided societies, explained the problem to me, the question of what to do about wokeness "rearranges the chairs at the ideological dinner party in interesting ways." Because it injects limiting ideas about race and religious identity into the antiracist and secular discourse, it also opens the door to a kind of left-illiberalism that it has been traditionally virtuous from a liberal position to oppose. And yet, simultaneously, "being anti-woke allows a proximity between the center and the far right; you start with a *colloque* about *le wokeisme* and you end up questioning foundational liberal principles like freedom of expression." (One month after the conference, the minister of higher education at the time, Frédérique Vidal, announced the establishment of an official government inquiry into French public universities in order "to assess what comes from militancy and opinion.")

These were some of the nuances and contradictions on my mind when I visited Blanquer one evening in March 2022. I wanted to understand why, precisely, *le wokeisme* was of such a pressing concern in a society that I had lived in now for ten years but only recently begun to suspect was and would continue to be far less willing to entertain the often farcical excesses that have proved so disruptive back where I came from. The moment I crossed the entrance to the Ministry of Education, in Paris's tony 7th arrondissement, I got a partial answer: there was a prominently placed portrait of Samuel Paty, the tragically beheaded high school teacher who has become a kind of icon of republicanism—a real-world martyr to the ultimate dehumanizing consequences of zealous group identification. Blanquer's voluminous ground-floor office, with a lit fireplace and expansive views of a walled garden, felt reassuring by comparison.

Blanquer is bald-headed, matter-of-fact, and fluent in English. It was while studying at Harvard in the 1990s that he first became aware of the PC culture that was the test run for today's crisis. While sympathizing with many of the aims of political correctness, he told me that he began to suspect the practice of treating women and minorities as different and special was ultimately antithetical to equality. "In the history of ideas, it's not the first time that when you push an idea to the extreme, it becomes its contrary," he said. When I asked him why he suggested in the past that the battle against wokeness has already been lost, he admitted that it was only "a provocation—I never think we'll lose." I told him about my impression after watching Rokhaya Diallo speaking at the Tocqueville Conversations that wokeness seemed impossible in France. "Well, the situation is that if you speak with the population in general, they are not with Rokhaya," he acknowledged. "Ninety percent of the people, even the Muslim people or people of different minorities, would be against her. But among the elites, this sector is winning each day some parts of the market in academic and media life."

When I asked him if there were some specific cases of cancel culture in the French context that approached the level of James Bennet at *The New York Times,* or Greg Patton, the professor of business communication at USC who was investigated for pronouncing a word in Chinese that merely sounded like the n-word, he paused for a moment. Eventually, he mentioned a production of *The Suppliant Maidens,* by Aeschylus. In 2019 there were American-style protests over a ludicrous claim that the ancient Greeks had dabbled in blackface. But these protests were unsuccessful and far from popular, and when I attended the opening-night performance, the minister of culture was there in attendance in a sign of solidarity against the attempted cancellation. In the typical American debate, this would have been the moment that the claim is made that cancel culture doesn't exist.

Blanquer conceded all of this, then made an unexpectedly compelling case to shift these realities to his rhetorical advantage. He flipped the debate on its head: wokeness, cancel culture, whatever you want to call it, these forces operate successfully in the United States and other parts of the Anglo world because that balkanized model of multiculturalism is fundamentally vulnerable. The French, in his estimation, are not invincible, but have the advantage of a model of republicanism that is better equipped to weather the tumultuous new ideological currents. His bold idea was to create "laboratories of the Republic" and *export* them to America. This was what President Macron meant when he insisted there are other ways of conceptualizing the multiethnic society that don't depend on the American emphasis on identity politics. "Instead of having Americans invading France," Blanquer said, "we will create institutions to provide explanations about secularism, about the republican approach, and to tell *The New York Times,* are you able to have a real debate about that instead of caricatures about France?"

I liked this idea, which I found quixotic in the best way, and left the ministry, pausing once again to consider that tragic portrait of Samuel Paty. "In France, *wokeisme* is probably extremely limited and contained, but it can kill," Chaouat would later remind me, erroneously conflating identity politics *tout court* with murderous fundamentalism while accurately exposing the existence not of a binary but of a continuum. Staring at that poor teacher, I could not argue with his conclusion: "[Wokeness] can be very dangerous when it's a matter of supporting people who claim that there is [such a thing as] blasphemy."

. . .

In 1975 the French philosopher Michel Foucault published *Discipline and Punish: The Birth of the Prison,* marking his turn from earlier historical and structuralist work into the explicit analysis of power, establishing himself as one of the most influential thinkers in the English-speaking world for decades to come. In Foucault's telling, power is not just something that is possessed (the way a king might possess the power to dominate his subjects) but rather something far more diffuse, flowing through society. While present everywhere, it is anything but evenly distributed, pooling in certain areas while remaining precariously shallow in others.

This was a groundbreaking vision, and one that informs our American sense of reality today more than ever before: in place of any particular oppressor there is instead a vague, slightly conspiratorial sense that there is some *them* out there, systematically sowing oppression.* The field of critical race theory, which was popularized and demonized after the summer of 2020 as "CRT," and which grew out of critical legal studies in the 1980s and 1990s, inherited this tendency along with other core Foucauldian tenets, such as the centrality of embodied experience and the impossibility of neutral, objective perspective. But it is not new. Twenty years after *Discipline and Punish,* the collection of essays *Critical Race Theory: The Key Writings That Formed the Movement* was released, already looking

---

* This mode of analysis is recognizable, for example, in the sociologist Eduardo Bonilla-Silva's highly influential 2003 study, *Racism Without Racists: Color-Blind Racism and the Persistence of Racial Inequality in America.* Both Bonilla-Silva's understanding of "color-blind racism" and Foucault's theories of power emphasize ways in which power operates through discourse, ideology, and governance to perpetuate systems of inequality and oppression irrespective of individual agents.

retrospectively on the discipline. Six years after that, *Critical Race Theory: An Introduction* appeared for broad use in survey courses, announcing the field's arrival.

Most Americans, of course, had never even heard the term "CRT" until Donald Trump, Donald Trump Jr., Tucker Carlson, the activist Christopher Rufo, and various other reactionary and opportunistic figures began invoking it as a catchall bogeyman in the raging culture war of the 2020 election cycle.* But over the past decade, plenty had become acquainted with its key assumptions, premises, and modes of inquiry in the massively popular works of racial literature that dominated the publishing industry since Ta-Nehisi Coates's epoch-defining memoir *Between the World and Me* paved the way for DiAngelo's *White Fragility,* Ibram X. Kendi's *How to Be an Antiracist,* and *The New York Times Magazine*'s alternate history and school curriculum, *The 1619 Project.* At the same time, as the digital manners and meme culture that developed organically on activist-centric Tumblr migrated to media-saturated Twitter, the jargon of academe—that "critical" preference for "bodies" instead of "people," "white supremacy" instead of "prejudice," "patriarchy" instead of "sexism," among many other previously esoteric constructions—became the lingua franca of social media at the precise technological and cultural moment in which social media in turn became the communications tool to dominate the Western zeitgeist.

Many commentators have observed that these ideas and others along with them, "French theory," have volleyed back and forth across the Atlantic, between Europe and America, adapting and

---

* Rufo himself stated this plainly on Twitter on March 15, 2021: "We have successfully frozen their brand—'critical race theory'—into the public conversation and are steadily driving up negative perceptions. We will eventually turn it toxic, as we put all of the various cultural insanities under that brand category."

mutating over time as they spread through new populations and return in modified form.* But the mutual influence and regard stretches back further still. Late in *Democracy in America,* there is a short, thought-provoking passage titled, with typical nineteenth-century flair, "How Americans Counteract Individualism by the Doctrine of Self-Interest Properly Understood." Here, Tocqueville already depicted the aristocratic European order that had produced him as morally outmoded. "When the world was controlled by a small number of powerful and wealthy individuals, they enjoyed promoting a lofty ideal of man's duties," he writes. By contrast, "the inhabitants of the United States almost always [know] how to combine their own well-being with that of their fellow citizens." This pragmatic, quotidian doctrine of self-interest properly understood, he concedes, does not inspire the kinds of grand gestures and virtuous sacrifices that attain the dimensions of noble beauty. On the contrary, the American way vulgarizes the ethical ideal, preventing the rare few from rising significantly above "the ordinary level of humanity." Nonetheless, he concludes that of all the moral philosophies it is the one best suited to the needs of contemporary citizens; were everyone to adopt the American habits, "gross depravity would be less common." And so, he encourages his French audience to look seriously at the New World not as something foreign but as a harbinger of the future.

It is no exaggeration to say that "wokeness" is also a destroyer of virtue and beauty. It makes a slogan of the ineffable, betrays every secret, spoils the ending of every tale. The politics of identity

---

* The process was once memorably explained to me as akin to eating at Pizza Hut in Italy. Yes, it is pizza, which is a style of food with origins in Naples. But it was altered in America, and the combination of dough and cheese and tomato sauce that ricocheted back across the Atlantic from the New World had become something else entirely.

that undergirds the obsession with social justice obliterates every marker of individuality and subordinates every psychological ambiguity to the stark and inflexible dictates of abstraction. It smacks of determinism—trapping our present in a soul-crushing and neverending past that likewise steals the innocence from any collective future. Despite all of that, I have had to ask myself whether any amount of the ideology is healthy at all. Like a controlled burning of the underbrush that prevents the wild conflagration later, is it the case that a limited American-style turn counteracts the divisions of identity precisely by recognizing the divisions of identity?

I am convinced that the authentically color-blind society is the final destination every Western society must assiduously direct itself toward. But there will be painful and counterintuitive stops as we attempt to get there. In a classified memo published on WikiLeaks, the former U.S. ambassador Charles H. Rivkin laid out the pragmatic, self-interested rationale for that minority recruitment program Diallo had participated in years ago: "French institutions have not proven themselves flexible enough to adjust to an increasingly heterodox demography. We believe that if France, over the long run, does not successfully increase opportunity and provide genuine political representation for its minority populations, France could become a weaker, more divided country, perhaps more crisis-prone and inward-looking, and consequently a less capable ally."

I was haunted by these words as I watched the results come in for the French election in 2022. For the time, Macron, and thus the liberal center, was able to hold.* But an identity-driven extrem-

---

* More recently it has begun to crumble again, as the cordon sanitaire against making alliances with the far-right National Rally party was breached for the first time in the European elections of 2024, provoking Macron to call snap parliamentary elections that resulted in the ascendancy of both the far-left and far-right coalitions and a departure from the prior centrist majority.

ism flourished, with the nationalist Le Pen coming in second and the Muslim Brotherhood–endorsed Mélenchon, who captured some 70 percent of the Muslim vote, virtually tied with her in third place. There is a surprising amount of overlap between the latter two, most notably an indulgent and infuriating irresponsibility when it comes to Vladimir Putin.* Both have long records of advocating "non-alignment" and disparaging NATO and the European Union at a time when Russian forces are massing on the Continent and France has become the de facto leader of the European Union. Macron cannot run again. Were either of these two—or alternatives channeling similar forces—to assume the presidency in the future, the catastrophe would be enormous.

"We wish to retain everything and often lose the lot," Tocqueville had cautioned in that essay, before seeming to anticipate the overwhelming self-absorption that defines the politics of identity in a democratic society. "No power on earth can stop the increasing equality of social conditions . . . from disposing each citizen to become wrapped up in himself." If the question then is not how to stamp out but how to responsibly channel these impulses as we consider the flawed but understandable myopia of group identity, I can't help but think of Winston Churchill's famous apocryphal quip about liberalism: you have no head if you wholly embrace it, but if you categorically reject it, you have no heart either. *Le wokeisme*, or whatever one wants to call it, is a problem because of what it gets wrong—most notably the subordination of individual to group identity and the fetishization of racial and other differences. The glaring fallacy that there can ever be a *single* problem with a single solution. But it is even more of a danger because it is so often *par-*

---

* Tribal polarization is, of course, also powerfully undermining support of Ukraine and opposition to Putin in America.

tially true. There really are limitless past oppressions to stew over,* and some not insignificant number of them continue to affect us in new and sometimes subtle ways.

A priori, it is hard to deny the superiority of the French model of universal citizenship—*liberté, égalité, fraternité*. In practice, the American reflex of "speaking-as-a" does manage to perceive real experiences that otherwise can be dismissed altogether and, when suppressed long enough, put us all at risk—even if the partial truths they reveal may ultimately obscure more than they can ever illuminate. It would be a mistake for either culture to mold itself wholly in the image of the other. I am convinced that the future belongs to the open, multiethnic, liberal society that finds a firm yet flexible third way to fully face the truth and synthesize the two.

* Victimization Olympics is a game truly anyone can play. Even Vladimir Putin has taken a page out of the playbook of historical grievance, painstakingly making his case for the invasion of Ukraine with a detailed list of slights stretching back to the ninth century. And he has self-published a kind of delusional Russian *1619 Project*, reimagining his own country's true history and founding.

CHAPTER EIGHT

"Cancel Culture" and Its Discontents

In March 2022, one month after launching his war of aggression that collapsed city blocks, murdered, pillaged, displaced, and raped civilians by the thousands, and snapped Ukraine into existential territory no European nation has known since World War II, Vladimir Putin claimed during a televised meeting with leading cultural figures that "the West" was "trying to cancel" Russia. More specifically, he said it was attempting "to cancel a whole 1,000-year culture, our people."

It was certainly true that Russia had been disinvited or banned from the Champions League men's soccer final and the Formula One Grand Prix, as well as the European Broadcasting Union's Eurovision song contest. The Royal Opera House had also rescinded an offer of residency for Moscow's Bolshoi Ballet, which had planned to stage twenty-one performances over the summer. The Mariinsky Orchestra, of St. Petersburg, likewise would no longer be welcome to perform at Carnegie Hall, a venue at which the distinguished conductor Valery Gergiev, a friend and supporter of Putin's, had been replaced. In Europe, the Munich Philharmonic also split with Gergiev for failing to condemn the invasion. As did the Verbier Festival in Switzerland, which asked him to resign as music director of the Verbier Festival Orchestra. In the Netherlands, the Rotterdam Philharmonic threatened to scrap him too. Russian artists pulled themselves out of the Russian Pavilion at the Venice Biennale—a *self-cancellation*—and Warner Bros., Disney, and Sony stopped releasing their films in Russian cinemas. The second-ranked men's tennis player in the world at the time, Daniil Medvedev, along with all the other Russian and Belarusian players on tour, was forbidden to compete at Wimbledon that summer. Even esteemed *dead* Russian cultural figures had become verboten overnight—posthumous guilt by association—with the Cardiff Philharmonic Orchestra removing Tchaikovsky from its program.*

But then Putin said something genuinely outrageous, though telling in the extreme. He directly compared the ostracism of the Russian state in the realms of culture and diplomacy to the ongoing controversy surrounding the British author J. K. Rowling's statements on the subject of women's rights and transgender people. "Recently they canceled the children's writer Joanne Rowling," Putin said, "because she—the author of books that have sold hundreds of millions of copies worldwide—fell out of favor with fans of so-called gender freedoms."† He was referring, of course, to Rowling's public interventions into fraught but necessary debates about women's rights and dignity and transgender inclusion in previously

---

* This move was widely criticized at the time. Putin compared it to Nazi book burning in the 1930s.

† Rowling immediately distanced herself from Putin's comments. "Critiques of western cancel culture are possibly not best made by those currently slaughtering civilians for the crime of resistance, or who jail and poison their critics," she tweeted to her more than fourteen million Twitter followers, adding the hashtag #IStandWithUkraine.

single-sex categories and spaces, such as prisons, restrooms, changing rooms, and sporting competitions. Whether or not Rowling,
who is one of the most successful and beloved living writers and a
billionaire, was or really ever could be "canceled" is a matter of dispute. But by 2020, she undeniably became the subject of ferocious
online abuse after she quote-tweeted an article titled "Creating a
More Equal Post-COVID-19 World for People Who Menstruate." The
comment she appended read, " 'People who menstruate.' I'm sure
there used to be a word for those people. Someone help me out.
Wumben? Wimpund? Woomud?"*

Putin in particular, and Russia in general, had long been viewed
by certain fringes of the European and American right wing as a
bastion of traditional white male virility[†] for his strict stance against

---

* In the ascendant social justice framework that extends—perhaps most
powerfully—well beyond race into questions of sexuality, gender, and biological sex, the simple act of questioning such neologistic constructions as "people
who menstruate" was seen by many as an explicit statement of transphobia.
Prior to this, in December 2019, Rowling had also drawn backlash for express-
ing support for Maya Forstater, a researcher who was fired from the Centre
for Global Development after she expressed skepticism of proposed changes
in U.K. law that would allow people to self-identify their gender. Forstater had
argued that biological sex should be the sole determinant of gender and that
trans women should not be recognized as women in all circumstances, particularly in potentially vulnerable contexts such as women's single-sex spaces.
In July 2023, as was reported by the BBC, Forstater "was found to have experienced discrimination while working for the Centre for Global Development
(CGD). . . . In their decision on Friday, three London judges said Ms Forstater
should receive compensation of £91,500 and interest of £14,904.31." "Maya
Forstater: Woman Gets Payout for Discrimination over Trans Tweets," BBC,
July 1, 2023.
[†] In contradiction of the even more traditional prejudice that holds that Slavs
are not really "white."

"gay propaganda" and other instances of liberal decadence. Was not, he seemed to suggest, the invasion of a sovereign country really just another strike against the stifling consensus of monothought imposed by the hegemonic, totalitarian liberal order? This was an extraordinarily cynical rhetorical ploy, as preposterous given the scale of the slaughter and transgression meted out by the Russian state as it was unintentionally elucidating regarding the genuine severity of abuse that ordinary, nonviolent public and private figures were being subjected to for all manner of alleged wrongthink in the West. The shunning, scapegoating, and loss of reputation and livelihood were in many cases of the same order of magnitude for the children's author who objects to the neologism "people who menstruate" as for the conductor who stands in solidarity with the murderous dictator. A similarity that should in fact give us pause, if not for the reasons that Putin intended.

In June and July 2020, in the heated days and weeks after watching the video of George Floyd's death in Minneapolis and corresponding with American friends about the bizarre and chilling institutional and cultural developments that had followed it, I was part of a group of five writers who drafted and organized "A Letter on Justice and Open Debate." That document was ultimately signed by more than 150 artists and intellectuals, some of whom were very famous, from the far left to the center right of the political spectrum—including most dramatically Rowling herself, but also Salman Rushdie, Noam Chomsky, Cornel West, Francis Fukuyama, and Margaret Atwood—and published on the *Harper's Magazine* website on July 7. The Harper's Letter, as it became known, made an extremely simple point: justice and freedom are inextricable values and, in a democracy, one cannot exist in the absence of the other. "Our cultural institutions are facing a moment of trial," the letter argued in simple and clear terms.

> Powerful protests for racial and social justice are leading to overdue demands for police reform, along with wider calls for greater equality and inclusion across our society, not least in higher education, journalism, philanthropy, and the arts. But this needed reckoning has also intensified a new set of moral attitudes and political commitments that tend to weaken our norms of open debate and toleration of differences in favor of ideological conformity. As we applaud the first development, we also raise our voices against the second. The forces of illiberalism are gaining strength throughout the world and have a powerful ally in Donald Trump, who represents a real threat to democracy. But resistance must not be allowed to harden into its own brand of dogma or coercion—which right-wing demagogues are already exploiting. The democratic inclusion we want can be achieved only if we speak out against the intolerant climate that has set in on all sides.

The letter identified "an intolerance of opposing views, a vogue for public shaming and ostracism, and the tendency to dissolve complex policy issues in a blinding moral certainty." And it stressed that "the restriction of debate, whether by a repressive government or an intolerant society, invariably hurts those who lack power and makes everyone less capable of democratic participation. The way to defeat bad ideas is by exposure, argument, and persuasion, not by trying to silence or wish them away." Despite its frankly anodyne message—truly the bare minimum for a liberal, open society—the text proved powerfully divisive and was viewed three million times on the *Harper's* website alone, translated and reprinted in leading newspapers around the world, from *Le Monde* in France to *El País* in Spain, *Die Zeit* in Germany, *La Repubblica* in Italy, *Reforma* in Mexico, and also in publications in Japan and the Netherlands. Though it purposefully avoided use of the term, the letter immediately became part of an explosive and ongoing debate around the subject of "cancel culture" that continues to this day.*

"Free thinking is not harmful to disadvantaged social groups," as one hundred Spanish-language intellectuals, including the Nobel laureate Mario Vargas Llosa, put it in their own open letter in support of the Harper's Letter. "On the contrary, we believe it is emancipatory and censorship, however well-intentioned it may want to present itself, is counterproductive." This is a position that proved extremely controversial at the time of the letter's publication and, to my chagrin and continuing surprise, has remained so in the years that have followed. The exploitative co-optation of justifiable concern over so-called cancel culture by some insincere voices on the right and in the middle, and by elected officials and public figures on all sides—of which Putin's comparisons are but the most extreme example—as well as those who simply wish to avoid accountability for misconduct of any kind, has muddied the debate.

Critics of the letter, a variety of whom were also leading advocates for the shift to "moral clarity" in theory and "antiracism" in practice—*reality itself is biased; therefore, debate must be restricted,*

---

* As is the case with "wokeness," I genuinely dislike this term and believe it obfuscates more than it clarifies, alluding as it does to a variety of complex and subtle practices and attitudes. I avoid it and try to use more specific language whenever possible. It is difficult for most people who use the construction even to define. Yet, like wokeness, it is a memorable and accessible shorthand that symbolizes *something* real and wrong operating in the culture. To use the cliché about pornography, most people know it when they see it.

and we should be the arbiters of what is permissible—attacked the letter and its signatories with a ferocity and disingenuousness few if any of us would have predicted. The backlash arrived in waves that concentrated not at all on the three paragraphs of content within the document but on the timing of its publication and various clusters of signatures appended to it, some of whose names were associated with other views and positions that violated or merely challenged the emerging social justice consensus. The letter was framed as anti-black and white supremacist not for what it *said* but because of the timing of its release. The presence of black and other non-white signatories—including myself—was dismissed as an irony, evidence of further racism (internalized and otherwise), not its reverse. Given how "marginalized voices have been silenced for generations in journalism, academia, and publishing," a surprising number of critics argued in a counter letter, the current silencing of new voices today is not a significant problem, as if an equality that is achieved by rendering *everyone* as insecure as oppressed minorities had once been were a desirable or effective vision for the future.

That was but the most obvious objection. It was possible to project really any grievance onto the defense of tolerance and freedom of expression in a time of widespread and ongoing moral panic. The inclusion of prominent Jewish names, such as Bari Weiss, meant the letter was also "a free pass for Zionists."* Through a third lens and assortment of signatures—not only but most prominently that of Rowling—the letter was read as nakedly transphobic. "The sheer number of signatories who have waded into the transgender debate

* Patrick Sullivan (@BasicMountain), "Remember when she signed that Harper's letter and people thought she meant something other than a free pass for zionists and terfs?," Nov. 13, 2020, 4:21 p.m., x.com/BasicMountain /status/1327270336291737600?s=20.

on the anti-trans side is astounding," the journalist Katelyn Burns began a viral thread on Twitter. "I read many of the references to specific gripes in the letter's text as specifically directed at trans critics." One prominent trans writer, Jennifer Finney Boylan, a columnist at *The New York Times* and now the president of PEN America—the preeminent group defending writers from censorship—herself came under attack for signing the letter. Within hours, she tweeted a particularly illuminating mea culpa. "I did not know who else had signed that letter," she wrote. "I thought I was endorsing a well meaning, if vague, message against internet shaming. I did know Chomsky, [Gloria] Steinem, and Atwood were in, and I thought, good company. The consequences are mine to bear. I am so sorry." Yet this apology could only underscore the letter's central thesis: there really *was* a pernicious and informal pressure to calibrate one's viewpoints and public statements to align not only with pre-approved values but with preapproved *proponents* of those values. Not all spokespeople are created equal. Guilt by association made allegiance to principle treacherous. "I signed the Harpers [sic] letter because there were lots of people who also signed the Harpers [sic] letter whose views I disagreed with," the writer Malcolm Gladwell publicly responded to Boylan, reiterating what once would have been obvious but could no longer be taken for granted. "I thought that was the point of the Harpers [sic] letter."

For the critics scorning the Harper's Letter, concerns about fairness, openness, and tolerance of divergent viewpoints were not simply overblown; the phenomenon they attempted to address—an atmosphere of censoriousness—did not even exist in the first place. Like a distorted mirror image of Putin's deranged grievance, these detractors denied their own power while selectively interpreting disputes to reinforce it. What was this phenomenon, then? How exactly was it distinguishable from mere "accountability"* for wrongdoing, and why was it so urgent to resist now—even as racism and other kinds of prejudice continue to require our attention, and when malicious and insincere opportunists exploit even valid concerns to insulate themselves from critique?

One week after the Harper's Letter, Ross Douthat published an elucidating opinion in *The New York Times,* attempting to make sense of what such a complicated social phenomenon entailed. In "10 Theses About Cancel Culture," Douthat writes, "Cancellation, properly understood, refers to an attack on someone's employment and reputation by a determined collective of critics, based on an opinion or an action that is alleged to be disgraceful and disqualifying." In this way, there is certainly a degree of validity to Putin's claim that some Russian culture workers like the conductor Gergiev were indeed being targeted for their incorrect opinions—vocally supporting a murderous invasion—and, as a direct result, having their livelihoods and reputations damaged. This is not quite the same thing as choosing not to platform state-backed Russian ballet troupes, a move that seems both unfair to individual ballerinas and wholly justifiable during war.† At the same time, we should be able to maintain the strength of our convictions and the stamina for nuance in order to acknowledge that the categorical banning of any and all Russian nationals from competing at Wimbledon or other sporting events amounted to an instance of anti-Russian backlash that *was* in fact excessive. Even, and perhaps especially, righteous

---

* Margaret Sullivan, "So You're Being Held Accountable? That's Not 'Cancel Culture,'" *Washington Post,* Jan. 31, 2021.

† "The Bolshoi still receives around 70 percent of its financial support from the Russian government, a company official said. No current performers have spoken out against the Russian invasion." "Russia's Bolshoi Ballet Aims to Perform Again in the West," Voice of America, Aug. 4, 2023.

rationales and justifications are susceptible to growing overly puni-
tive. It is for this reason that further qualifications of the phenomenon are necessary and debate and pushback are to be welcomed
and encouraged, not stifled or forbidden. "There is no human society where you can say or do anything you like and expect to keep
your reputation and your job," Douthat concedes. Social life is not
a free-for-all. There will always be well-established transgressions
beyond which most people and organizations simply will not wish
to venture. The right to free speech is sacrosanct and protected, at
least in America, but one abuses this power at one's own social and
professional peril.

The digital highway we must all traverse has only made the road
to peril exponentially more accessible, with uncountable on-ramps
into which we do not always realize we are merging. The internet
has fundamentally changed the way we cancel, and extended cancellation's reach into our most private arenas. As Douthat continued,

A skeptic might say that it wasn't liberalism but space and
distance that made America a free country—the fact that you
could always escape the tyrannies of local conformism by
"lighting out for the territory," in the old Mark Twain phrase.
But under the rule of the internet there's no leaving the village: Everywhere is the same place, and so is every time. You
can be canceled for something you said in a crowd of complete strangers, if one of them uploads the video, or for a joke
that came out wrong if you happened to make it on social
media, or for something you said or did a long time ago if the
internet remembers. And you don't have to be prominent or
political to be publicly shamed and permanently marked: All
you need to do is have a particularly bad day, and the consequences could endure as long as Google.

The only authentically liberal stance, then, is to resist cancel culture as well as its right-wing exploitation simultaneously. As the co-author and co-organizer who became the public face of the Harper's Letter, I have been criticized in ways that have astonished me—and have even lost some offline friendships and professional opportunities—which has led me to think long and hard about the complex pressures, assumptions, and risks of age-old human tendencies to scapegoat, ostracize, and publicly shame in a time of panoptical social media and economic scarcity (recall that purges are also jobs programs). If socialism is the redistribution of wealth, one could say that social justice orthodoxy is the redistribution of status and recognition through competing claims of oppression.

"Cancel culture" functions as one of the primary means by which that transfer is presently administered. It is not merely being fired, nor is it simply facing consequences for breaching well-established norms of manners and behavior. It is rather the process of making *an example* of someone who has violated or simply been accused of violating a still-evolving and usually contested taboo. "Celebrities are the easiest people to target, but the hardest people to actually cancel," Douthat further qualifies. This is why J. K. Rowling is the quintessential instance of the phenomenon. He continues:

> Their resilience explains why some people dismiss cancellation as just famous people whining about their critics. If someone has a big enough name or fan base, the bar for actual cancellation is quite high, and the celebrity might even have the opportunity—like a certain reality-television star on the campaign trail in 2016—to use the hatred of the would-be cancelers to confirm a fandom or cement a following.
>
> However, not everyone is a celebrity, and . . .
>
> Cancel culture is most effective against people who are

still rising in their fields, and it influences many people who don't actually get canceled. The point of cancellation is ultimately to establish norms for the majority, not to bring the stars back down to earth. So a climate of cancellation can succeed in changing the way people talk and argue and behave even if it doesn't succeed in destroying the careers of some of the famous people that it targets. You don't need to cancel Rowling if you can cancel the lesser-known novelist who takes her side; you don't have to take down the famous academics who signed last week's *Harper's Magazine* letter attacking cancel culture if you can discourage people half their age from saying what they think. The goal isn't to punish everyone, or even very many someones; it's to shame or scare just enough people to make the rest conform.

In this way, cancellation operates with the logic and velocity of a sucker punch: the target cannot protect herself and won't even know where the attack is coming from until it has already landed. When it is effective—as it was most powerfully in the case of James Bennet at *The New York Times,* or with regard to the leadership of the Poetry Foundation—it results in a coercive and widespread *onlooker effect,* enforcing a fake consensus,* which, ironically, functions less as a democratizing force than as an elite gatekeeping etiquette for both whites and non-whites who understand how to navigate the intricate codes of language.

That gatekeeping function, which revolves primarily around *statements,* not actions, is a feature and not a bug of the

---

* This fake consensus proved to be extraordinarily harmful to the left, blinding them to the extent of the resentment that propelled Trump back into office in 2025. See: *Private Truths, Public Lies: The Social Consequences of Preference Falsification,* by the economist Timur Kuran.

phenomenon—the foundation on which it generates so much of its real-world power. In 2023, when I profiled the playwright Michael R. Jackson, who happens to be black and gay and widely celebrated for his complex explorations of identity, he nonetheless returned repeatedly to the ways the evolving discourse around race, identity, and social justice stifles genuine viewpoint diversity, failing spectacularly to take into account the perspectives of flesh-and-blood black people, as opposed to their avatars and champions in the gamified alternate universe of social media. He spoke to me of his best friend, Kisha, who is a black woman running a day-care center in South Carolina. The two of them talk constantly about how initially compelling concepts like intersectionality* have turned into rhetorical class markers. "So many of these [concepts] don't have any practical applications to anybody's actual lives," he told me. "I bet you a garbageman has never had to do a diversity training," he said. "This only operates at a certain class level." Jackson said his mother—one of eight children, who left the Deep South, moved to the North, held down a job, raised a family, made a home—"would never call herself a feminist, let alone an intersectional one." Yet she is "one of the most powerful black women I know." The issue, as he saw it, boiled down to the fact that *more school* is always required to make use of these terms, or even to understand them, and as a result

---

* "'Intersectionality' was coined in 1989 by Kimberlé Crenshaw, a civil rights activist and legal scholar. In a paper for the *University of Chicago Legal Forum,* Crenshaw wrote that traditional feminist ideas and antiracist policies exclude black women because they face overlapping discrimination unique to them. 'Because the intersectional experience is greater than the sum of racism and sexism, any analysis that does not take intersectionality into account cannot sufficiently address the particular manner in which Black women are subordinated,' she wrote in the paper." Merrill Perlman, "The Origin of the Term 'Intersectionality,'" *Columbia Journalism Review,* Oct. 23, 2018.

they're deeply exclusionary. "You have to read more. . . . It's endless working and reading and studying," he said. "I feel like there's a scam inside of it that's meant to keep some people on top and some people on bottom." He went on, "It's all about these social-class associations, and you either have entrance into this country club or you don't, based on whether you subscribe to a kind of thought or belief system."

This is one major reason why the invocation of cancel culture has become such an effective and reached-for cudgel. As numerous political observers have pointed out in the years since Trump's surprise victory over Clinton, and in light of his consistent gains among black and Latino voters, it very well may help explain why the Republican Party has become more attractive to working-class Americans of all ethnic backgrounds, many of whom feel alienated from ever-shifting, frequently counterintuitive elite manners and etiquette. As *The New York Times* itself argued in a highly controversial 2022 editorial, the backlash to which only proved the persuasiveness of its findings, "For all the tolerance and enlightenment that modern society claims, Americans are losing hold of a fundamental right as citizens of a free country: the right to speak their minds and voice their opinions in public without fear of being shamed or shunned." Whether or not there has ever existed such a *right,* per se, progressives—such as one former staffer who tweeted, "If I still worked at the New York Times, I would seriously think about quitting today"* —are naive simply to dismiss the larger point. As the editorial continued,

> A full 84 percent of Black people polled shared the concern of this editorial that it was a "very serious" or "somewhat

* Adam Davidson (@AdamDavidson), X, Mar. 18, 2022.

serious" problem that some Americans do not exercise their freedom of speech out of fear of retaliation or harsh criticism. And 45 percent of Black people and nearly 60 percent of Latinos and white people polled reported that they'd held their tongues in the past year out of fear of retaliation or harsh criticism.

Such numbers are inconsistent with a healthy, multiethnic, and pluralistic country. One of the most disturbing and strange moments of the 2020 campaign season came not from Trump but from Joe Biden, three days before George Floyd's death reset the national conversation on race. In a remote interview from his basement in Delaware, Biden jokingly but revealingly told a popular black morning radio host who had just invited him to come back on the show for further questioning that essentially there was nothing more to say to black audiences. He had no greater case to make to win black votes, because, he explained, "if you have a problem figuring out whether you're for me or Trump, then *you ain't black*" (emphasis mine). While it is true that in 2020, according to research conducted by Pew, 92 percent of so-called single-race black, non-Hispanic voters would go on to vote for Biden, and just 8 percent backed Trump, the outright statement that racial authenticity *dictates* this pattern is not only insulting; it indicates a deeper mode of thinking and prejudice that contributes to a constrictive speech culture—one that is counterproductive and untenable in an increasingly mixed and dynamic society.

When we profess to care about diversity—a value it would be exceedingly difficult to find a prestigious institution not openly pledging allegiance to—what do we even *mean* by the term? Do we mean, effectively, that the same slate of views ought to be expressed by increasingly phenotypically varied, uniformly arrived, or upwardly mobile speakers with equal access to a set of preferences, dispositions, and tastes they were socialized into through exclusionary educational filters? Is that the mountaintop we are so assiduously climbing toward? Are we saying—as was the implication of the criticism that met Jennifer Finney Boylan and that was amplified in her swift capitulation—that there really are specific ideas and associations certain identity categories are *required* to shun or embrace in lockstep? Are we interested at all in the perspectives of those minorities *within the minority:* the Muslim with a critique of Islamism;* the young white woman who is concerned about due process in the era of #MeToo; the black Ivy League professor who balks at the new "antiracist" doctrine that reifies racial difference? Are these not also authentic points of view?

---

* One of the Harper's Letter signatories I was most proud to include was Kamel Daoud, an Algerian journalist and novelist who lives in Oran with a fatwa on his head. Daoud's acclaimed 2013 debut novel, *The Meursault Investigation,* is a brilliant and deeply humanizing retelling of Camus's *The Stranger* from the perspective of the brother of Meursault's nameless Arab victim. In his columns and interviews, however, Daoud made comments critical of Islam's role in Arab societies that caught the attention of an obscure Salafist imam, who accused him of apostasy and called for his murder on Facebook: "The apostate, infidel, Algerian, 'Zionized' writer, criminal, insults God. . . . We call on the Algerian system to condemn him to death publicly." Mohammed Aïssaoui, "L'écrivain Kamel Daoud fait l'objet d'une fatwa," *Figaro,* Dec. 17, 2014.

CHAPTER NINE

The Spectacle of January 6

Rodolphe and Celia had moved to Brooklyn a decade earlier, during the same season we'd relocated to Paris. Now when we all got together, it was as semi-foreign guests in our own former cities, caught between two not-quite homes rendered more clearly through one another's not-quite-alien experiences and interpretations. France was passively enduring the humorless COVID curfew President Macron implemented late the previous autumn—after a magnificently liberated summer—as the curve once again shot upward. During those miserable winter months, when even the grocers and pharmacies shuttered at 6:00 p.m. and the bars and cafés never opened, we rebelled in the only way available, surreptitiously hailing Ubers under false pretenses to gather in small groups and cook and drink in one another's curtained apartments.* It was an awful time to be in France, as sharp a contrast as imaginable to the early can-do spirit of that first wave of the pandemic. If there was any upside, it was the sense of stolen camaraderie such forbidden gatherings occasioned.

That particular January evening grew late. We were finishing the

---

* These were the days when everyone still dutifully tested before coming over.

wine when I realized I had missed several notifications, which were flashing across my phone with increasing frequency. All the various messages could be boiled down to some version of the same essential question: Are you *seeing* this? When I opened Twitter, the *this* was the entirety of my timeline. It was difficult at first to make sense of what we were watching. The video clips and images simultaneously looked funny, foolish, staged, spontaneous, fake, *hyperreal,* stupid, deeply pathetic—as well as genuinely alarming, terrifying even. I can think of few if any moments during which I have ever felt further—spiritually if not physically—from my beloved homeland, as we hunched over our respective smartphones, watching dozens of untrained bodies ineptly scale the sides of the Capitol (it was impossible at that moment to understand if these riotous hordes were even serious, or if this was some elaborate joke, as they struggled mightily to climb the walls lining the steps they could have simply ascended).

What was so impressive, watching the spectacle in both real and recycled time (short clips played over and over again ad infinitum on the internet), was its sheer artificiality. The event—serious as cancer for the body politic—seemed to have scant meaning or physical weight outside the self-referential generation of images. More than even the death of George Floyd, the pandemonium of January 6 fully inhabited our screens, seemingly existing in a space somewhere beyond the reality principle. Rioters wore costumes, draping themselves in tawdry Trump paraphernalia and gaudy Stars and Stripes; some came dressed up as Founding Fathers. They filmed themselves—mostly, it became clear, to prove to themselves it was really happening—and posted their videos to social media, ultimately, deliciously, incriminating themselves in the process.*

* "America's Winter Palace was stormed, but the result was not a revolutionary coup or a dual power stand-off. Instead, most of the insurgents— infantrymen for the American lumpenbourgeoisie, from New York cosmetics

Many wore expressions of stupid disbelief as they meandered through the halls of Congress, marveling like tourists.

"How is this possible?" we all said, pantomiming disbelief. The visuals were appalling, their implications outlandish—a cascade of profanity, disrespect, and failure. We caught our first glimpses of the memes being born that day: the cartoonish shaman; the even-keeled man with ominous-looking zip ties on his waistband; the unshaven fool with his feet up on Speaker Pelosi's desk; the brazen San Diego veteran felled by a single bullet as she miscalculated her too-dramatic entrance. The brave and stranded lone police officer improbably holding back a mounting stampede. How is this *possible*? But the truth is that we knew exactly how this sham of protest was not only possible but inevitable. If we forced ourselves from the soothing habit of stubborn belief in normative decency, good sportsmanship, and democratic fair play, we'd have to admit to ourselves and each other that there was nothing shocking at all about such a debacle, not anymore. It was bound to happen in a country so inflamed by ignorance, divorced from principle, spoiled by tribal affiliation, and deformed by mutual mistrust and conspiratorial thinking. We stared at our screens with a reluctant comprehension.

This would be the second time—the first was September 11—that I felt the full force of "spectacular society" as Guy Debord intended it. "Everything that was directly lived has receded into representation," he writes in the first of his theses. The melee in Washington, a minuscule part of society, now stood in for the whole, morphing into a memeified performance of America's polarization writ large. Our experience eavesdropping on the scene from Paris was identical to the overwhelming majority of the country, the

salesmen to Floridian real estate agents—were swiftly arrested *en route* home, incriminated by their livestreams and social media posts." Anton Jäger, "Political Instincts?," *New Left Review,* March 19, 2024.

99.9999 percent of Americans who also never glimpsed what happened on January 6 but were now submerged in the day's fragmentary images and forced to develop a meaningful political response to it. Obviously, the event—exponentially amplified through the *pseudo-event* on our devices—could do nothing but supercharge existing divisions. "The spectacle is not a collection of images," Debord continues, "it is a social relation between people that is mediated by images."

The pathetic insurrection, whipped up by the cheapest internet conspiracy and the most outlandish lies and innuendo about a "stolen" election—all originating in the mouth of the entertainer-president—was but a physical manifestation of the social media era's much larger and more serious and sustained assault on Truth. Donald Trump might have personified this subversion, but it has been for many years now atmospheric, "a pervasive air of unreality," as Christopher Lasch already noted, extending far beyond his person or the movement he represents and very much implicating large and influential swaths of the progressive left as well. On virtually every major debate, from race to gender to epidemiology to foreign policy, who among us has not at some time or another experienced the longing to subordinate facts to feelings, ideology, and propaganda? "In a world which really is topsy-turvy," Debord strikes the target once more, "the true is a moment of the false."

After that disquieting dinner, in the days and weeks to come, many more ignominious details would surface. As David Remnick summarized the contours of the riot in his introduction to the congressional report, "On January 6, 2021, thousands marched on the Capitol in support of Trump and his conspiratorial and wholly fabricated charge that the Presidential election the previous November had been stolen from him. Demonstrators breached police barricades, broke through windows and doors, and ran through the halls of Congress threatening to exact vengeance on the Vice-President, the Speaker of the House, and other officeholders. Seven people died as a result of the insurrection. About a hundred and fourteen law-enforcement officers were injured."*

For years now—certainly since the Obama breakthrough—a resentful and sporadically deadly impulse has been cultivated on parts of the right, animated by the reactionary belief that a multi-cultural society is in essence an anti-white society. This was most clearly on display on August 11, 2017, in Charlottesville, when white supremacist protesters garbed in khaki pants and polo shirts gathered under the Unite the Right banner and stomped across the University of Virginia's campus. The occasion was the planned removal of a statue and the renaming of a park, both of which had honored the Confederate general Robert E. Lee.† The protesters car-

---

* These numbers have been disputed. See Robert Farley, "How Many Died as a Result of Capitol Riot?," FactCheck.org, accessed March 2, 2025, www.factcheck.org.

† This was at the beginning of an ongoing moment of almost obsessive revision and cleansing of monuments to the past. Trump posed a not completely objectionable thought experiment when he countered a reporter's question about the removal of the statue of Robert E. Lee:

> **Reporter:** Should that statue be taken down?
> **Trump:** Excuse me. If you take a look at some of the groups, and you see—and you'd know it if you were honest reporters, which in many cases you're not—but many of those people were there to protest the taking down of the statue of Robert E. Lee.
>
> So this week it's Robert E. Lee. I noticed that Stonewall Jackson is coming down. I wonder, is it George Washington next week? And is it Thomas Jefferson the week after? You know, you really do have to ask yourself, where does it stop?
> **Reporter:** George Washington and Robert E. Lee are not the same.
> **Trump:** George Washington was a slave owner. Was George Washington a slave owner? So will George Washington now lose his status? Are

ried lit tiki torches and chanted, "End immigration," "Blood and soil," and "You will not replace us; Jews will not replace us."* It was in many ways a distinctly *un-* or even *anti-*American vision. In fact, it recalled the Nazi theorist Carl Schmitt, who famously argued that "all right is the right of a particular *Volk.*" In his 1932 essay, *The Concept of the Political,* Schmitt asked, "Who is a people's friend,

---

we going to take down—excuse me, are we going to take down statues to George Washington? How about Thomas Jefferson? What do you think of Thomas Jefferson? You like him?

Reporter: I do love Thomas Jefferson.

Trump: Okay, good. Are we going to take down the statue? Because he was a major slave owner. Now, are we going to take down his statue?

So you know what, it's fine. You're changing history. You're changing culture.

However, as one of the Unite the Right's organizers, Nathan Damigo, stated under oath, "the truth is the rally was never about the Lee statue." In his own admission, it was a "pivotal moment for the pro-white movement in America."

* The formulation initially caught observers by surprise. There are 7.5 million people of Jewish descent in the United States, about 2.4 percent of the population. What did these white identitarians mean by "*Jews* will not replace us"? This was the first time many Americans had encountered in the mainstream the European logic and rhetoric of the "great replacement" theory, in which antisemitic conspiracies and tropes play a necessary role. In this telling, rootless, cosmopolitan Jews purposefully undermine and *dilute* strong and supposedly cohesive white nations through socialism, on the one hand, and the homogenizing forces of the neoliberal marketplace, on the other—both of which inevitably lead to the importation of masses of desperate and dependent black, brown, and yellow immigrants. Jews are also understood here to orchestrate a godless culture of sexual license that further subverts the traditional white family through queerness and miscegenation. Those on the "antiracist" left who hold that Jews are simply white miss this crucial nuance.

and who is an enemy?" For Schmitt, to define one's enemies was to identify one's inner self. "Tell me who your enemy is, and I'll tell you who you are," he wrote elsewhere. In a ludicrous fit of playacting as Germans, the organizers of the rally in Virginia saw in Trump a unifying folk emblem as well as a champion for their collective grievances and bulwark against their enemies, who were so rapidly transforming *their* country.

There is no doubt that white nationalists were energized by the emergence of Trump. David Duke spoke candidly about what his political ascendency meant for their cause, linking the rally to the president in the most explicit terms. "We are determined to take this country back. We're gonna fulfill the promises of Donald Trump," Duke said opportunistically in Charlottesville. "That's why we voted for Donald Trump because he said he's going to take our country back."* Trump himself was loath to distance himself too explicitly from the antidemocratic, paranoid, and violent energy surging through his base, speaking with uncharacteristic ambiguity as he denounced an amorphous "hatred, bigotry and violence on many sides."[†]

---

* Dan Merica, "Trump—Once Again—Fails to Condemn the Alt-right, White Supremacists," CNN, Aug. 13, 2017.

[†] It is illuminating to remember the degree to which Trump's commentary was at odds with other leading Republicans in 2017. Senator Orrin Hatch of Utah, then the most senior Republican in the Senate, tweeted, "My brother didn't give his life fighting Hitler for Nazi ideas to go unchallenged here at home." The ideas being promoted at the rally, he continued, "are fueled by hate, & have no place in civil society." Senator Marco Rubio of Florida tweeted, "Very important for the nation to hear @POTUS describe events in #Charlottesville for what they are, a terror attack by #whitesupremacists." And Senator Cory Gardner of Colorado put the matter in even starker terms: "Mr. President—we must call evil by its name. These were white supremacists and this was domestic terrorism."

To this day, most of the discussion around Trump's statements on the rally get hung up on one line—which like much of his speech was convoluted and ridiculous—about "very fine people on both sides."* But before he made those inept comments, he said something else worth revisiting:

> I will tell you something. I watched those very closely— much more closely than you people watched it. And you have—you had a group on one side that was bad, and you had a group on the other side that was also very violent. *And nobody wants to say that, but I'll say it right now. You had a group—you had a group on the other side that came charging in, without a permit, and they were very, very violent.* (Emphasis mine.)

Despite the "hatred and bigotry" of the white nationalists, which is a detail of enormous magnitude, one complicating reality a great number of Americans primed to be sympathetic to Trump's candor also latched onto was that there was, indeed, violence on more than one side. To acknowledge this fact is not in itself to condone the racists who came to Charlottesville for the express purpose of provoking the nation, nor is it to draw any false equivalence between the murderous resentment of James Alex Fields Jr.—the white nationalist who drove his car through a crowd and killed a white counterprotester named Heather Heyer—and the left-wing groups that met this bigotry head-on, armed and bracing for a conflict their own presence helped ensure. "The organizer of the 'Unite the Right' rally, Jason Kessler, was heckled, punched and forced

* Much ink has been spilled on this topic in an attempt to portray Trump's remarks as having been misrepresented and taken out of context. That is somewhere between ambiguous and unconvincing.

to flee a news conference by an angry crowd," *The New York Times* reported.

> Groups that identify as anti-fascist . . . have been physically confronting neo-Nazis, white supremacists and, in some cases, speakers who merely challenge the boundaries of political correctness on college campuses across the country.
>
> In Charlottesville, about 20 members of a group called the Redneck Revolt, which describes itself as an anti-racist, anti-capitalist group dedicated to uniting working-class whites and oppressed minorities, carried rifles and formed a security perimeter around the counterprotesters in Justice Park, according to its website and social media.
>
> The group, which admires John Brown, a white abolitionist who led an armed insurrection in 1859, issued a "call to arms" on its website: "To the fascists and all who stand with them, we'll be seeing you in Virginia."

There is no question that Trump was demonstratively not the leader to rise to the occasion and guide the nation to anything like a higher moral plane, but an honest and self-critical grappling with the complexity of violence, intolerance, tribalism, political extremism, speech intimidation, and coercion is something America has been in desperate need of for years now and has not come close to receiving from either major party since at least candidate Obama's "A More Perfect Union Speech," all the way back in 2008.

What we have been given repeatedly instead is the language and rhetoric of social justice. It is de rigueur within academia and mainstream media to redirect all manner of conversation away from a focus on isolated incidents so that we may take into consideration the more expansive *contexts* within which to properly understand them.* We are constantly encouraged to think critically about current events in terms of their historical context. In Virginia, specifically, this might have meant that in a discussion of the removal of statues now associated with a racist past, even acts of vandalism against such public property would be more productively reframed within the context of a larger struggle against racial oppression. Likewise, we are urged to rethink acts of sabotage by environmental activists—to pipelines, for instance, or the defacement of beloved paintings in national museums—as a necessary form of resistance or awareness raising in the fight against climate change. What might appear to be *mere* vandalism today, the thinking goes, is in fact a necessary correction of a historical wrong when placed within this larger contextual framework. So, too, are we invited to think in terms of the broader sociological context of cultural and economic pressures acting upon individuals when it comes to drug offenses. When thinking about Appalachian communities brought to a standstill by the omnipresence of opioids or people in inner-city communities like George Floyd's, we might consider the bigger picture of high unemployment rates and low educational attainment, in addition to whatever we think of individual agency and self-control. Viewed this way, through a more expansive lens of intergenerationally limited social mobility and lack of financial resources, drug addiction and other pathologies are frequently seen as the symptoms of deeper structural insecurity. In the context of criminal justice more broadly, for some activists, this means taking holistic account of systemic bias *tout court,* in order to reconsider even violent and highly antisocial transgressions as the inevitable and even pitiable response to prior cruelty. There are countless such

---

* See, for instance, the Princeton historian Kevin Kruse's contribution to *The 1619 Project:* "How Segregation Caused Your Traffic Jam."

versions of the tendency. The point is always quite simple: events themselves—even when clearly unethical or explicitly against the law—are not to be considered strictly on their own terms, within an intellectual vacuum.

But what was the greater context informing the ignorant and angry mob of Americans who chose to follow a demagogic carnival barker and lay siege to government property in January 2021, going so far as to erect a hangman's gallows on the National Mall, in pursuit of "justice"? Some of them, such as the Oath Keepers and other highly organized militias, were neither naive nor amateurs and have been meticulously preparing for armed revolt. They had been "standing by," as Trump himself instructed them to do. That was their context, and these militias constitute a different category altogether. There were, however, many other men and women in attendance who were neither organized nor trained but had been gorged on an outlandish diet of riots and looting in Ferguson, Minneapolis, Kenosha, Portland, Seattle, and many other theaters of open lawlessness and rebellion besides, all of which were frequently condoned.

It is not only unrealistic but downright fantastical to presume such evocative and sustained depictions of bedlam enacted throughout the country would exert *no influence* over the strained and warped American psyche at a time of heightened tension and pandemic. And it is improbable to think there could be no possibility of "fiery but mostly peaceful protests" being perverted and seized upon by a demagogue's propagandized followers. On the contrary, many of the January 6 rioters, however idiotic, *believed* and continue to believe they were operating from a place of their very own crystalline "moral clarity"—precisely the reason such a juvenile and subjective lens could never provide the basis for a responsible and pluralistic politics. The January 6 insurrection—far more symbolically destructive and politically dangerous—was nonetheless a gross apotheosis of a kind of increasingly common tendency, visible on the social justice left for years now, to make the country's politics in the street whenever feeling sufficiently unheard.* How difficult is it really to imagine that the populist right had aped this flamboyant reflex—or found their justification in it, no matter how twisted or cynical the logic—from the ritual of witnessing the not just tolerated but quite often celebrated lawlessness that defined the previous summer?

What happened on January 6 at the Capitol was a proxy for a far more profound sickness we feel everywhere around us, regardless of our tribalized political alliances: there is something deeply wrong in our society, and there has been for some time now. The unique threat to American, and global,† democracy that Trump and his movement represent cannot be excused or downplayed; it

---

* To be clear: This is not at all to suggest that January 6 was spawned by what came before it, or that it is merely derivative of the pandemonium of the summer of 2020. At the same time, it is not entirely qualitatively different, either. Rather, it is a more advanced point along a continuum of societal failure.

† "Which is the real Europe? The mostly peaceful, democratic, and united continent of the past few decades? Or the fragmented, volatile, and conflict-ridden Europe that existed for centuries before that? If Donald Trump wins the U.S. presidential election in November, we may soon find out. Trump flirted with pulling the United States out of NATO during his first term as president. Some of his former aides believe he might really do it if he gets a second. . . . A post-American Europe would struggle to meet the threats it faces—and might even revert, eventually, to the darker, more anarchic, more illiberal patterns of its past. 'Our Europe today is mortal. It can die,' French President Emmanuel Macron warned in late April. In an America First world, it just might." Hal Brands, "Trump's Return Would Transform Europe," *Foreign Policy* (Summer 2024).

may very well mark a pivotal moment in the country's decline. "History reproducing itself becomes farce," Jean Baudrillard echoed Marx with a twist. "Farce reproducing itself becomes history."

After the ignominy of 2021, Trump's return to power in 2025 represents that aphorism's darkest fulfillment. The weeks that followed January 6—during which he finally faced bipartisan condemnation in the Senate, a slew of resignations in his administration, a second impeachment in the House, and banishment across social media—were, in retrospect, a passing moment of sobriety. With the knowledge and experience accumulated over the eight years since he stunned himself with an Electoral College victory over Hillary Clinton, the responsibility for such a regressive development lies at the feet of his supporters and enablers alone as well as those in power who failed to thwart his improbable rehabilitation.

If the purpose is to *understand* the political and moral disaster in which we now find ourselves—and not merely to signal our enlightenment in relation to it—an unsentimental assessment of the social justice left, and the agenda-setting institutions that repeatedly caved and pandered to its excesses, is not only reasonable but obligatory. For that also has rendered for millions of Americans the disastrous illusion of Trump ever more plausible. And not just plausible but *desirable,* in the way that it is desirable in the mind of a gambler to seek his own ruin at the roulette wheel, after having already sustained irrecoverable losses.

Afterword

When I started writing this book in the spring of 2021, the momentum behind the social justice movement that reached its zenith in the summer of 2020 seemed unquestionable, irresistible. In a society in which George Floyd so publicly and lamentably died on camera, our notions of inclusion, safety, harm, and agency had expanded profoundly. We were now far beyond discussions of police brutality, even as our sense of the complexity of human life had been so powerfully diminished, squeezed into the space of a raw dichotomy. Actions, policies, and ideas had been decisively reconfigured as either racist or antiracist. The entire country and much of the world beyond it was now filtered through opposing binaries: villain/victim, oppressor/oppressed, colonist/indigenous, white/"person of color." Whatever gray area might have still been thought to exist between these poles was either a folly or a luxury; whichever it was, we couldn't afford it. And as has been the case throughout the history of the United States, broad struggles for justice and recognition that were initiated by and on behalf of black Americans were further extended to other minorities. It was not only explicit physical violence or interpersonal bigotry but also subtler forms of exclusion and bias that needed to be addressed now with fervor. POC, BIPOC, Native Americans, AAPI,* Latinos, LGBTQ+, women, disabled people, Muslims, the undocumented, the neurodivergent—the language, manners, and policies of our dominant institutions, amplified by the social internet, would seek to rectify the discrimination presently understood to be faced by all of them.

Then, on October 7, 2023, three years into the era of racial reckoning, soul-searching, and institutionalized "moral clarity" epitomized by the pandemic summer of George Floyd, the surprise slaughter of twelve hundred men, women, and children in Israel, as well as the abduction of at least 250 more, remade the culture and politics of the United States all over again. More specifically, the glaring inconsistencies and hypocrisies the massacre and the relentless Israeli response exposed within American universities, media organizations, and popular culture achieved something I had not believed was possible, at least not in the near term. "The Great Awokening," or whatever we may call that period that began in the wake of the death of Trayvon Martin and culminated in the summer of 2020, had been abruptly bookended that autumn. The conflict in Gaza—and more specifically the contested position of Jews as a category within "whiteness"—fundamentally broke the emergent social justice consensus.

The utter velocity with which pro-Palestinian voices responded—

---

* The inclusion of Asians here is somewhat conditional. While there has been in recent years a growing awareness and celebration of the superficial visibility of "Asian American" identities in literature, television, and cinema, there has also been a countervailing desire to downplay the specific challenges and biases faced by these communities. When it has been inconvenient, such as during disputes over academic achievement and meritocracy, or with regard to racialized hate crimes during COVID, Asian Americans could also be ignored or dismissed as honorary participants in whiteness.

many even before there was any sort of counteroffensive to object to, and when the only concrete fact was the dead—seemed incredible. Just three days after the indiscriminate slaughter of hundreds of mostly Jewish civilians by Hamas, a group identifying itself as the Chicago chapter of Black Lives Matter tweeted a stylized meme of a paraglider's silhouette under the exuberant caption "That is all that is it!" In the image, which was viewed hundreds of thousands of times, a Palestinian flag flaps above the swooping figure; below, in capital letters, it reads, "I STAND WITH PALESTINE." The use of motorized parachutes and hang gliders to descend on civilian populations, most notably the Supernova Sukkot music festival, was of course never a matter of conjecture. Yet the denial, justification, and even the glamorization of that violence began immediately—before the bodies had even cooled or the hostages had been counted. This baffling response to videotaped butchery of the variety popularized in the previous decade by the terrorist group ISIS exposed a shocking moral blindness—a sudden and lazy unwillingness to bear witness—among large swaths of the population that had previously organized themselves around a sweeping commitment to racial, ethnic, sexual, and religious justice.*

* While it is true that Black Lives Matter is and has always been a decentralized organization, and the Global Network renounced the Chicago statement, the substance of the group's renunciation is worth examining closely. The BLM Global Network described the Chicago statement as unrepresentative of the "official" viewpoint of the group: "The actual/real BLM is only ONE Twitter/ IG account and website and people see for themselves we have not issued any pro-Palestine press release on either outlet." The response went on to characterize the BLM Chicago account as "independent" and "without any association with our company at all." This framing was not entirely convincing, however, because it conveniently elided the fundamental decentralization of the movement and presumed a top-down messaging that has never existed. To the contrary, one of the most salient differences between the movement

Of course, it was not only Israeli civilians who were attacked that Saturday morning. Nor was it even simply Jews or people who could be categorized, however tenuously, as "white"* who lost their lives in Hamas's rampage. For one excruciating example, there was the videotaped lynching† of a twenty-one-year-old black African farming intern from Tanzania named Joshua Mollel. Militants surrounded him, stabbed him, stood on his chest, and riddled his body with bullets while shouting, "God is great." When he was already lifeless, they blew his head clean off his body.‡ Mollel was not the only African murdered that day, either. Hamas's massacre was both diverse and inclusive. According to NPR, some thirty-nine Thai migrant workers were slaughtered, and more than two dozen more were abducted.

It is a terrible irony that a movement that had always drawn its force from the infectious language of *visual* moral outrage—the videotaped imagery of victimization, unsafety, and gratuitous violence—had to render itself so willfully incoherent in order not to see what had happened on October 7. Putting aside, momentarily,

---

for black lives and the civil rights movement of the 1960s has always been the former's deliberate decentralization and lack of hierarchical control.

* The majority of Israeli Jews are of indigenous Middle Eastern Mizrahi ancestry, some 44.9 percent of the total population compared with the next largest Jewish subgroup, the European-descended Ashkenazim, who make up just 31.8 percent. (See Noah Lewin-Epstein and Yinon Cohen, "Ethnic Origin and Identity in the Jewish Population of Israel," *Journal of Ethnic and Migration Studies* 45, no. 11 [2019]: 2118–37, doi.org/10.1080/13691 83X.2018.1492370.)

† Unlike the numerous misuses of this term in recent years, what happened to Joshua Mollel was the *Merriam-Webster* definition of a lynching, that is, "to put to death (as by hanging) by mob action without legal approval or permission."

‡ They brought his remains back to Gaza, bloody and naked, on the back of a pickup truck.

the more obvious abomination of declaring, even if only by omission or implication, that some Jewish lives actually are disposable, an activist movement that was predicated on the notion that black lives *matter* had to work especially hard to stifle the cognitive dissonance of viral footage of a helpless black man being destroyed by Palestinian militants. This was motivated ignorance, a purposeful turning away from easily accessible facts. The BLM Global Network simultaneously disavowed the Chicago chapter's tweet while also insisting, "We are not getting involved in this Israel/Palestine situation." In that way, it was representative of a larger social justice movement whose worldview could not honestly account for the shameless violence of Hamas and did not wish to do so.*

That social justice movement that sprang from the haunting audio of Trayvon Martin's frightened screams, the jarring photos of Michael Brown's splayed corpse,[†] and the awful videos of Eric Garner's, Tamir Rice's, and Philando Castile's last moments had repeatedly demonstrated the simple and devastating force of a cell phone connected to the internet. Hamas understood this power, too. The militants were executioners, certainly, but they were also cinematographers, filming and posting triumphant footage of their

---

* It is not completely unlike the way contemporary discussions of slavery eschew consideration of the scale or severity of the Arab slave trade or the reality of slavery in some African countries in the present day. "CNN appears to show youths from Niger and other sub-Saharan countries being sold to buyers for about $400 (£300) at undisclosed locations in Libya," the BBC reported in November 2017. Amid all the relentless introspection into the legacy of slavery that was sparked by the publication of *The 1619 Project* in 2019, I am unaware of any substantial, high-profile discussion of such atrocities occuring right now.

† As well as, crucially, the mythologized but erroneous rallying cry of "Hands up, don't shoot!" that did so much to oversimplify and obscure our national conversation about race and policing.

crimes, as if they were performing both Derek Chauvin's and Darnella Frazier's* roles in tandem. What's more, video of the October 7 pogrom did not surface only to be subsequently denied. There were no attempts to cover up the revolting evidence or to blame it on rogue "bad apples." This was no tragic error of judgment, as those who take life in America so frequently maintain. On the contrary, the group documented their own atrocities for the express purpose of disseminating the footage and winning sympathy and praise for their deeds. What was the response to this gesture in America, among so many who had spent the previous years deploring the most negligible instances of *symbolic* violence, when confronted with mass videotaped slaughter of innocents? Far too often it was simply to refuse to engage with Hamas on the group's own clearly articulated terms. There was instead a vaguely cosmopolitan desire to evince solidarity with a faraway rebellion while remaining ensconced in a cotton-padded provincialism.†

---

* Frazier was the seventeen-year-old who recorded the video of George Floyd's death and uploaded it to Facebook and Instagram.
† The ne plus ultra of this tendency would have to be Ta-Nehisi Coates's sudden return to the ideological arena with the publication of his 2024 essay collection, *The Message*. In the book's largest section, which documents his ten-day trip to Palestine in the summer of 2023, he manages not even to *mention* Hamas. He does not address October 7 at all. "This is a choice—and a conspicuous one at that, especially for an author who had long positioned himself 'against sentiment divorced from evidence, against a world that escapes footnotes,'" Jennifer Szalai noted in *The New York Times Book Review* ("Ta-Nehisi Coates Returns to the Political Fray, Calling Out Injustice," Sept. 29, 2024). As Daniel Bergner wrote:

> Coates goes beyond allying himself with the Palestinian cause. He identifies entirely with it. He and the Palestinians share the suffering of "conquered peoples." It is almost as if he feels that through his embattled attachment and identification, he can free his own psyche

The BLM Chicago infographic might have been particularly crude in its delivery,* to the surprise of many Jews (as well as many gentiles), but it was not substantively out of sync with a whole slew of American reactions to the massacre that were filtering through mainstream institutions and circulating on the internet, even as the day's horror was still unfolding. Some of these were not provincial at all but motivated by flagrantly illiberal internationalist politics. On the very morning of October 7, as the world glimpsed naked corpses paraded through the streets like trophy game, the Yale historian Zareena Grewal tweeted, "My heart is in my throat. Prayers for Palestinians. Israel is a murderous, genocidal settler state and Palestinians have every right to resist through armed struggle, solidarity #FreePalestine." When it was pointed out that, Israeli soldiers aside, many civilians had also been targeted, Grewal, a tenured professor of American studies, of ethnicity, race, and

---

from "the long shadow [of slavery]." And this personal urgency may elucidate Coates's staggering omission. His essay, in a book published near the one-year mark of Hamas's October 7 attack, contains nothing about that day and nothing about the war since. . . .

Why leave this out? Wouldn't Coates have wanted to argue that Israel's bombing campaign has amounted to genocide or ethnic cleansing? Wouldn't he have wished to conclude his case in this way? Probably, but in doing so he would have been compelled to at least note Hamas's murders, rapes, dismemberments, and kidnappings of civilians, even if only in the swiftest summary, and this would have marred the purity of the essay. ("The Problem with Moral Purity," *Atlantic*, Sept. 24, 2004.)

* So much so that it was quickly deleted—though the disavowal was far from unequivocal: On October 11, after the post was removed, BLM Chicago (@BLMChi) clarified, "When we say Free Palestine, y'all say anti-Semitic & Hamas. Israel's terrorism created Hamas & Zionism is a betrayal of the peace of Judaism not those shouting against its genocidal effect on Palestine." X, Oct. 11, 2023, 5:49 a.m., x.com/BLMChi/status/1712088041748156749.

migration, and of religious studies, did not hesitate. "Settlers are not civilians," she tweeted. "This is not hard."

Najma Sharif, a Somali American writer with bylines in unusually fashionable publications,* also went viral when she tweeted, "What did y'all think decolonization meant? vibes? papers? essays? losers." The real scandal of her question lay in its unflinching honesty and the ideological reality it so succinctly conveyed without sugarcoating. Here again was the crucial distinction between esoteric and vulgar meanings, which we had grown so accustomed to conflating. In all the euphemistic talk of "decolonizing" reading lists, curricula, cafeteria menus, journalism, art collections, historical scholarship, and whatever else one could imagine, many of us had lost sight of the most basic truth that Camus understood when he rejected the kind of "justice" that would place bombs on the tramway alongside his mother.† Sharif and Grewal might have been shockingly callous in their remarks, but they were also far more candid and clear-sighted about the underlying meaning of words and ideas that had been popularized and diluted in the wider social justice conversation, which had broken out of the academy and gone global in the era of social media.

"The decolonization narrative has dehumanized Israelis to the extent that otherwise rational people excuse, deny, or support barbarity," the British historian Simon Sebag Montefiore observed at the end of October:

> It holds that Israel is an "imperialist-colonialist" force, that Israelis are "settler-colonialists," and that Palestinians have

---

* Ranging from *Soho House* magazine to *Highsnobiety, Teen Vogue, Paper,* and *Dazed*.
† "I believe in justice, but I will defend my mother before justice."

a right to eliminate their oppressors. . . . It casts Israelis as "white" or "white-adjacent" and Palestinians as "people of color."

This ideology, powerful in the academy but long overdue for serious challenge, is a toxic, historically nonsensical mix of Marxist theory, Soviet propaganda, and traditional anti-Semitism from the Middle Ages and the 19th century. But its current engine is the new identity analysis, which sees history through a concept of race that derives from the American experience.*

Where there was not outright celebration of the atrocities taking place, in a strange echo of Trumpian reasoning that the left has betrayed repeatedly, the message arising from other, more respectable sources often amounted to a version of *there's violence on many sides*. In *The New York Times,* on October 7, in a short article titled "Gaza Has Suffered Under 16-Year Blockade," the opening paragraph reads, "For some Gazans, Saturday morning's surprise Palestinian attack into southern Israel seemed a justified response to a 16-year Israeli blockade. Others worried that the coordinated attack would only add to Gaza's misery as the tiny enclave braced for a large-scale response from Israel." Conspicuously, no one, according to this narrow framing, was particularly worried about what it meant in flesh-and-blood terms to mow down, maim, rape, abduct, and murder men, women, and children at random for sins attributed to their nation (or the nation they simply happened to be standing in when the militants found them). The article, written

* Simon Sebag Montefiore, "The Decolonization Narrative Is Dangerous and False," *Atlantic,* Oct. 27, 2023.

by the *Times*'s Middle East correspondent, did not even describe in passing the massacre. In a Twitter thread also on October 7, Agnès Callamard, the secretary-general of Amnesty International, called on "all parties to the conflict to abide by international law and make every effort to avoid further civilian bloodshed." Three didactic tweets later, she wrote, "Israel has a horrific track record of committing war crimes with impunity in previous wars on Gaza." Callamard never referred to Hamas by name.* At Harvard, a coalition of Palestinian solidarity groups whose members concealed their identities issued a statement holding "the Israeli regime entirely responsible for all unfolding violence." From the *Crimson:*

> "Today's events did not occur in a vacuum," the statement reads. "For the last two decades, millions of Palestinians in Gaza have been forced to live in an open-air prison. Israeli officials promise to 'open the gates of hell,' and the massacres in Gaza have already commenced.
>
> "In the coming days, Palestinians will be forced to bear the full brunt of Israel's violence. The apartheid regime is the only one to blame."

At NYU Law School, Ryna Workman, the president of the university's Student Bar Association, wrote in a message to the group that "Israel bears full responsibility for this tremendous loss of life," *The New York Times* reported after the message drew widespread scrutiny. "This regime of state-sanctioned violence created the conditions that made resistance necessary. . . . I will not condemn Palestinian resistance." (Workman would graduate the following semester in a

---

* Agnes Callamard (@AgnesCallamard), X, Oct. 7, 2023, 4:24 p.m., x.com /AgnesCallamard/status/1710752942578368793.

stole emblazoned with the phrase "Black Lawyers Matter," a caption underneath the image declaring, "Long live the student intifada.")

In light of such speech, a further fracturing became noticeable. Suddenly, even among those who would previously have been opposed to it, there was a newfound appetite for silencing free expression, neutralizing viewpoint diversity, and canceling the livelihoods and career prospects of the upwardly mobile activists who had so thoroughly married institutions to their values in the summer of 2020. Soon, it was not only the protesters who were engaged in blunt identitarian politics but also some ostensibly liberal Jews and their allies. On the same day of their comments, Workman, for one highly visible example, was repudiated by the dean of NYU's law school and had their job offer at a white-shoe firm rescinded—a comeuppance that was roundly celebrated on social media, despite being a textbook instance of cancel culture. At the same time, a highly influential mix of financiers and corporate executives who were alleged to be coordinating with one another via private text message groups sought a list of members of the Harvard student organizations behind the open letter so that, according to a tweet from the hedge fund billionaire Bill Ackman, their most outspoken participant and a former Hillary Clinton supporter turned Trump fanatic, "none of us inadvertently hire any of their members."* By

---

* "Ackman, the CEO of Pershing Square Capital Management, tweeted he has been approached by 'a number of CEOs' asking for the names of the student organizations to ensure 'none of us inadvertently hire any of their members,' arguing students 'should not be able to hide behind a corporate shield when issuing statements supporting the actions of terrorists.'

"Jonathan Neman, the CEO and co-founder of healthy fast casual chain Sweetgreen, responded to Ackman's post on X, saying he 'would like to know so I know never to hire these people,' to which healthcare services company EasyHealth CEO David Duel responded: 'Same.'

"DoveHill Capital Management CEO Jake Wurzak also supported Ack-

October 12, a truck with a billboard attached to it drove around Harvard's campus displaying the names and photos of the students who signed the letter along with the caption "Harvard's leading antisemites."

A dualistic social justice worldview and the DEI bureaucratic superstructure tasked with implementing it simply could not incorporate the fluid and ambiguous nature of contemporary Jewish American identity to anyone's satisfaction, which forced a large and influential number of people to pick sides.* No comfortable axis point could be found for Jews along the intersectional matrix of privilege and grievance. Plenty who had long conceived of themselves as assimilated now began to explicitly self-categorize in reductive terms of group membership. Pro-tribalism, pro-identity politics arguments arose from quarters that had only yesterday been passionately anti-tribal. That is not to imply that this was a unanimous reaction, and Jewish Americans remain anything but a monolith. Many continue to make up the most vociferous voices advocating for the Palestinian cause, decrying Zionism. Yet antisemitism remains core to both Islamism and white supremacist ideology; the far right in America as well as numerous European countries never received the memo that Jews had been inducted into whiteness. More concretely, in 2023 the director of the FBI, Christopher Wray, warned that antisemitism was reaching "historic levels," noting that despite constituting just 2.4 percent of the U.S. public, Jews account for nearly 60 percent of all religious-based hate crimes.

When some Jews, many of whom thought of themselves as

---

man's plea to release the names of the students." Brian Bushard, "Billionaire Ackman, Others Pledge They Won't Hire Harvard Students Who Signed Letter Blaming Israel for Hamas Attack," *Forbes*, Oct. 10, 2023.

* In truth, this worldview flattens and oversimplifies all identities.

true liberals and allies in the ongoing quest for social justice, now brought their own claims of discomfort and discrimination forth for consideration, there arose an urgent question: Would Jews, too, be allowed into the tent of DEI protection alongside the rest of the vulnerable and marginalized? Would the bias response hotlines that had become a feature of campus life pick up their calls? Or would the ultimate goal now be to adhere to more universal, hands-off values that in recent years had been so flagrantly neglected?* The

---

* A controversy over Halloween costume etiquette at Yale is illustrative of the way such situations had only recently been handled. From the Foundation for Individual Rights and Expression (FIRE):

On October 30, 2015, Erika Christakis—then the associate master of Yale University's Silliman College—responded to an email from the school's Intercultural Affairs Council that asked students to be thoughtful about the cultural implications of their Halloween costumes. Christakis, an expert in early childhood education, questioned what she and some Silliman students perceived as an intrusion into the expressive rights of college students that compromised their autonomy. Her email was nothing if not a respectful invitation to students to have a dialogue about challenging issues. She wrote:

I wonder, and I am not trying to be provocative: Is there no room anymore for a child or young person to be a little bit obnoxious . . . a little bit inappropriate or provocative or, yes, offensive? American universities were once a safe space not only for maturation but also for a certain regressive, or even transgressive, experience; increasingly, it seems, they have become places of censure and prohibition. And the censure and prohibition come from above, not from yourselves! Are we all okay with this transfer of power? Have we lost faith in young people's capacity—in your capacity—to exercise self-censure, through social norming, and also in your capacity to ignore or reject things that trouble you.

The response from Yale students shocked the nation. Angry students accused Christakis and her husband, master of Silliman College,

answer came swiftly. Schools that had rushed to issue definitive statements on every ethical controversy from the Kyle Rittenhouse verdict to the scandal of awkwardly executed cafeteria offerings* were overnight committed to circumspection and institutional neutrality, an about-face that was understandably infuriating—even if it was always the correct position.

By the time the presidents of Harvard, the University of Pennsylvania, and MIT flew to Washington to testify before grandstanding

---

Nicholas Christakis, who defended her email, of failing to create a "safe space" for Silliman residents. Others demanded they resign or the university remove them from their positions. On November 5, 2015, FIRE President and CEO Greg Lukianoff recorded video of students confronting Nicholas Christakis on the Yale campus. ("Halloween Costume Controversy," FIRE, thefire.org/research-learn/halloween -costume-controversy.)

As Conor Friedersdorf summarized that video in *The Atlantic:*

"In your position as master," one student says [to Christakis], "it is your job to create a place of comfort and home for the students who live in Silliman. You have not done that. By sending out that email, that goes against your position as master. Do you understand that?!"

"No," he said, "I don't agree with that."

The student explodes, "Then why the fuck did you accept the position?! Who the fuck hired you?! You should step down! If that is what you think about being a master you should step down! It is *not* about creating an intellectual space! It is *not*! Do you understand that? It's about creating a home here. You are not doing that!" ("The New Intolerance of Student Activism," Nov. 9, 2015.)

* "Michele Gross, Oberlin's director of dining services, said in a statement on Monday that 'in our efforts to provide a vibrant menu, we recently fell short in the execution of several dishes in a manner that was culturally insensitive.'

She added: 'We have met with students to discuss their concerns and hope to continue this dialogue.'" Katie Rogers, "Oberlin Students Take Culture War to the Dining Hall," *New York Times,* Dec. 21, 2015.

members of Congress about antisemitism on their campuses, it was inconceivable that the new preference for institutional neutrality and viewpoint diversity over moral clarity would go uncontested. Even a casual observer would know that Harvard, like most of America's elite schools with the notable exception of the University of Chicago, had staked out for years now positions on urgent and complicated moral questions as a matter of habit. In June 2020, the school's then president, Lawrence Bacow, issued an official university statement that concluded, "The Harvard community is deeply distressed by the killings of George Floyd, Breonna Taylor, Tony McDade, and many more Black Americans at the hands of those who have promised to protect communities and uphold the rule of law. Black lives matter, and we must use this moment to confront and remedy racial injustice." As dean of the Faculty of Arts and Sciences, Claudine Gay had also released a rousing statement on the death of George Floyd, one that did not hesitate to name his killer or describe the encounter as unequivocally racist:

> Like many of you, I have watched in pain and horror the events unfolding across the nation this week, triggered by the callous and depraved actions of a white police officer in Minneapolis. We have been here before, too many times, and that familiarity is part of the heartbreak and outrage of this moment. Even as the global fight against the pandemic has forged new bonds and inspired acts of profound generosity, we are confronted again by old hatreds and the enduring legacies of anti-black racism and inequality. It's a familiarity that makes me deeply restless for change. Part of that change is the work we do here to learn and listen across lines of difference and to build a community grounded in trust and respect. Part of that change is our work to trace the roots of inequality

and its pernicious effects and to equip our students with the understanding and insight needed to create a better world. Now is the time to lean into our mission, with resolve and a new sense of urgency.

And in June 2022, Russell Phillips, as director, wrote on behalf of Harvard Medical School Center for Primary Care staff and faculty a partial reaction to a legal decision that not only millions of conservative Americans supported but even some of the most esteemed liberal jurists acknowledged was a probable outcome based on previously flawed jurisprudence:*

> We are devastated and concerned over the Supreme Court's ruling in *Dobbs v. Jackson Women's Health Organization* on June 24, 2022. For nearly half a century, the right to abortion has been upheld and protected as a federal constitutional right. It is consistent with the right to privacy and autonomy over one's body. As described by the American Medical Association, the overturn of *Roe v. Wade* is "an egregious allow-

---

* "[Ruth Bader] Ginsburg cautioned against the idea of thinking that the 1973 Roe v. Wade ruling, which declared abortion was a constitutional right, was enough to guarantee women's reproductive freedom. Ginsburg was a lifelong staunch advocate for abortion rights and gender equality, but from her early days she had criticised the Supreme Court's handling of the abortion issue.

"She believed that the Roe v. Wade case had based the right to abortion on the wrong argument, a violation of a woman's privacy rather than on gender equality. This, she thought, left the ruling vulnerable to targeted legal attacks by anti-abortion activists."

Myles Burke, "In History: How Ruth Bader Ginsburg Foresaw the Threat to Abortion Access in the US," BBC, March 18, 2024.

ance of government intrusion into the medical examination room, a direct attack on the practice of medicine and the patient-physician relationship, and a brazen violation of patients' rights to evidence-based reproductive health services." Moreover, the Court's decision will disproportionately impact disadvantaged women and birthing persons in our country and only worsen existing health disparities.

And yet, two days after the bloodbath that had claimed many hundreds of civilians in Israel, Claudine Gay, now Harvard's president, along with the university's deans, issued an unusually milquetoast response emphasizing "our common humanity" and "goodwill in a time of unimaginable loss and sorrow." She "did not explicitly condemn Hamas or rebuke the student groups" that had preemptively faulted Israel for the slaughter, as the Harvard legal scholar Jeannie Suk Gersen noted in *The New Yorker*. "When [Gay] defended free speech in response to calls to curb anti-Israel or antisemitic statements, critics cried hypocrisy, noting that Harvard intervenes in incidents of alleged racist and sexist speech, under the rubric of harassment and discrimination policies."

Then, on December 5, 2023, Representative Elise Stefanik, a Harvard alumna and theatrical Trump supporter—hardly a high-minded defender of liberal values—publicly called the bluff, daring President Gay and her peers to speak to the nation on behalf of Jews from a place of moral clarity equivalent to previous occasions:

QUESTION: Dr. Gay, a Harvard student calling for the mass murder of African Americans is not protected free speech at Harvard, correct?
GAY: Our commitment to free speech . . .

QUESTION (*interrupts*): It's a yes or no question. Is that okay for students to call for the mass murder of African Americans at Harvard? Is that protected free speech?

GAY: Our commitment to free speech extends . . .

QUESTION (*interrupts*): It's a yes or no question. Let me ask you this. You are president of Harvard, so I assume you're familiar with the term intifada, correct?

GAY: I've heard that term, yes.

QUESTION: And you understand that the use of the term intifada in the context of the Israeli-Arab conflict is indeed a call for violent armed resistance against the state of Israel, including violence against civilians and the genocide of Jews. Are you aware of that?

GAY: That type of hateful speech is personally abhorrent to me.

QUESTION: And there have been multiple marches at Harvard with students chanting, quote, There is only one solution: intifada, revolution, and, quote, globalize the intifada. Is that correct?

GAY: I've heard that thoughtless, reckless, and hateful language on our campus. Yes.

QUESTION: So based upon your testimony, you understand that this call for intifada is to commit genocide against the Jewish people in Israel and globally. Correct?

GAY: I will say again, that type of hateful speech is personally abhorrent to me.

QUESTION: Do you believe that type of hateful speech is contrary to Harvard's code of conduct, or is it allowed at Harvard?

GAY: It is at odds with the values of Harvard.

QUESTION: Can you not say here that it is against the code of conduct at Harvard?

GAY: We embrace a commitment to free expression, even of views that are objectionable, offensive, hateful. It's when that speech crosses into conduct that violates our policies against bullying, harassment, intimidation . . .

QUESTION (*interrupts*): Does that speech not cross that barrier? Does that speech not call for the genocide of Jews and the elimination of Israel? When you testify that you understand that is the definition of intifada, is that speech according to the code of conduct or not?

GAY: We embrace a commitment to free expression and give a wide berth to free expression, even of views that are objectionable.

Though Gay and the other presidents—who were all advised by the same law firm—did provide robotically competent, legally justifiable responses, there was something both eyebrow raising and off-putting about the performance, which was wholly devoid of emotional resonance. Each of them struggled mightily to model coherent moral leadership or to articulate a compelling vision of what an intellectually serious community's ethical standards should be.

As Israel bombed Gaza with both U.S. support and a scale of collateral damage that has shaken many ardent supporters of the country's right to self-defense, by the spring of 2024 there was again the sense that Americans were failing to grasp the situation's shifting moral dynamics. "We are fighting human animals, and we are acting accordingly," Israel's defense minister, Yoav Gallant, famously declared. Flamboyant new outrages exposed fresh and inscrutable blindnesses and hypocrisies as a reinvigorated social justice movement and its opponents continued to filter an ancient and tragic foreign conflict through our own highly specific and self-referential lenses. I say reinvigorated, but resurrected might be more fitting. A broad skepticism and fatigue had already set in, bending the consensus enough for the events of October 7 to break it. DEI and professional managerial class "antiracism" procedures and practices were by this point commonly viewed as not just ineffective but measurably counterproductive.* Claudine Gay was forced to resign spectacularly at Harvard†—something that had only recently seemed impossible—as was Liz Magill at the University of Pennsylvania. MIT's president survived the fallout from the congressional hearing, but the school had already quietly been reversing its post-Floyd experimentations, notably reinstating its standardized testing requirement—temporarily jettisoned in the interest of racial equity—and acknowledging that diversity had actually *dropped* in its absence.‡

Despite the pogrom that prompted the invasion, Gaza's devastation and the civilian death toll it exacted, rising into the tens of thousands, altered the American scenario further. At the outset of

---

* A pioneer of implicit bias research, Mahzarin Banaji, published an op-ed in *The Wall Street Journal* in September 2023 that argued, "The typical DEI training doesn't educate people about bias and may even do harm."

† Technically, on the basis of dozens of acts of minor plagiarism.

‡ "Our research shows standardized tests help us better assess the academic preparedness of all applicants, and also help us identify socioeconomically disadvantaged students who lack access to advanced coursework or other enrichment opportunities that would otherwise demonstrate their readiness for MIT," Stu Schmill, MIT's dean of admissions, acknowledged. "We believe a requirement is more equitable and transparent than a test-optional policy."

the conflict, Isaac Herzog, Israel's president, used language strikingly reminiscent of the Yale historian Zareena Grewal to cast "the entire nation" of Palestinians as "responsible" for October 7. "This rhetoric of 'unaware, uninvolved civilians,' is not true," he continued. "They could've resisted, they could've fought this evil regime that took over Gaza," he concluded even as he hedged, "There are also innocent Palestinians in Gaza. I am deeply sorry for the tragedy they are going through." The ferocity of Israel's reaction, which frequently amounted to collective punishment, catalyzed and reoriented the American social justice left around a single galvanizing struggle*—even as it provoked equally motivated opponents and alienated many potential allies and moderates. The new intersectionality, born of the same old social justice Manichaeanism, spotlighted ever more complicated and paradoxical alliances, such as the movement that organizes itself under the slogan "Queers for Palestine."† Such cluelessness on the part of left-wing activists in turn allowed far too many onlookers to absolve themselves of the necessary effort to grapple with the vicious math of retaliation: in less than a year, some 2 percent of the entire population of Gaza had been eradicated.

* There has been no such outcry, for example, about the Taliban's ban on women's voices being heard singing or reading in public. Associated Press, "Taliban Bans the Sound of Women's Voices Singing or Reading in Public," CNN, Aug. 22, 2024.

† Prior to the war in Gaza, the Palestinian territories ranked among the least hospitable to homosexuality globally. Despite Israel being the only Middle Eastern society in which gay rights are robustly safeguarded, such activists nonetheless reject celebration of this discrepancy as "pinkwashing," or using LGBTQ+ rights to promote a progressive image that is not otherwise merited. The 2024 edition of the LGBTQ+ Pride Flag, which is updated annually, was revised to prominently feature Palestinian colors. It is impossible to picture the blue and white of Israel ever receiving similar treatment.

Over the course of the spring, as protests and encampments dominated elite college campuses across the country, and some administrations cracked down in reaction,* "in many students' eyes, the war in Gaza" became linked to a litany of other preoccupations, "such as policing, mistreatment of Indigenous people, racism and the impact of climate change," Jeremy W. Peters reported in *The New York Times:*

> They described, to a striking degree, the broad prism through which they see the Gaza conflict, which helps explain their urgency—and recalcitrance.
>
> Ife Jones, a first-year student at Emory University in Atlanta, linked her current activism to the 1960s civil right [*sic*] movement, which her family had participated in.
>
> *"The only thing missing was the dogs and the water,"* Ms. Jones said of the current pushback to demonstrators. (Emphasis mine.)

That last admission is perhaps as efficient a distillation of post-2020 activist rhetoric as one is likely to encounter. The sheer presentism and lack of perspective evinced by a student enrolled at one of the

---

* This institutional response on free speech grounds was frequently hypocritical, "though not in the way the protesters think," as Steve McGuire noted in *City Journal*. "University administrators have historically been lenient toward those demonstrating for causes they support; they have used prejudicial admissions and hiring to create left-leaning campus communities; and they insist that social-justice activism is essential to their institutional missions. They have thus allowed their campuses to become ideological tinderboxes." Is it any wonder the students become confused when administrators balk at the inevitable explosion?

nation's top-tier universities would be comedic if it were not so tragic. The dogs and the hoses—which is to say the entire pre-civil-rights society arrayed behind them—were not so many details in the older generation's story. What this student unintentionally admits is damning: the only thing missing in her struggle *is the oppression.*

If such a distinction were still dubious, Johannah King-Slutzky, a PhD student in English and comparative literature at Columbia University, permanently clarified it. As part of the group that broke into Hamilton Hall,* King-Slutzky addressed television reporters and demanded the university deliver what she termed "basic humanitarian aid" to prevent the protesters suffering "dehydration" or "starvation" during their voluntary occupation.

In that fraught moment, it became evident that some of the world's safest and most demonstrably privileged young people had so fully adhered to the oppressor/oppressed dichotomy that they not only glamorized but cannibalized the latter's reality. Activist students at Columbia, who had channeled the spirit of the 1960s and sparked a mimetic chain reaction of tent encampments from UCLA to Dartmouth, were now explicitly "role-playing to satisfy

---

* Hamilton Hall was famously occupied in April 1968 during the demonstrations over gentrification in Harlem and complicity with the war in Vietnam. A multiracial group of Columbia students barricaded themselves inside, holding the acting dean, Henry S. Coleman, hostage. Black students renamed the building Malcolm X Liberation College and promptly expelled their white classmates, who went on to occupy other buildings on campus. Inspired by this, in April 2024, a mix of students, staff, alumni, and outside agitators protesting the Israel-Hamas war occupied Hamilton Hall again. They renamed the building Hind's Hall after Hind Rajab, a six-year-old Palestinian girl killed by the Israel Defense Forces. The NYPD cleared the hall on the evening of April 30, 2024. See John Yoon, "Hamilton Hall Has a Long History of Student Takeovers," *New York Times,* April 30, 2024.

their fantasies," as the Iranian activist Elica Le Bon observed in her viral Twitter analysis of the spectacle:

> Here, the students have appropriated the suffering of Gazans and are cosplaying as living through humanitarian crisis. In their American make-believe story where Ivy League infrastructure sets the scene, the students play Gazans and the school administration plays Israel. Israel (the school) is blocking their "basic humanitarian aid" in this play, and if they don't receive it soon, they will "die of thirst and starvation" (appropriating exact experiences of Gazans). They also destroy upper class buildings and claim them as "liberatcd" while the students repeat chants in zombie-like chorus, playing the roll [sic] of "freedom fighters" destroying Israeli infrastructure and claiming them freed. . . . You don't see this in lower tier schools from kids of lower socio-economic standing because they aren't plagued with the guilt of privilege that they're seeking to launder through Middle East role plays of feigned suffering. . . . Meanwhile, these Ivy League students who can have much more than a glass of water and as much food as their stomachs can take are commanding the attention of the media and the entire American audience, while actual Gazans who need humanitarian aid are ignored.

The lavish self-indulgence of these demonstrations notwithstanding, and despite their measurable failure to persuade the majority of Americans of the correctness of their position,* the student activists

* According to YouGov research, "Three-quarters of Americans have heard about the recent arrests of pro-Palestinian protesters demonstrating on college campuses throughout the country. Nearly half of people oppose the protests, while around one in four support them. Few support demonstrators'

couldn't help but reveal a skin-deep commitment to free expression and viewpoint diversity among far too many liberals, so-called heterodox thinkers, and conservatives. Some of the same politicians, cultural observers, and everyday Americans who downplayed or excused the January 6 insurrection or posed as free speech absolutists during the racial reckoning now found themselves in the insupportable position of calling for the silencing—and in some cases imprisonment—of people they merely disagreed with, applauding violent police interventions against even peaceful protest.* Such hypocrisy was counterbalanced by an abiding inability among progressives to comprehend that at least some of the images of the nationwide "student intifada"[†] were startlingly reminiscent of the lawlessness of the Capitol Hill riots. As social justice–oriented a figure as the Reverend Al Sharpton was bitterly mocked and derogated by the left for stating a simple and obvious truth: "How do the Democrats, how do all of us on that side, say January 6 was wrong if you can have the same pictures going on, on college campuses?"[‡]

---

calls for divestment, and one in three believe college administrators have not responded harshly enough to the protesters." Taylor Orth, "What Americans Think About Recent Pro-Palestinian Campus Protests," YouGov, May 2, 2024, today.yougov.com.

* In Texas, the Republican governor, Greg Abbott, sent in a hundred state troopers, some on horseback, to UT Austin, where they arrested some fifty students. "Students joining in hate-filled, antisemitic protests at any public college or university in Texas should be expelled," he wrote on Twitter. It was an extraordinary contradiction for a governor who, during the unrest of 2020, signed a bill to enshrine new free speech protections on college campuses.

[†] While it was certainly a protest of national scale, it is more accurate to call it an Ivy Intifada, because the real commotion was almost entirely restricted to private colleges and flagship state universities.

[‡] Philip Lewis (@Phil_Lewis_), X, May 2, 2024, 7:55 a.m., x.com/Phil_Lewis_/status/1786001459835761019.

The long arc of the American moral universe, wherever it may ultimately bend, has been warped grotesquely beneath the competing heat and pressure of the on- and offline movement for social justice and the right-wing illiberalism it both feeds off and nourishes. From the abnormally harmonious days of Obama's election, through the tumult of the pandemic, to the disruption of the Gaza encampments in the tense months preceding Trump's third and most threatening bid for the presidency, one dismal truth that spans the political chasm has become all too obvious: a remarkable and increasing number of Americans believe themselves not only justified but *entitled* to resolve political disagreements by force if they sense themselves at an impasse. Genuine liberals, as well as their moderate and center-right partners, have no choice but to reclaim the abandoned moral high ground. We must identify and disown the means of extremism—even when they manifest themselves in pursuit of ends we may agree with. That is the most basic prerequisite for democracy.

This book, I have only realized in the writing, is fundamentally not about a comparatively privileged* and influential slice of humanity's penchant for fashionable manners and neologisms, or radical new theories about identity and justice. That hunger for novelty is but a symptom of a far more tragic and devastating tendency to forget the fragile blessings of the liberal society. It has been our puzzling fate not just to inherit but to voluntarily repeat the mistakes of previous generations—to flirt with their hatreds and prejudices and to romanticize their limitations and grievances. In a free and open society, we have deliberately swerved from the path of incremental improvement onto a

---

* And multihued.

Sisyphean cycle of exhaustion. We arrive again at the base of the mountain. If the coming years of struggle back up it are to teach us anything, let it be the reprise of an insight that was already evident at the founding—vigilant memory is the shadow price of liberty.

Acknowledgments

Summer of Our Discontent would not have been possible without the indefatigable efforts of Andrew Wylie, a man whose energy and belief are as infectious as his knowledge of the industry is reassuring. Within weeks of our first meeting, I found myself holding a new proposal. I am also grateful to Erroll McDonald at Knopf, who believed in this project and fought for it at a fraught cultural moment when that was not necessarily the path of least resistance. His erudition, judgment, and patience (and then lack of patience) were crucial at every step. The sheer amount of wisdom and experience both of these men bring to publishing is something to behold.

Life is fuller, with many more responsibilities than the last time I wrote a book. I am grateful to the American Enterprise Institute for welcoming me as a scholar and for the yearslong, multifaceted support. I owe enormous thanks to Robert Doar and Yuval Levin for bringing me in and allowing me the slow time and stability to think. Thank you to Nicole Penn and the entire SCCS department, who have been so insightful and kind. The workshopping sessions were highlights for me—demonstrations of an unusual degree of personal and intellectual interest and generosity from the entire community that I won't forget. Noah Rosenfield was the Platonic ideal of a research assistant. (I cried tears of joy for him and pity for myself when I learned he was leaving for Yale.) A special thank-you to Jane Brady Knight, who, during the two times we overlapped, went above and beyond as an advocate and friend.

I am indebted to Edward Hirsch, André Bernard, and the John Simon

Guggenheim Memorial Foundation for critical support that was made possible by the generosity of Wendy Belzberg and Strauss Zelnick. At a time when I needed more than anything to believe this project could receive a fair and open-minded reading in the wild, this specific fellowship was an extreme shot in the arm. What this institution means to artists, scholars, and writers, year in and year out, cannot be overstated. Immense thanks to Henry Louis Gates Jr. for modeling the life of the mind and reading my proposal.

I owe continuous thanks to the entire American Academy in Berlin, where it has been an honor first to come as a fellow and then to serve on the board. A special *vielen dank* to my dear friend Kati Marton.

I owe a decade's worth of thanks to Antoine Flochel, Colombe Schneck, and Alexander Maksik for the extraordinary literary community (and endless Spanish ham) these three make possible at Can Cab—a magical place I feel is literally too good to be true every time I'm lucky enough to be there. *Muchas gracias,* Antoine, for making this dream retreat tangible.

This book is the direct result of the pandemic, a bizarre and punishing time that was also more than redeemed through the ties of kinship and friendship that it strengthened. *Merci mille fois* to the greatest lockdown companions I could have ever hoped for: Jordan Mintzer, Sophie Toporkoff, Christopher Silva, Tamara and Dimitri Mintzer, and, most of all, Valentine, Marlow, and Saul. Those quiet days in Brézéan spent watching movies, doing chores, and shooting baskets are ones I will always cherish.

The private correspondence that kept my faith during this period was with four writers who exemplify lucid thinking and moral integrity, as well as selfless commitment to liberal values. It resulted in an important public statement. George Packer, Mark Lilla, Robert Worth, and David Greenberg (maybe the single most effective emailer I have ever witnessed), thank you, brothers, for inviting me to get involved. Two of the best years of my professional life were spent at *Harper's*. I have profound admiration and gratitude for Christopher Beha and Rick MacArthur, both of whom immediately understood the need—and had the courage—to publish "A Letter on Justice and Open Debate," lending it the imprimatur of the magazine that had motivated me to first want to be a writer. Deep thanks to

Giulia Melucci for her enthusiasm and relentless efforts to get it out into the world.

I also want to thank Violet Chernoff for her research assistance and keen intellect.

There are many friends, writers, and minds—too many to list—who came into my life and enriched it during this period, whose time and conversation focused my thinking, made me laugh, and simply helped me feel less alone. A heartfelt shout-out to you all. And a profound thank-you to Rikki Schlott for so much careful reading, conversation, and moral support along the interminable final stretch.

I owe the sincerest thanks to Leon Botstein and Roger Berkowitz for making me a professor and allowing me to follow my truest intellectual interests at the Hannah Arendt Center at Bard College. And to Robert Boyers and Adam Braver, who have provided a warm and inspiring summer base for my nonfiction teaching at the New York State Writers Institute at Saratoga. It is a privilege to be able to read and discuss words and ideas with students and peers—one I don't take lightly and that has taught me more than I have been able to transmit.

Books are infrequent, but newspapers, magazines, and journals keep a writer going. Some ideas, themes, and passages here began in essays over the years. I have had the fortune to be edited by some of the smartest people I've ever met who have also frequently been incredibly thoughtful and kind. Profound gratitude to Willy Staley, Jessica Lustig, and Jake Silverstein at *The New York Times Magazine;* Chris Beha and Timothy Farrington at *Harper's;* Daniel Zalewski at *The New Yorker;* J. Oliver Conroy at *The Guardian;* Jason Farago at *Even;* and Jeff Goldberg, Denise Wills, Adrienne LaFrance, Yoni Applebaum, Juliet Lapidos, Don Peck, Jack Segelstein, and Honor Jones at *The Atlantic,* where I have been extremely lucky to find a home.

Finally, thank you to my parents, who took the time to make me a *reader* before I was a writer, and to my big brother, Clarence, who forced me to learn to argue and make my skin thicker.

A Note About the Author

Thomas Chatterton Williams is a staff writer at *The Atlantic* and the author of *Losing My Cool* and *Self-Portrait in Black and White*. He is a visiting professor of humanities and senior fellow at the Hannah Arendt Center at Bard College, a 2022 Guggenheim fellow, and a visiting fellow at the American Enterprise Institute. He was previously a contributing writer at *The New York Times Magazine* and a columnist at *Harper's Magazine*. His work has appeared in *The New Yorker, London Review of Books, Le Monde,* and many other places and has been collected in *The Best American Essays* and *The Best American Travel Writing*. He has received support from New America, Yaddo, MacDowell, and the American Academy in Berlin, where he is a member of the board of trustees.

A Note on the Type

This book was set in Charter, the first digital typeface designed at Bitstream by Matthew Carter in 1987. Charter is a revival of eighteenth-century Roman type forms with narrow proportions and a large x-height. The square serifs were originally intended to maintain crisp letterforms on the low-resolution personal printers of the 1980s. However, the typeface has remained popular because of its eloquent modern design.

Composed by North Market Street Graphics,
Lancaster, Pennsylvania